LANSDOWNE
Through the Years

LANSDOWNE
Through the Years

EDWARD NEWMAN

HODDER
HEADLINE
IRELAND

Copyright © 2006 Edward Newman

First published in 2006 by Hodder Headline Ireland

1

The right of Edward Newman to be identified as the Author of the Work has been asserted by him in accordance with the Copyright, Designs and Patents Act, 1988.

A CIP catalogue record for this title is available from the British Library.

ISBN 0340 92400 4
[13-digit ISBN 978 0340 92400 6]

Typeset in Caslon by Anú Design, Tara
Cover and text design by Anú Design, Tara
Printed and bound in Great Britain by CPI Bath Press

Hodder Headline Ireland's policy is to use papers that are natural, renewable and recyclable products and made from wood grown in sustainable forests. The logging and manufacturing processes are expected to conform to the environmental regulations of the country of origin.

Hodder Headline Ireland
8 Castlecourt Centre
Castleknock
Dublin 15
Ireland

A division of Hachette Livre UK Ltd, 338 Euston Road, London NW1 3BH, England

Contents

Foreword

Edmund Van Esbeck

The Lansdowne Road ground holds a very special place, not alone in the annals of Irish rugby, but also sport in Ireland on an even broader scale. Since the middle of what historians refer to as the Victorian era, the tumult and the shouting that are an integral part of the big sporting occasion have echoed around the ground in Dublin 4.

We owe an immense debt to the man who started it all, Henry William Doveton Dunlop. A noted athlete in his day, he had a vision of creating a sporting complex in the Dublin area. With that in mind, he purchased a twenty-one-year lease on the ground from Pembroke Estate at an annual rent of £70. He was the founder of The Irish Champion Athletic Club and the committee of the club raised £1,000 for the purpose of enclosing and levelling the ground, laying down a running track and erecting a pavilion. Dunlop's dream had been realised. In addition to his main interest and prowess in athletics, he was also the founder of the Lansdowne Rugby Club in 1872, thus the very tangible rugby connection from the outset of the ground as a sporting theatre.

It was in Lansdowne Road that the first athletics international in history took place when Ireland met England in 1875. By that time, Ireland had entered the international rugby arena but, in fact, Lansdowne Road was rejected as being unsuitable by the rugby authorities as the venue for the first international played in Dublin. The game was played instead at the Leinster Cricket Ground in Rathmines.

When Ireland played England for the second time in Dublin, on 11 March 1878, Lansdowne Road was the venue and, since that match, every senior international played in Dublin has taken place at the ground.

Dunlop eventually sold the lease to Harry Sheppard, who was honorary treasurer of the IRFU, but Sheppard died a young man in 1906 and his mother sold the lease to the IRFU for a nominal sum. The lease was extended and, thus armed, the IRFU set about major development, which has been ongoing through the years. Today, however, it is no longer able to meet the needs of the current era and so the grand old aristocrat of rugby stadia is about to be demolished and replaced by a grand new structure incorporating all the amenities deemed imperative in the modern game. It is, in the circumstances, opportune to reflect on that very brief history of the ground and how it came into the possession of the IRFU.

One man who has made a major contribution to the ongoing development of the ground is Ronnie Dawson, assuredly one of the great figures in the history of the game in this country. A former captain of Ireland and captain of the Lions, a former Ireland and Lions coach, and former president of the IRFU, he was also one of Ireland's representatives on the International Rugby Board. An architect by profession, he used his professional expertise on a voluntary basis to help maintain the ground and oversee improvements. He is owed an immense debt of gratitude for a magnificent contribution.

Lansdowne Road has, of course, been the venue for soccer internationals and international athletics, but this publication deals with some of the happenings, the days of great joy and indeed occasions of acute disappointment, for those rugby players who were centre stage at a ground unique in the annals of rugby football, the oldest international rugby stadium in the world.

Generations of Irish rugby followers will have their special memories and, on a personal level, I will never forget the excitement of my first visit to Lansdowne Road almost sixty years ago. I was, at the time, a schoolboy living in Cork, and was brought by my late brother Frank to see Ireland play Australia in December 1947. Ireland lost comprehensively that afternoon, but there was some compensation in the fact that I had made the pilgrimage as I saw my hero, Jack Kyle, play for Ireland for the first time.

We were not to know it on that December afternoon but the Irish rugby team was about to enter a 'golden era' with Kyle at the heart of the triumphs of a Grand Slam, two Triple Crowns and three championships between 1948 and 1951. It was my good fortune to have been at those matches.

Through the years that followed, those of us who write about rugby for a living were able to view the drama from a position of great advantage – the press box, situated ideally in line with the halfway line, initially from the old East Stand and then, from 1974, from the West Stand.

Lansdowne Road has for long now been the mecca for a multitude, its situation is ideal and as one old rugby international once said to me, 'You know, it was not just the rugby and the atmosphere, but it was also a social meeting place for so many of us.'

Many have played a part in the history of the ground. In *Lansdowne Through the Years*, Edward Newman is concerned in the main with those who wore the green and enjoyed glory and, at times, disappointment.

Through the years, there were great occasions to savour and to relive as long as memory holds. Victories over the big powers of the southern hemisphere, Australia and South Africa and a famous draw against the All Blacks. But it is what is now known as the Six Nations Championship (and which was initially the International Championship) that has always had a special place in the game in these islands. The Triple Crown and Championship wins at Lansdowne Road in 1982 and 1985 are especially precious memories as is the 2004 Triple Crown success achieved at the ground.

Each person will hold their own memories. In the pages that follow, some of the great players who displayed their talents on the old green sward give us the benefit of their memories. In giving those men the opportunity to share their experiences with us, Edward Newman has served us well.

The changes have been immense since the days when Dunlop saw his dream come true when the affluent arrived in their horse-drawn carriages, the rest by train and tram. Now, we look back with great affection on the days that are gone and look forward with great expectation to a time when, in its new life, the stadium will retain the unique atmosphere that has pervaded the great old ground.

History gives value to the present hour and its meaning.

Edmund Van Esbeck
July 2006

Introduction

Edward Newman

Lansdowne Road has been at the epicentre of Irish rugby for 130 years; a venue for epic matches and great tries and individual feats. There is no more vibrant a sight than when it's brimful with hordes of supporters and there is nothing more uplifting than the raucous sound created inside as an Ireland player hurtles towards the tryline at either the Lansdowne Road or Havelock Square End. Lift the lid on the past and there's Willie Duggan handing his cigarette butt to the referee as he takes the final of fourteen steps from the Lansdowne tunnel. The emotion locked between the shaky boards of this old structure when John Pullin's England walked onto the hallowed turf in 1973 and the crowd rose to their feet for a five minute standing ovation. They travelled amidst threats from paramilitary groups as the Troubles worsened in Northern Ireland. 'We may not be very good but at least we turn up,' were the famous words from Pullin in his post-match speech at the dinner reception at the Shelbourne Hotel, to which men wept as they stood again, as they had hours earlier at Lansdowne, to applaud the England captain and his team.

When the crowd is in full voice, when its roar is at its most throaty, and especially when Ireland are winning, there is no greater venue in world rugby. Players from both Ireland and abroad echo this sentiment and mean it. One of Irish rugby's most iconic figures Keith Wood has called the famous Lansdowne Roar 'the beat'. On 31 December 2006, when Leinster host Ulster in a Celtic League game, the beat will be silenced, at least temporarily, as the stadium undergoes radical redevelopment. The wrecking ball will bring over 130 years of rugby, sadly but inevitably, to dust and rubble but the memories will remain steadfast, locked inside this most valuable piece of Dublin real estate – sixteen acres in the most expensive suburb in Ireland. And how fitting – or is it serendipity? – that Leinster and Ulster who played the first game at the stadium, an inter-provincial match in 1876, will also play out the last.

So many words have been used to describe what Lansdowne Road is and what it represents.

It is at one time unique and magical and timeless. For the home team, it is a citadel and, for visiting teams, it has come to be known as the lion's den.

There might be similarities with other old and atmospheric grounds – like the ivy-covered Wrigley Field home to the Chicago Cubs baseball team or Carisbrook in Dunedin, New Zealand – but Lansdowne stands as a queen amongst them. Will there ever be its like again? Certainly, the time has come to move on as rugby undergoes rapid change in the professional era and the rugby supporter seeks the best and most comfortable surroundings. In this regard, Lansdowne is outmoded, but the atmosphere generated inside through three different centuries should not be lost amidst development. The dawn of the multi-purpose corporate stadium has made old Lansdowne (ironically built as a multi-purpose complex) redundant, but the hope is that the distinctive atmosphere that has pervaded the ground since it held its first international between Ireland and England in 1878 will not be lost within the new structure. One can only wonder whether the brain-child behind Lansdowne Road, Henry William Dunlop, ever envisaged that his stadium venture would evolve into a structure that would house epic rugby matches.

Early in its history, Lansdowne hosted teams from the southern hemisphere and none came bigger than the visit of the first All Blacks – 'the Originals' – captained by Letterkenny native Dave Gallaher in 1905. The Originals played thirty-two matches and won thirty-one on their tour of Great Britain and Ireland, but such was their popularity that, when they arrived on these shores, the IRFU decided to make the international an all-ticket affair – and Lansdowne became the first stadium in the world to host an all-ticket international. A powerful All Black side overwhelmed the Irish 15–0 and, on their tour, they kept twenty-four of their opponents scoreless. In total, the All Blacks scored 830 points and conceded only thirty-nine. The All Blacks returned in the autumn of 2005 and, having visited the birthplace of Dave Gallaher in County Donegal, overwhelmed Ireland 45–7, a performance and a result almost in homage to the Originals.

Lansdowne Road is also closely linked to world history. The British cavalry from nearby Beggar's Bush barracks originally used this sixteen-acre site to graze and water their horses. And they indulged in a bit of rugby there too. The morning after the outbreak of the First World War in August 1914 rugby players, mainly from Wanderers and Lansdowne clubs, enlisted there for service. A monument to mark this occasion stands behind the ivy-coated South Terrace and a plaque to the Wanderers and Lansdowne players who were part of the first 'pals regiments' hangs beside the Wanderers bar. In September 1914, it was decided that all club games and representative matches should be suspended for the duration of the war, though schools and inter-provincial matches did continue and all competitions, as well as a full international programme, were not played again until the 1919–1920 season.

While relations had dipped to an all-time low between Ireland and England during the War of Independence and, despite the parlous state of Dublin, the England rugby team fulfilled its fixture in 1920 travelling to Lansdowne and winning the Five Nations game 11–14. (It had moved from a

Four Nations to a Five Nations Championship in 1909 and France won their first game on their first visit to Lansdowne in March of that year.)

When the IRFU was secure in its tenancy, it set about a major rebuilding and planning programme for the stadium. The ground was swung on its axis from an east–west to a north–south alignment and a covered stand was erected on the west side of the ground and an uncovered stand to the left of it – this cost £6,000 and was finished in time for the visit of Scotland in February 1908, a game Ireland won to mark the occasion. In 1928, the east side of the ground was fitted with a stand.

Meanwhile, the West Stand ran its course in 1955 when it was decided to build a modern two-tier structure, one which arched over the railway line that served the busy suburban route to Sandymount, Blackrock and southeast Dublin. In 1974, the lower tier of the West Stand under-went major renovation and, in 1983, it was decided that the old East Stand should be demolished to be replaced by a modern structure. One man who has devoted a huge amount time to the development of Lansdowne Road is former Ireland and Lions captain Ronnie Dawson. An architect by profession, Dawson served on the IRB for twenty years as well as a term as the President of the IRFU.

Internationals were suspended again after the outbreak of the Second World War but, three years after the end of the war, the coming together of a golden generation of Ireland players resulted in Ireland's first (and to this day only) Grand Slam in 1948. Ireland played only one game in that Grand Slam year in Lansdowne Road – a 6–0 win over Scotland – before the title was claimed with a 6–3 win over Wales in Ravenhill, Belfast.

In the late 1940s and 1950s, great athletics meets were hosted at Lansdowne Road. The late Dutch sprinter Fanny Blankers-Koen, who won four gold medals at the 1948 London Olympics, ran in Lansdowne, while, in the late 1950s, Ronnie Delaney, who won a gold medal in the 1,500 metres at the 1956 Melbourne Olympics, displayed his athletic prowess on the Lansdowne track.

While at the epicentre of Irish international rugby, Lansdowne Road has provided the pulse for Irish soccer's glory days especially throughout the Jack Charlton era from 1986 to 1995. During the Englishman's tenure, the Republic of Ireland qualified for a European Championship (1988) and two World Cups (1990 and 1994) – with many of the most epic qualification games played out in the Dublin 4 venue. There's no doubt that Lansdowne Road has been the focal point for the fostering of Irish international football teams and the theatre for some of football's greats. Indeed, during the Charlton years, Irish football reached its apogee, and Lansdowne was at the heart of its glory years.

It has become a field of dreams for schoolboys from the province of Leinster where Junior and Senior Schools cups have been fought out at the venue. And while playing host to its tenants Lansdowne FC and Wanderers FC through the decades, Lansdowne also opened its doors to the club game in this country with many All-Ireland League finals being played there. Leinster Senior Cup games have also been hosted there and in the 2005–2006 season the inaugural AIB

All-Ireland Cup final was won by Cork Constitution in Lansdowne Road.

Lansdowne has also been a venue for concerts – a stand-out one being the visit of U2 in August 1998. They brought their infamous and somewhat brash Pop-mart tour and post-modern gig to the oldest stadium in the world but it didn't look out of place.

The players in this book describe the ground as a theatre of dreams – and of broken dreams. They describe how a passionate Lansdowne crowd could, at different times, make them run ten seconds faster and help them play above their abilities. Many of Lansdowne's great days have been recounted in great detail by the players – Ireland's golden years between 1948 and 1951; how Ireland nearly beat and should have beaten the All Blacks in 1963 and 1973; Ollie Campbell's twenty-one points helping 'Dad's Army' to the 1982 Triple Crown – the first to be won at Lansdowne Road; Michael's Kiernan's drop goal that gave Doyler's boys the 1985 Triple Crown; Donal Lenihan's inner torment at losing to a last-minute try to Australia in the 1991 World Cup quarter-final; Irish rugby's dark ages; the transition to professionalism and its associated problems; Ronan O'Gara's splendid kicking single-handedly beating Australia (2002) and South Africa (2004); Brian O'Driscoll's hat-trick against Scotland in 2002; our current golden generation and their Triple Crown successes in 2004 and 2006. Brief snapshots of what are voluminous memories from inside the ground.

The fans have played such a crucial part in making Lansdowne, as the Welsh great Ieuan Evans says, 'vibrant and raucous'. Bill McLaren says that Irish fans were philosophical about their rugby football – that win or lose a good time was had by all. McLaren felt the Irish 'kind of skidded along'. It is felt by others that the supporters, especially those on touchline seats or East Stand terrace, must have had a mischievous quality about them too. Former England hooker Brian Moore remembers one particular day where he got a dose of Lansdowne 'hospitality', 'England were playing at Lansdowne Road. At the bottom of a ruck five yards from our line, I felt an Irish hand grab my ankle. All I could think was he is going to try and sprain my ankle, but he pulled his hand away and with it my boot. He promptly turned around and threw it into the crowd. Sure enough, when I, as you can imagine, politely asked for my boot back they refused. The referee ordered play to continue – a five-yard scrum with only one boot! Eventually, the boot was thrown back at me and we carried on.'

I'm sure Brian Moore will look back wistfully at that moment and smile and say – 'that's Lansdowne and that's the Irish'. Keith Wood says that Lansdowne 'seems to live for the big occasion; it comes to life struggling one last time to hold its place'. When the current stadium shuts it doors for the final time on 31 December 2006, it will forever hold its place in people's hearts. That's a guarantee.

Edward Newman
August 2006

To my mother Marie and
my father John

The View from the Pitch

Ollie Campbell

Fly-Half
1976–1984

Before he scraped the Lansdowne Road mud from his boots and placed it in a plastic bag for keeps after Belvedere College won the Leinster Schools Senior Cup in 1971, before he talked his way into Lansdowne Road to witness the emotion and magic of the historic Five Nations game between England and Ireland in 1973, Ollie Campbell sat in the West Upper alongside his father, James Oliver, bewitched by the All Blacks who fashioned a 6–5 victory over Ireland in December 1963.

It might be expedient to say that Campbell was deeply influenced by the genius of the All Blacks full-back Donald Clarke, but the truth is that he became a keen student of Clarke's kicking game. He would always look back on that winter's afternoon in 1963 as a pivotal moment in his life. It was the day Clarke left an indelible mark on his psyche and, more importantly, on his kicking game, which he would put to good use in kicking Ireland to a Triple Crown in 1982.

'From the moment my father took me to see them, I would have had a fascination with the whole All Blacks mystique – what they stand for, what they mean. So there is just something about the All Blacks. Even the name – it's not just New Zealand, it's the All Blacks. They've rarely disappointed.'

Twenty years after he first set eyes on those famous black shirts, he was touring with the Lions in New Zealand 'playing in all these grounds that I'd only ever read about or seen briefly on TV'. Their aura of invincibility had gone around the world like the wind – and Campbell was caught in the slipstream. For ever. 'The 1963 side was captained by Wilson Whineray who, to this day, would be considered one of the great captains of New Zealand rugby – he's certainly an MBE if not a Sir Wilson Whineray for his services to New Zealand. He has been very successful in everything he has done. You also had Colin Meads, you had Stan Meads and Donald Clarke at full-back. Donald was probably the first really great kicker – he kicked the old-fashioned way with the toe and that. For many years, he was actually the biggest man who ever played for New Zealand, even though he was a full-back – he was a colossus. Those were the sort of names that caught my eye.

'Johnny Fortune got a try for Ireland but, if I remember right, it was a fairly late, long penalty by Don Clarke that actually squeezed victory for the All Blacks. The Irish side that day included Willie John McBride, Ray McLoughlin, Noel Murphy and Tommy Kiernan – the last two would also have a massive influence on my career. So in many, many ways that first day was really a defining day for me in my life, in my career and how things evolved after that.'

The visit of the All Blacks in 1963 lodges lovingly in Campbell's memory but when the modern batch arrived on these shores for a test in November 2005, the bond with the All Blacks grew even stronger. Players like Keven Mealamu and Jerry Collins took a breather from their hectic schedule (which included a visit to Letterkenny, County Donegal, to the birthplace of Dave Gallaher, captain of the 1905 Originals – the first All Blacks) to drop out to Campbell's beloved Old Belvedere on Angelsea Road to meet some of the kids.

It was Gareth Edwards who said that 'rugby is really a simple game and it's only the coaches who make it complicated' and, thankfully, Campbell didn't have three different kicking advisors at province, national and Lions level to blunt his edge. He was old school and self-taught, untainted by opinion and input from others. For someone who never kicked a ball at school, who hadn't done so much as a 22 drop-out or a halfway kick and who had never punted or place-kicked at school, his record at test level was the result of sheer hard work. He was nineteen before he assumed kicking duties on an Old Belvedere thirds side, the captain presuming that if he was at fly-half, he was also a kicker.

But Ollie was fifth place-kicker on the Belvedere College side that won the 1972 Leinster Schools Senior Cup, special days for the north Dublin school completing, as it were, back-to-back titles.

Campbell's first appearance at Lansdowne was in the 1971 final, as a fifth year and a fringe player who was only fleetingly involved in senior rugby that season and played in only five friendly games. Tony Duane was injured in the last minutes of the semi-final cutting short his season and, on cup final day, Campbell was told two hours before kick-off that he'd be playing. Not much time to notify family, but the short notice carried long-term benefits – there was no room for nerves but plenty of space for free expression. 'Only afterwards do you realise what a huge occasion it was. It all happened a bit quickly. But that was my first time playing in Lansdowne Road and, as I've mentioned many times before, I kept the mud from the boot in a plastic bag for a long, long time afterwards.'

The coach at the time was a Jesuit Jim Moran who would have played things very calmly, very coolly, and he said that Ollie should play the match, rather than the occasion. 'That would have been very much his mentality at that time, "It's just another game of rugby." I was very proud of the medal. There wouldn't be anything near the media hype that is there now. And, today, you add in the satellite station Setanta – it's now on television. The exposure would be just more modest in my time.'

The following season, he had the medal in his pocket and the temperament to match the emotional longevity of a cup final campaign as well. Belvedere faced Terenure in the final, their long-time adversaries. 'They had beaten us solidly at U9s, U10s all the way up, twice a year, every year. OK, we beat them at U16, but they had half their team playing for a senior team that day. It didn't look good when, in Senior Cup year, we lost to Terenure before Christmas, 25–3. In the final, we were losing 10–3 after twenty minutes and we were looking at another drubbing by this Terenure team. Suddenly, we turned it around. Whatever happened, we won 20–10. Michael Hickey, who would be a brother of David Hickey – of the Dubs teams of the 1970s – was a superb place-kicker. He could kick them from anywhere and, in fact, that day against Terenure, he kicked four penalties from all sorts of angles and distances and that helped us win the cup. He was the man of the match. They're great memories and there's nothing that I experienced or achieved in my subsequent career that surpassed the experience of representing the school and winning a couple of cup medals.'

Ollie returned to Lansdowne Road in 2005 to watch his alma mater lift the Leinster Schools Senior Cup for the first since his team of all talents walked the steps of the West Stand in 1972.

'Over half the 1972 team live outside of Ireland now. It was a sign of our era I suppose, but we got as many as we could for a function in Old Belvedere before the match and then we walked down from Anglesea Road. We all agreed afterwards that the sweetest sound we had ever heard was the sound of the final whistle going in Lansdowne Road that day. We said we can get on with our lives now but, suddenly, then we are consigned to history!'

Campbell scored his first try at the ground in 1973 in a provincial schools victory for Leinster, but later came a memory that still burns brightly within him.

The occasion? England's visit to Dublin during the Troubles. 'There was such emotion, gratitude and admiration all rolled into one for the English team that day. That was certainly a very poignant moment.'

In 1973, it was England's turn to travel to Lansdowne and John Pullin's side arrived despite paramilitary threats (in 1972, Wales and Scotland refused to play at Lansdowne because of the threats players had received). Campbell shouldn't even have been there that day. He had no ticket. 'My dad was allowed to drive down Lansdowne Road, drop myself and Albert Horton, an elderly man, outside and I was only to talk my way in, bring Mr Horton up to his seat and then leave the ground. But I didn't leave. I ended up sitting on the steps of the West Upper and, as long as I'll live, I will never forget the applause when the English team ran out. It really does to this day send a shiver up my spine, and I also remember how Ireland captain Willie John McBride, sensing what was happening, held back his team from running out so that the applause rang out even more.'

Campbell made his entrance on the international stage in January 1976 against Australia – he arrived like a whirlwind, but left the field with a whimper. The loud thud within his head was the sound of his kicking game imploding, but, in a game of inches, the misses just came down to sheer fractions.

The circumstances surrounding the disclosure of his first cap came at the Shelbourne Hotel twenty-four hours before the game and were rather casual. Typical old school. He says he was probably eating a steak when Roly Meates gave a tap on his shoulder and said, 'Ollie, Barry's out [Barry McGann], you're in for tomorrow. Congratulations.'

The week before, he played for Old Belvedere against Galwegians on a pitch that would have resembled the Battle of the Somme, a match that should never have gone ahead. 'Probably the worst match that I played in my life and that was my preparation for playing at Lansdowne Road the following week!'

He was glad of a calm dressing room and felt humbled amongst the legends. The pre-match speeches from Meates and captain Mike Gibson were less of the chest-thumping variety and more intrinsic motivation, to use modern parlance. The tendency, it seemed, around that time would have been to signal your intent through loud passionate blasts from the heart. 'Roly was very quietly spoken, a cerebral guy in his approach to rugby as was Mike Gibson, which was fantastic. On that particular day, it was very low-key which, to be honest, suited me much better than the rabble-rousing stuff that would often have gone on around that time.'

The game? Best forgotten if you were Ollie or Irish. 'And it wasn't even a full house. They beat us 20–10. I had a 100 per cent record with my kicking – I missed four out of four! But they were all by just a fraction. I was dropped and I didn't play for Ireland again until the infamous Australian tour of 1979. It was the only team I was ever dropped from, from when I started Under-9s until I retired. I was one of five new caps that day – Johnny Cantrell, Phelim McLoughlin (got his one and only cap aged thirty-four) and John Robbie who is a great friend of mine. Johnny was twenty and I was twenty-one. I have a photograph at home and the two of us look like twelve year old kids. I'd be thinking sometimes, "What were we doing there?"'

This time there was no mud collected and preserved to go alongside his Belvo souvenir, just

6

a thought that glory was fleeting and obscurity was forever. Ollie wasn't too inclined to read news-papers when he was playing, but the temptation to reach for the experts' views was too great to resist the following Monday. 'I was in the College of Commerce in Rathmines at the time. I remember going to college on the Monday after the match and it took all day to even open *The Irish Times*. I told myself that there wasn't much good that could be said. I remember reading the report from the bottom to the top – literally starting at the bottom and working my way up through it. I said it to the writer, Ned Van Esbeck, over Christmas 2005 – I'd never said it before and I thought it was about time that I did – that he didn't even mention my name, which was fantastic because he really couldn't have said many positive things. So the fact that I was young, the fact that it was my first cap, I was only twenty-one and all the rest of it. It wasn't the fact that I missed a few kicks that we lost – we were outplayed. I really appreciated what Ned did and I've never forgotten that. After reading it I said, "What a relief to not even to be mentioned." If I'd been aware of any criticism out there, well, I would have been affected by it. It all happened a bit quickly. I was too young and wasn't ready and I'd be the first to admit it.'

He also wasn't ready when a mysterious brown envelope came through the letter box six months later. 'Today you're formally presented with your cap at a function the evening after the

Ollie Campbell was at first-centre, Tony Ward at out-half in this Five Nations match against England in 1981. Campbell is being tackled by Steve Smith (9) and John Scott of England. Ireland lost 6–10.

Despite risks to personal safety as the Troubles raged in the North, England travelled to play Ireland in the Five Nations on 10 February 1973 at Lansdowne and, since that day, there has always been a special welcome for England for their biennial date in Dublin.

In 1972, Scotland and Wales had refused to travel to Dublin because of fears for their players' safety and their decision rankled deeply within the IRFU and, especially, with Ireland's players who felt that the Grand Slam was within their grasp, as they had already beaten France and England away.

Before John Pullin brought his team to Ireland, lock Peter Larter opted not to travel because, being an RAF officer, he felt threatened. Full-back Sam Doble also asked to be excused. Neither played for England again.

Willie John McBride also played a part in helping bring English and Lions luminary David Duckham to Dublin. Duckham's wife, Jean, feared for his safety but, after a phone conversation with his Lions team-mate, England's most celebrated player of the time decided to travel. In fact, McBride pleaded with him to go and, in his autobiography, said that the match would have been postponed if Duckham didn't travel. 'What David and Jean did at that time for the future of rugby football was incalculable,' he wrote.

On the day, Willie John held his team back under the West Stand to allow England to run first onto the green paddock of Lansdowne to receive a standing ovation and rapturous applause that lasted for five minutes.

That Pullin's men came to Dublin demonstrated almost Churchillian valour and courage in the face of threat and provocation. England lost the match 18–9, but, at the post-match dinner in the Shelbourne Hotel, Pullin uttered the immortal words, 'We may not be very good – but at least we turn up' which drew an impassioned applause from the black-tie gathering.

9

match. I got my cap in a brown envelope in the post with not so much as a compliment slip in June of that year – that would have been quite standard as well. So things have moved on a lot. And to show how long ago it was, after winning your new cap, you were allowed keep your jersey and your socks. But, if it wasn't your first cap and if you wanted to keep your jersey, it cost £10 and your socks cost £3.'

When he arrived home from Australia after kicking Ireland to two test wins in 1979, Campbell was a home-town hero. But he had taken the place of Tony Ward on tour so the battle for the Number 10 shirt intensified and the attention their relative merits drew as out-halves was the talk of the nation – and divided the country. Before the 1980 Five Nations, due mainly to their heroics Down Under, Ireland were tipped to win the Triple Crown but, after losing away to England in Twickenham, Scotland came to Lansdowne Road. The pressure was back on Ireland. And back on Ollie. 'We were tipped to win the Triple Crown that year because of what we'd done to Australia. Against England, we got a bit of a pasting really – 24–9 – so that was hopes of a Triple Crown blown to pieces.'

Ireland beat the Scots 22–15 thanks to Campbell's three penalties and drop goal and a conversion from Terry Kennedy's try. 'That would have been my first win for Ireland at Lansdowne Road. We beat Wales at home that year as well. Wales were probably still the team to beat and that was at the end of their long decade of dominance, so I'd say beating Wales carried more kudos to beating Scotland – that was certainly one not to forget.'

The Campbell–Ward debate raged yet again before the following year's Five Nations. Campbell started at 10 for the French game but, after a loss and in an effort to accommodate two of the brightest talents of the same era, Ward returned to out-half and Campbell moved to the centre. But it proved a difficult championship for the Irish as they went on to lose all their games narrowly.

'As Moss Keane says, "It was Ireland's best ever whitewash." I think we were in the lead in every game at half-time and we only lost every game by a score. Tommy Kiernan had taken over as coach at that stage and he was quite fantastic during that period. He kept saying we were doing the right thing, it's only a question of time, the wins will come, keep doing what we're doing. He was absolutely just fantastic.'

Going into the 1982 campaign, Ireland were aiming to bring a seven-game losing streak to an end and Campbell returned to out-half for that year's Five Nations. 'We beat Wales but nobody was talking about a Triple Crown – the only thing was the sheer relief of having broken a long, losing sequence. We went to England two weeks later and won 16–15, with Ginger McLoughlin's famous try. A fortnight after that, we had Scotland at home and, suddenly, the chance of a Triple Crown, which we hadn't done for thirty-three years – and we'd never won a Triple Crown at Lansdowne Road – seemed possible. So, all that again happened quite quickly and out of the blue. The only change in the pack that went on the tour to Australia in 1979 was Donal Lenihan in the second row so the pack was seasoned, they knew what they were about. In the backline, I

I crossed the line … at last: Ollie Campbell scores his first try for Ireland in front of the Wanderers Pavilion on 19 March 1983. Ireland beat England 25–15, Campbell scoring 21 points – a try, conversion and five penalty goals.

was the only one remaining from 1979, so suddenly I'm one of the veterans.'

He tried to put the atmosphere out of his head and one of his memories is for the whole of the second half playing into a gale-force wind. 'We only turned around 15–6 at half-time. So it wasn't a big enough lead. Most of the game seemed to have been played down the East Stand side. I don't think anyone on the East Stand sat down for the whole match – and, naturally, they were all standing up on the lower terrace – singing "Cockles and Mussels". I've often said it, but they sort of willed us to victory. They just would not have accepted anything but a victory and I think they were as responsible as anyone on the pitch for us winning that match.'

He remembers, too, the sound of silence after John Rutherford's try levelled matters. He says it was like having the television at full blast and suddenly pressing the mute button. 'If you go back to the first half and the John Rutherford score: a lineout about the halfway line on the East Stand side, Roy Laidlaw made a brilliant break fed John Rutherford and went racing under the posts. You could hear a pin drop. This wasn't in the script because that made it 6–6. We turned over 15–6 ahead, then Jim Rennick and Andy Irvine missed a couple at the start of the second half which would have made it a very uncomfortable ride in the second half, but we came through and it was just euphoria. Looking back on it now, a 21–12 win seems comfortable and, by and large, we were in control for most of the game but when Jonno went over for that try…

'I was brought up on the Grand Slam and Triple Crown winning teams of 1948 and 1949, the Jackie Kyles, the Karl Mullens, the George Nortons, the Bill McKays, the Des O'Briens – it's almost like I was there. My dad would talk particularly about Jackie Kyle, and all of my life they were my heroes, they were up on a pedestal – imagine winning a Triple Crown, a Grand Slam – and then you're on the next team to actually win a Triple Crown. That certainly wasn't lost on me – being the first Irish side to win a Triple Crown in Lansdowne Road for only the fifth time in Ireland's history.'

Many say it was Campbell's Triple Crown. He kicked six penalties and a drop goal that afternoon against Scotland, but his meticulous attention to detail had brought the man who would eat sleep and drink rugby to undergo intensive surgery to his place-kicking before Triple Crown day.

'I remember against England I hit a ball from about forty yards just to the left of the post. I hit it absolutely beautifully just hoping the wind would draw it in. And it never moved an inch and I was furious with that. So when we got back on the Sunday, I went straight to Anglesea Road with my five balls in the boot of the car, and I was probably out for a couple of hours just practising exactly from that spot. So, for whatever reason – and I had never done it before and never did it since – but 90 per cent of the kicks I took that day in the Scotland match were from that one spot on a field where I missed against England. Three minutes into the Scottish match – penalty for Ireland. Where is it from? From exactly the same spot as the one I missed in Twickenham! My feeling was that I could hit it with my eyes closed after I had hit two or three hundred from exactly that spot. Put it down, over the bar and we were away. So I suppose that day did make sense of all the practice.'

Campbell's late father, who played as a Louth county minor as well as being a prop with Suttonians, hardly ever missed an international at Lansdowne Road – and his enthusiasm rubbed off on young Seamus Oliver. Campbell talks of how his father 'got a great kick' out of his career and how it was his father who set those Lansdowne dreams alight when he tossed a new leather rugby ball to him in their back garden when he was six years old and said, 'If you catch this, you can keep it.' Campbell did.

One of Campbell's other earliest memories was going out on the pitch after the matches as a young lad. While his dad was having a couple of drinks in the Lansdowne or Wanderers pavilion, Ollie would be out on the field mainly using a pair of gloves rolled up as the ball and, if there were other kids around, that was fine. They'd knock around and it just seemed to go on for hours in the dark. Only the lights from the two pavilions kept their game alive. Ollie would always be Mike Gibson – drop kicking and grubber-kicking and running as any kid would do and then his dad would come out and they'd go home – but not for long.

Eye on the ball: Campbell, in classic pose, as Phil Orr and Willie Duggan admire his artistry.

Ciaran Fitzgerald

Hooker
1979–1986

Your imagination might not need too much prodding to picture Ciaran Fitzgerald pacing the dressing room under the West Stand at Lansdowne Road before either of the Triple Crown deciders against Scotland (1982) or England (1985). An army officer by day, in the dressing room Fitzie was equally adept at drilling his team, bringing presence and charisma and force of will to the entire Ireland squad.

You can't help but conjure an image of the Ireland hooker finger-wagging and giving instructions when he paced the room to gee up each player. Or an index finger pointed to his temple stressing the importance of mental toughness and of keeping your head when all around others might be losing theirs. And then, for good measure, you must factor in an appropriate level of 'colourful' language to capture the importance of it all.

Before Big Jack Charlton, Mick McCarthy and the giddiness of a soccer World Cup in Italy, Ireland had Ciaran Fitzgerald – rugby's Captain Fantastic. He was the original of the species and Lansdowne Road will hardly see his likes again.

No holding me back: Ciaran Fitzgerald breaks from a forest of white shirts during Ireland's Triple Crown match against England on 30 March 1985.

Lansdowne Road was packed and giddy for the Triple Crown decider in 1985. The win – for a few weeks at least – dimmed the horrible reality of economic depression and rising unemployment, symptoms of Ireland's lumbering economy of the 1980s. The nation's self-esteem was at an all-time low but at least Fitzie and his boys raised hope.

To underline Fitzgerald's legendary motivational skills we got a snapshot on television during that 1985 Triple Crown decider. It came in a moment of the match when Ireland was struggling. You didn't need to be the world's most qualified lip reader to interpret his immortal words during an interlude in the second half when he bellowed, 'Where's your f***ing pride?'

You almost stood to attention yourself.

It wasn't a premeditated outburst, but it came nevertheless from the heart and perhaps that vignette – as well as the free-flowing style of rugby they were encouraged to play – captured the free-spiritedness of Mick Doyle's team, a coach who inspired his players to be themselves. As Hugo MacNeill, who played full-back on that Triple Crown winning team, said, 'Doyle caught the spirit of an already confident group, he lit the touchpaper … it was youth gone mad, given its head.'

16

They didn't play in a straitjacket; it was rugby from the heart – just like Fitzie's moments of motivational genius.

Tony Ward describes Fitzgerald as the greatest-ever Ireland captain, and how can you dispute that – to lead Irish teams to two Triple Crowns (1982 and 1985), a share of the championship (1983), and a championship (1985) in the space of five years is a fine achievement.

Many considered the Connacht man the perfect choice as captain. From a province that has always been the poor relation when it came to international selection, Fitzgerald brought a new dimension to his role as captain. He empowered those around him to play with a cause.

His rise to instant recognition, to an elevated plateau in the story of Irish international sport, is part fairytale, part romance. As a boy growing up in Loughrea, County Galway, he joined the local boxing club and, if in later years showed fighting qualities as a rugby player, he was a real scrapper inside the ring, winning two All-Ireland championships. He was an avid GAA fan and attended each of Galway's three-in-a-row All-Ireland football wins between 1964 and 1966 in Croke Park. On the field, he distinguished himself as a promising hurler at Garbally College and, in 1970, impressed the Galway minor selectors who put him on a team alongside Iggy Clarke and Sean Silke in an All-Ireland minor final against Cork, where he marked Martin O'Doherty.

It was during his early teenage years that he remembers travelling to Lansdowne for the first time, and the game left an indelible mark on the young sportsman.

'I came up with my father, a friend of his and his son. I remember watching Wales play Ireland. I must have been thirteeen at the time. I hadn't played rugby, but I remember watching it from the South Terrace and saying something to my father like, "I could play that, I'd like to play it." That was my first introduction to rugby really.'

After being knocked out of the Connacht college's senior hurling competition early in his Leaving Cert year, Fitzgerald was approached to try his hand at being hooker for the school team. 'They were stuck for a hooker to play against Blackrock. It was my last year in Garbally – they weren't allowed play cup rugby at the time because the local bishop felt that the rugby ethos was a corrupting influence on our Catholic sensibilities. I remember playing that match – I didn't have a clue what the rules were but I remember reading offside and other laws of the game going up in the bus. We played Blackrock and gave away loads of penalties. I played a couple of matches that year and then I went on to UCG and played with them in the Connacht League. It wasn't long then until I was making my mark with Connacht.'

Fitzgerald made his senior home debut for Ireland against Scotland in 1980. He wasn't too intimidated by Lansdowne – he even went as far as to say he was inspired by the environment. 'I don't think I ever got that nervous about any match. I always felt going out that I couldn't wait to get out there and the first thing you notice – as anyone will tell you – is the roar. Lansdowne Road is so compressed, the crowd is really in on top of you. And I will always remember that. I remember saying to myself, "How could you not play well in an environment like this?"

They always say that the good players on a stage like that would be better players whereas the guys who are not as mentally strong will suffer a bit because they get distracted because it's just one big roar. And, in my time anyhow, the one thing about Lansdowne Road was the constant roar. I think the proximity of the touchline seats as well added to the atmosphere.'

As a hooker, he had the onerous task of communicating calls to his lineout jumpers and a scrum-half in the Lansdowne din. Amidst the relentlessness of test rugby, he smiles at the proximity of the fans, of how he found himself stopping for a chat with some supporters or with the person who was handing back the ball. Often he had to coax back a ball – a priceless piece of memorabilia – from a supporter's grasp. 'In the old days, when there weren't ball boys, the ball would be in amongst the crowd. You wouldn't get it back immediately, you then would have to interact with them, nod or something like that. Only then was it brought back to you again. Even when you're knackered in the second half, it had to be done. I would always remember comments from people encouraging me and that would lift me further because I would be going in to get the ball whereas other lads wouldn't get as close to them.'

Fitzgerald remembers days in Lansdowne when the noise level reached such a pitch he could only communicate lineout moves by hand signal or through his scrum-half who would then relay the information to his jumpers. 'It was difficult in Parc des Princes and Cardiff Arms Park when it was full din, but I just think that Lansdowne Road is a far more intimate ground than any of the other ones because of the proximity of the people. I think it's a reason a lot of the visitors used to hate playing in Lansdowne. One reason was because the Irish used go bananas there. The passion in the old days was a huge factor and the Lansdowne crowd was always part of that. And the breezes around Lansdowne Road were unlike any other ground. You'd think you're playing with the wind and suddenly it's coming against you.'

Fitzgerald played in an era when there was little, if any, of the finely choreographed lineout moves of today. Organised mayhem might be one description of the old days. 'It was a bit of a lottery. In those days, there was no lifting in the lineout. As the late Mick Doyle used to say, "You were pushing in the lineouts and jumping in the scrums."'

Fitzgerald's first outing at Lansdowne Road in January 1980 passed off smoothly when Ireland triumphed 22–15 against Scotland. He says his mother didn't go to Lansdowne but stayed behind in the Shelbourne Hotel lighting candles and saying decades of the rosary.

He believes the tour to Australia the previous summer – where he earned his first cap – steeled him for what lay ahead in the Five Nations and he felt he had earned some respect from his team-mates, grizzled old warriors like Willie Duggan, Phil Orr and Fergus Slattery. 'The benefit for me going into Lansdowne Road is that I had been with the Ireland team for six and a half weeks out in Australia. I felt when I came back that I was a hardened tourist, a member of the squad and because of that had earned a bit of respect from the other guys as well. I didn't feel like the novice or young garsún going out in the first match. I was confident I could deliver on the first day as well. For me, it was a much easier transition. I wasn't afraid going out that I was going to make a clown of myself in front of all these people who knew me.'

He scored a try in the Welsh match at Lansdowne Road that March, and remembers the volcanic eruption after he crossed the line. Ireland won 21–7. His mother's candles were burning brightly in the Shelbourne that afternoon.

Fitzgerald missed the entire 1980–1981 season after dislocating his shoulder in a club match with St Mary's. The 1981 Five Nations saw Ireland lose all their games with a combined total of just thirteen points, but Fitzgerald could not believe how Ireland had suffered a whitewash given the possession they enjoyed in each outing. When he returned the following season, Fitzgerald took over the captaincy from Fergus Slattery. He had an inclination there would be a change and prepared himself mentally in case he was chosen.

He remembers a group of players low on morale and noticed that many were annoyed by the criticism of their play and a pack labelled 'Dad's Army'. 'A lot of fellows were coming to the end of their careers. The Mossies [Keane], the Willies [Duggan], the John O'Ds [O'Driscoll], the

Running from the madding crowd: Euphoria breaks out as Fitzgerald and Michael Kiernan make their way through the crowd and down the steps under the West Stand moments after winning the 1982 Triple Crown.

Slatts [Fergus Slattery] of this world were clearly fed up. They were pissed off because there was dog's abuse that year and people didn't want to finish up like that.'

The timing of Fitzgerald's coronation as captain could not have been better. Yes, he was younger than many of his peers and his army background might have allowed him to slip on the mask of a sergeant major. But he didn't dictate. Fitzie admonished players without alienating them. He inspired but was never insipid. He once described himself as 'sensitive to people and curious about people', and his people skills coupled with Tom Kiernan's coaching brought about a first Triple Crown in thirty-two years. More importantly, it was the first Triple Crown to be won at Lansdowne Road.

'There's no precedence for captains – everyone is different, there's no captaincy school in the IRFU. From my point of view, I wanted to get Moss Keane, Willie Duggan, Slatts, all these guys moving and once they moved everything else happened and fellows followed them. They weren't difficult to motivate because they were all pissed off, labelled "Dad's Army" or "on the scrapheap", "gone". I used say, "Is this the way we're going to finish or not?" Even though I was relatively youngish – more than they were – they accepted that what I was saying was the way to go. I didn't feel shy about saying it because, at the end of the day, the older guys weren't going to finish like that and the younger guys like Trevor Ringland and Paul Dean could create once the guys did it up front. Those were the tactics.'

A look at the video of the 1982 Scotland match shows Fitzgerald impressing upon Ginger McLoughlin, the Shannon prop, to give one more big scrum for the cause.

For many, 1982 was Ollie Campbell's Triple Crown, his six penalty goals and one drop goal propelled Ireland to a 21–12 win over the Scots. 'That day against Scotland everyone was up for it, so it was a question of keeping it as cool and as calm as you could and then, in the last few minutes before leaving the dressing room, you would hit the few vocals or whatever. You'd be pulling some fellows off the ceiling and some fellows you'd be doing the opposite to. Everybody is different and people had their own routines. You'd know when guys were uptight – they'd go to the same spot and things had to be the way they always wanted them. Fellows slot into their own zone because you have to get to a certain pitch mentally before you get out of the dressing room. Because once you get out there, the first ten or fifteen minutes of any match like that, you have to be really impervious to any noise, injuries or pain.

'Were Scotland as formidable as us? I think we had the stronger pack. I think the biggest thing about Scotland that day was that they were very good on the offside line or killing ball on the ground and we had to be fairly physical in the loose. There was absolutely no problem that day – I'll never forget the sight of Scots going down on the ball and being rucked out of it. Irish fellows were hitting rucks harder than I had ever seen. And, even with that, the Scots still put their bodies on the line. I think most of Ollie's penalties that day came from them killing the ball or coming in from the side. And that's the sort of day it was – they were a difficult team to put away. Scotland had very good teams right through the 1980s and they played a very fast game. And that's what you had to deal with.'

Fitzgerald's favourite Lansdowne memory was the 1985 Triple Crown win. He was injured in 1984, a season when Ireland got the Wooden Spoon. But the arrival of Mick Doyle brought with it sweeping changes and a new attacking philosophy. The country liked Doyler's way and got behind the arrival of a new generation of Ireland players. 'There was only Donal Lenihan and Phil Orr left from 1982 and all the rest were young guns with Paul Dean at out-half, Brendan Mullins, Michael Kieran – they were all young and talented, new kids on the block, full of enthusiasm, who had a great attitude to the game and didn't see a problem with doing anything. It was probably the most enjoyable year I played rugby because there was no expectation from anybody. We were just a side that had come together. You could see in the training there was a special thing developing there from within inside the squad, not from outside. Mick, in fairness, let it all develop and let us do our thing. So the more we played together and trained together, the more we developed as a unit.'

Ireland's rugby that season, particularly away from home in Murrayfield and Cardiff Arms Park, was a thrilling concoction of fifteen-man rugby. Here was a team playing with a real *joie de vivre*, which coloured matches with spontaneity and splendidly worked tries. 'Looking back at the tries scored that season, they were ahead of their time in terms of skill. We had a vision to look for those sort of the scores. If 1982 was all about forward strength, in 1985 we had a young pack and real dynamic back-row in Carr, Spillane and Matthews and loads of speed in the backs. In Cardiff, we lost the battle up front, but the backs played some brilliant rugby that day. It was all teed up for the last day. And I'd say the only pressure that came on the lads was for the last match because people realised that we could actually play good rugby. All of our games that year were won against the odds. The first match over in Murrayfield was ding-dong. They had the upper hand near the end and we produced a score in the last five to eight minutes with Trevor Ringland's try in the corner. That was a well executed try.'

On to Lansdowne Road and those immortal words – 'Where's your f***ing pride' – one wonders where they came from. 'I don't even like repeating it. Very rarely would I repeat it. I just knew my own thought process at the time. I really felt we were backed into the corner. We were trying to keep the tide out because, physically, they were a much bigger team and the match was played in real wet heavy conditions. We were getting out-mauled in the second half, smothered nearly. Guys were getting tired and you could see it. I don't know where that came from. It might have been out of pure desperation. There was nothing else there to think of. And that's about it.'

Michael Kiernan's drop goal won Ireland the Triple Crown and Fitzgerald will forever remember the scenes in the immediate aftermath of that win. If Munster have built up a special rapport with their fans in today's European Cup, then this team gripped the imagination of the success-starved Irish in the 1980s. 'After the win in 1985, I never experienced anything like it.

I got in under the stand to be interviewed after the match, trying to get my breath back again. The next thing a security guy comes in and says, "Ciaran, you're going to have to go outside." And I said, "Serious – what for?" "You're going to have to go outside, Ciaran, because the crowd want you outside." I had never heard that one before at a rugby game. I remember going outside and up to that VIP place, standing up on the plastic chairs to just acknowledge the crowd and what they did. I nearly broke my neck because these chairs were flipping and I was wearing my big boots. You'd associate speaking to the crowd with Croke Park rather than Lansdowne. The crowd, the support, the ground, everything – I'll always especially remember that one.'

For someone who understood the importance of club, Fitzgerald fondly remembers St Mary's Leinster Senior Cup win over Lansdowne in 1987. Business commitments forced Fitzie to retire from international rugby, but Mary's filled the void. 'We were against a very fancied Lansdowne team who had beaten us in a league match by thirty-odd points three weeks beforehand. We had a team of kids playing against them. It was totally against form at the time. All the Mary's supporters went bananas afterwards. It was my last outing with them at Lansdowne and it meant a lot to me to be playing in the cup win. To win it at headquarters was something special too.'

Fitzgerald was coach of the Irish team in 1991 and almost masterminded the greatest of all victories against Australia in that year's World Cup quarter-final at Lansdowne Road.

In his efforts to cultivate a lasting team spirit, Fitzgerald took the team out of the city centre to Finnstown House in Lucan for the duration of the tournament, organised a weekend away in Kerry where the players were spotted playing hurling in Sneem GAA grounds. He recalls Kerry Radio trying to make a big deal out of it and stirring up some controversy that the Ireland team entered the field without getting permission. Fitzgerald says they got the go-ahead from Sneem GAA officials and the squad enjoyed a good game of rounders there.

'Everyone was up for the Australia match – I think silly mistakes cost us at the end. We didn't have a star-studded team from 1 to 15, but it was great squad, a great group of people. People were critical of Neil Francis in his ability to take pain and pressure but I thought that was one of his best matches for Ireland. There were guys like Donal [Lenihan] beside him and Dessie Fitzgerald in front of him and Philip Matthews behind and they were real winners in terms of being mean and hard and that's what you had to be.'

When Gordon Hamilton discovered untapped reserves of energy late in the second half to run in for what seemed to be a match-winning try, Ireland looked safe. And then … the restart. 'I said all we need to do is put this away. I knew the clock was ticking away. But Australia came down field and the rest is history.'

Hamilton's try was, however, one of the great Lansdowne moments. 'Gordon was a very good footballer. He came from a junior club. We picked him up and he came up to the standard very quickly. To score a try the way he did against an Australian side that had all the bells and whistles of running rugby was a great achievement. I couldn't believe it – to see this fellow passing down through the centre. I remember sitting in the stands and seeing this fellow going and saying, "Jesus Christ, we're going to score here!" I couldn't talk after that match. As a player, you'd always have something to say. It's worse as a coach. As a player, at least you're out there and you're doing it. When I went to the dressing room, I felt I had to say something though. As a coach, you have to be up for the guys, you're trying to get them back on their feet and give them credit where credit is due and all of that. I remember going to the after-match function at the Berkeley Court and Bob Dwyer was there. It was early afternoon and I couldn't eat. I was putting salad into a plate at this buffet knowing I wouldn't eat it and Dwyer comes over to me and starts talking about the match to me. I was in no mood to talk and was trying to be polite to him. But that's sport. He could not believe the performance of the Irish. After Gordon's try, he thought it was over and talking to [Michael] Lynagh afterwards, he couldn't believe it either. He was captain and he was trying to come up with a move. They didn't have a move. He couldn't think. Suddenly, the ball arrived in their hands and they played the skip which they usually do in training. They thought they were gone as well.'

Today, Fitzgerald works as co-commentator for RTÉ Radio on international days at Lansdowne Road. He enjoys analysing but admits he has his hands full trying to keep animated commentator Michael Corcoran from jumping out of the broadcasting box during moments of high drama. 'Often, he belts somebody beside him with a microphone. Someday, I'll have to tie him down or else get him a parachute because when he does go over the side, he is going to have a big fall!'

Mick Galwey

Lock

It's every Kerry boy's dream to win an All-Ireland football medal and, at only nineteen, Mick Galwey was part of the panel when the Kingdom defeated Tyrone in the 1986 final. It seemed Croke Park would become his field of dreams, but in little over five years, he was running out on Lansdowne Road in an Ireland shirt.

When invited down to Castle Island RFC in his late teens to help alleviate the club's problems in the lineout, the Currow native admits he developed an instant passion for the game. He was, what you might have then called, a Kerry dual player, torn between Gaelic football and rugby, but it wasn't unusual for lads in Currow and Castle Island to mix their days between the round and oval ball. Those whom he respected at the time advised him that, if he remained loyal to rugby, he'd play for Ireland.

It was a crossroads in his young career and his head was spinning about which direction to take. For a Kerry lad so conscious of his GAA roots, he took the road less travelled. Yet he'd be following in the footsteps of his

25

Currow neighbours Mick Doyle and Moss Keane who had also represented Ireland in previous eras. 'Gaillimh' completed the trinity from this tiny parish in north Kerry to wear the green. 'It was a very hard decision to make because, to be honest, a lot of the people would have felt I owed something back to the GAA because of the fact that I won an All-Ireland medal. But I felt I owed it to myself. Looking back, I certainly made the right decision. Kerry didn't win another All-Ireland for another eleven years – I doubt if I would have made any major difference! My rugby career took off on a gradual rise.'

Mick Galwey earned his first cap for Ireland against France at Lansdowne Road on 2 February 1991. He was driving from Kilkenny to Kerry when he turned the radio dial to the 2FM news and learned that he had made the team. His heart pumping with excitement, he stopped the car in Clonmel to ring home and his friends at Castle Island RFC. They had all heard the news bulletin just like him.

He remembers he made his debut alongside five others: London Irish scrum-half Rob Saunders, Simon Geoghegan of Connacht, NIFC's Gordon Hamilton, Brian Rigney of Greystones and Brian Robinson of Ballymena.

The phone calls from well-wishers poured in during the week but he particularly remembers the advice from neighbour Moss Keane and only wished that his neighbour from Currow had played in his era, his easy humour and Kerry ways would have calmed Mick's nerves.

He got advice from other unexpected sources too. At a function in Ballymena the week before his debut, he and Brian Robinson got chatting to Syd Millar and Willie John McBride. He was in exalted company but Millar's words resonated with him afterwards. 'He said, "Best of luck next Saturday. Forget about the ball for the first ten minutes!" That's coming from a fellow who has been there and done everything. I would have known Syd Millar from what I saw and read – as a player for Ireland and the Lions and he coached and managed as well.'

The team stayed in the Westbury Hotel the weekend of his first cap and Galwey will never forget walking up Grafton Street towards St Stephen's Green and the crowd opening before them as the team made their way onto the bus. 'As a young fellow, I remember seeing the bus driving to the match and being on it this time was a great thrill. I roomed those couple of nights with John 'Packo' Fitzgerald – he was kind of a mentor of the time. In fairness, he looked after me.'

The nerves were jangling around inside him in the dressing room under the West Stand beforehand. 'All these emotions were saying to me "This is it, this is my chance, this is what it's all about, this is what I've been waiting to do for a long time."' It was more than a baptism of fire for Gaillimh, particularly against the notoriously abrasive French. In the 1980s, he had watched near anarchy break out at a ruck and, the previous season, he had watched the intensity of the exchanges between Ireland and France on television. Galwey is not afraid to admit that forward exchanges in his early days were barbaric. 'Everything happened out there. Obviously, gouging and kicking fellows was unacceptable but it happened in some matches.' He knew his debut would be a memory to stay with him for ever, but the French stud marks tattooed onto his back were a decoration he did not expect to be living with for a few weeks afterwards. For his first lineout, he put Millar's words into action. It was a case of getting your retaliation in first. 'I remember France had this big brute of a fellow, Michel Tachdjian, and he did all kinds of damage in their previous match in Paris against Scotland. I remember the first lineout was going across the top. I just barely got him before he got me. It was just as well I went across because, otherwise, my head would have been taken off. It was a case of protecting yourself and laying down the marker. In fairness, the match carried on then. I remember getting a few right slaps during the match, serious slaps, like, knees into the head, a boot into the back of the head – there were no video refs there that time, no touch judges flagging, no citing commissioners. It was a hard game. You had to learn how to survive. It was the law of the jungle out there.'

Currow's Mick Galwey makes his Ireland debut against France on 24 January 1991. 'I remember getting a few right slaps during the match.'

Galwey and Ireland survived until half-time taking a surprise 10–6 interval lead, but if they dared to dream, they were given a dose of reality when Serge Blanco 'an artist in motion' was instrumental in spoiling Galwey's Lansdowne debut. The Biarritz and French full-back set up the decisive try that consigned Ireland to a 13–21 defeat. 'We actually did very well against France that day. I know they beat us towards the end, but it was the norm at the time against such French sides. We certainly put up a great battle. But my biggest memory remains that it was a hard game.'

Galwey was part of Ciaran Fitzgerald's World Cup squad in the autumn of 1991, but wasn't amongst the first-choice locks for the tournament. He played in Ireland's second group match against Japan at Lansdowne Road, a game Ireland won 32–16. 'Ralph gave as good a kicking display as I have seen in a long time. He kicked twenty points [four penalties and two conversions] while Noel Mannion scored two tries and Brian O'Hara got the other.' Donal Lenihan was picked at 4 in the lineout in the final pool game against Scotland and also in the World Cup quarter-final against Australia, but Gaillimh never felt excluded from team preparations. He noticed a great spirit develop within the squad, a bond that grew stronger even after a getaway trip to his native County Kerry. 'We came back from Scotland on a Sunday, flew to Dublin, and from there to Farranfore in Kerry. We checked into Parknasilla outside Kenmare for a bit of R and R,

27

because, after the Murrayfield match, it took the lads about three days to recover. We also played a game of rounders in Sneem GAA pitch and I was saying to myself, "I was here three or four years ago playing Gaelic football for Currow." Then we went back up to Finnstown House in Lucan to prepare for the Australians.'

Ireland were within minutes of creating the biggest upset in world rugby after Gordon Hamilton ran in for a try that nudged Ireland 18–12 in front with only four minutes left on the clock. 'When Gordon Hamilton got his try, I was sitting on the bench. I wasn't subbing but I remember sitting alongside John Fitzgerald, and we were jumping up and down hugging each other because we felt we were going to have another three weeks of this. Unfortunately, Australia came back and got their try – a piece of Michael Lynagh magic – and it was one of the most disappointing atmospheres ever seen in Lansdowne Road. Would we have beaten New Zealand the following week or England in the final? I don't know. But some people were saying that, if we had beaten Australia, we would have won the World Cup.'

Galwey might never have worn a green jersey in Lansdowne Road again after suffering a serious neck injury in a club game in 1993. Six weeks before touching down in Currow Corner, he lay in a hospital bed in a neck brace. He was one of the first rugby players to have an MRI scan and was told by a doctor that he would never play rugby again. He was given the bad news on a Sunday morning but, five days later, was given the all clear and lined for Shannon on the Saturday.

'I missed training that week but was straight out of the brace and into a match. There was no time to feel sorry for myself, straight back into the action and thankfully, with a bit of luck, I got back into the Irish team. That scare certainly made me appreciate the game even more. Being told that you won't play again because of an injury – that's your worst nightmare.'

He played against France at Number 8 but partnered Paddy Johns in the second-row against Wales. 'Eric Elwood had just made his debut a fortnight earlier against Wales in Cardiff where we won 19–14. Simon Geoghegan was at his best at the time, as were Philip Danaher, Vincent Cunningham and Michael Bradley, who was captain. We had a very good backline.' The Johns–Galwey partnership was renewed for the England match, but they were facing a formidable duo in Martin Bayfield and Wade Dooley.

> ### CURROW CORNER
>
> Where the West Stand meets the Havelock Square End of Lansdowne Road, the corner area of the field is known as 'Currow Corner'. Mick Doyle touched down on this famous piece of real estate against Wales in 1969; Moss Keane repeated the deed on the same patch against Scotland in 1980 and, in 1993, Mick Galwey scored a famous try there against an England side aiming for a Grand Slam.

Down in Currow Corner: Galwey helps secure Ireland an unexpected 17-3 win over England by scoring the game's only try in 'Currow Corner'. 'I didn't realise it but my sister Mary was sitting near the corner. She jumped over the railing and gave me a kiss.'

'I wasn't an out and out lineout jumper, Paddy Johns was at 2 marking Martin Bayfield, I was at 4 marking Wade Dooley, they were big men. To put it mildly, we got stuck in.'

There was also a strong Munster contingent in the pack and Galwey felt at home. 'Terry Kingston was playing, Claw [Peter Clohessy] was there, Pat O'Hara was there – what a great player O'Hara was. He was what I'd call "a player's player". There was a head-to-head with himself and Peter Winterbottom – Winterbottom made the Lions after. But they both had a clash of heads. Winterbottom went down and got umpteen stitches across his head. But O'Hara got up and played on. I'm not saying that incident defines O'Hara but that's the sort of fellow he was.'

Elwood was having one of those dream days for an out-half, Galwey remembers, and the Connacht man, with five minutes remaining, arced over a drop goal to push Ireland into a 12–3 lead. Then one of Galwey's favourite moments arrived when he notched a try to put the seal on an unexpected Irish victory. 'I remember there was a ball tapped back off a lineout. Phil Danaher was marking Will Carling in the middle of the field. Carling was trying to go around him, Danaher tackled him, turned over the ball. I remember Ritchie Wallace took it on, one or two of the backs then I took it on and arrived at the next ruck. Michael Bradley decided to go down the blind, I just happened to be in right place at the right time, I took the pass, drove over and I remember Tony Underwood on top of me making the last ditch tackle.'

There was an outbreak of emotion from the touchline seat when supporters spilled onto the field to share in Galwey's moment. Amongst the giddy throng was his sister Mary who had flown in from New York the morning of the match. She rushed over to give her brother a hug and, as it turned out, it was the closest Galwey got to a conversation with his sister for another eight weeks. 'I didn't realise it but my sister was sitting near the corner. I left a ticket for her in the Berkeley Court – it would have been for the centre of the West Stand. Anyway, the ticket got mislaid or someone robbed it. Then she met someone on the street and bought a ticket off him for face value. She ended up down in the corner. She got so excited that, after I scored the try, she jumped out over the railing. She's embarrassed by it to this day but I thought it was a lovely moment.

'After beating England in 1993, I remember being carried off the pitch, some poor misfortunate under me. Eric Elwood was too. It doesn't happen anymore. That's the way it has gone and there will be no going back. I remember seeing Ireland winning Triple Crowns there and seeing Moss Keane even being carried off the pitch.'

Mick Galwey has been dropped a total of fifteen times from various Ireland teams but, from 2000 to 2002, he was a more regular figure on the Irish team and played a big part in helping Ronan O'Gara, Peter Stringer and Shane Horgan find their feet on their international debuts against Scotland in 2000. Galwey had been dropped again for the previous match against England but was recalled for the Scotland game a week later at Lansdowne Road. 'Thankfully, I never got bitter and, thankfully, I never threw in the towel. I look back on it now and at the time it was hard to take. It got to me, maybe I didn't show it but I was lucky to have Shannon and lucky to have Munster. Sometimes, there were players there who you felt you were better than them, sometimes there were things happening with Ireland you would love to have been involved. The most important thing now is that I kept my dignity about me, I kept going and I got my chance again and I came back and, eventually, I was put out to grass. But my time was up at that stage. I was happy enough to walk away from it. I was thirty-five years of age and I had done my bit. Then, I knew I wasn't good enough to lead Ireland to the next World Cup.'

Gaillimh's recall for the Scotland Six Nations game in 2000 came on the back of sterling individual performances on a Munster side cutting a dash in the European Cup. 'Munster had done well, and Ronan, Peter and John Hayes got capped together against Scotland as well as Shane Horgan and Simon Easterby – it's great to see that they're still the backbone of the present Ireland team. At Twickenham, I came on at half-time, scored a try and was picked then for the next match. If we hadn't beaten Scotland, the likes of the O'Garas, the Stringers and these lads, including myself, would have suffered as well. Because I knew if we didn't win that day, I would never have played for Ireland again, but we did. We went 10–0 down and I thought "here we go again" – I was involved with Irish teams where you go 10–0 down and you wouldn't come back but there was something special about that team. We came back, we played well right to the end.'

It was thought that Ireland coach Warren Gatland had taken a major gamble in blooding so many new players, but it paid rich dividends. 'He often took gambles, some of them paid off, some of them didn't. But we all knew if we f****ed up that day, I knew I would never touch the grass of Lansdowne Road ever again. I was brought back because Munster were going well and the public were saying, "Bring Galwey back." That was putting fierce pressure on me. Thankfully, it worked out.'

Galwey took another kick in the guts when he was dropped for Ireland's trip to Murrayfield in September 2001 in the Six Nations, delayed because of the outbreak of foot and mouth disease in Ireland and Great Britain in the spring. 'At the start of the season, I was part of the teams that beat Italy and France and then for the next match back against Scotland in Murrayfield, Warren Gatland dropped me. In fairness to him, he said he was planning for the next World Cup. Scotland won and

Munster lift-off: John Hayes (left) and Peter Clohessy (right) lift Mick Galwey to win a lineout against Scotland in the 2000 Six Nations at Lansdowne. Peter Stringer (9) looks on.

then, the following weekend, Munster were playing Harlequins over in England. I played well, Warren came up to me and shook my hand and said, "We'll see you at training next week." I said, "Fair enough, I'll be there." I admire him for saying what he said. He told me straight up that he got it wrong, no other Irish coach had ever done that. We played Wales in the Millennium Stadium and beat them, and the following week faced England at Lansdowne Road.'

This was another one of those momentous Irish occasions on a day when England were going for the Grand Slam. Ireland denied them. Galwey might not have got a try but he played an important part in the lineout that ended with Keith Wood charging over the line. 'It's one of those moments you do on the training ground over and over and over again. That it came off then was fantastic. It was an incredible try but a simple move. Keith Wood threw a long ball, I

31

32

Is there a more iconic photograph to capture the old looking out for the young on the field of sport? Mick Galwey helps settle the nerves of Peter Stringer and Ronan O'Gara by standing, literally, shoulder to shoulder with his Munster half-backs, and bear-hugging them during renditions of 'Amhrán na bhFiann' and 'Ireland's Call'. One Sunday newspaper carried a caption 'Goodfellas' over this photograph taken before the Ireland–Italy Six Nations match in Lansdowne Road on 4 March 2000, when Ireland won 60–13, including a record thirty points from O'Gara. 'It was a very special moment for them and it was a very special moment for me,' remembers Galwey. 'It just seemed like the most natural thing to do. They were standing for the national anthem and, of course, they were nervous, of course they needed help, but they played fantastic games that day.'

went up, passed it to Malcolm O'Kelly. Anthony Foley comes in and rips it, offloads to Keith Wood, David Wallace takes out the man at the back – illegally or whatever – and Keith goes in.' Ireland denied England the Grand Slam, Lansdowne erupted and Galwey was in the lap of honour that followed. He remembers England won the championship but they trooped off disconsolate.

The celebrations continued back in the dressing room when Taoiseach Bertie Ahern popped in to congratulate the Ireland team. 'To see Bertie coming in, you know you were doing something right then. Ronan tried to drag him into the centre of the crowd – there was champagne and craic. They're great moments to have.'

Galwey has been a towering figure in each of Shannon's eight All-Ireland League titles since the competition's inception in 1990. His steadfast leadership and motivational qualities were central to Shannon's historic four-in-a-row from 1995–1998, while, during his second coming as a provincial and international player, Gaillimh also helped the famous Limerick club to a further two titles in 2002 and 2004.

He took over the reins of coach at the start of the 2004–2005 season, and his influence over the next generation of Shannon players has been instantaneous – one of Irish rugby's most iconic figures has coached the Limerick club to two more AIL titles; a remarkable feat in anyone's language. 'Our biggest title win came in 1998 when we won the four-in-a-row and played against Garryowen, our biggest rivals, but the respect was very big between us. It was the first All-Ireland play-off

Gaillimh celebrates with Shannon supporters after the Limerick club completed an historic four-in-a-row beating Garryowen in the 1998 All-Ireland League final. This was the first AIL final to be played at Lansdowne Road.

final – there were close to 25,000 people at Lansdowne for the game. Club rugby was still big because European Cup rugby was still in its infancy. For example, in 2005 when we won it, there were only 5,000 people at the match.'

As an assistant coach to Munster in 2004 (or 'PR man!' as he says self-deprecatingly), he watched his beloved province, one he had captained to two European Cup finals (2000 and 2002), as they were defeated by Wasps in the 2004 European Cup semi-final at Lansdowne. Nobody understood or felt the heartbreak more than Gaillimh, but, as an occasion, he'll never forget the noise and colour; that the old ground never shook and felt so alive and vibrant as it did that beautiful April afternoon in leafy Ballsbridge.

Galwey, along with Peter Clohessy, provided the half-time entertainment during the 2006 European Cup quarter-final between Munster and Perpignan. The two great characters of Munster and Irish rugby tried their hands at some place kicking for charity and, though it might not have been pretty, Galwey loved being back again in Irish rugby's citadel on a big match day.

'Even taking the penalties that day, it was funny to be back there. You hear the noise, you see a kind of a blur of the crowd and it doesn't bother you – you actually get a good buzz out of it. Being back there for the quarter-final, it was like the old familiar buzz. It was a nice moment for myself and Claw and I enjoyed it. It was fun. Let's put it this way: if I was to stand up on a tee box and there were five people looking at me taking my shot, I wouldn't say I'd be nervous but you'd realise they are there. Whereas, when I was in Lansdowne, it was normal; it was like I never left the place. There is something special about the place. It just has a great name – L-A-N-S-D-O-W-N-E R-O-A-D. It is a fantastic name for a pitch, there's a great ring to it. It's a great place when you're winning – when you're losing it's the loneliest place in the world. Nobody can tell you otherwise.'

It was just another memory from Gaillimh's teeming vault.

Denis Hickie

Winger

1997–

In his teens, Denis Hickie became used to big occasions and raucous crowds in Lansdowne Road and, today, the beat of the 'Old Lady' still moves him. As a schoolboy, he played in front of 20,000, captaining St Mary's College to victory over Clongowes in the 1994 Leinster Schools Senior Cup Final.

It took two matches to produce a winner but, in the replay, Hickie, a full-back in his halcyon rugby days, proudly walked up the steps of the West Stand to collect the college's first title in twenty-five years.

Schoolboy rugby is the best possible preparation for the professional game, according to Hickie, but his coaches taught him one of the most valid lessons in life – humility. The emphasis, he says, was not on blowing your own trumpet at an individual or school level. Rugby and life lessons came from his coaches and stood him in good stead when he took the leap up to professional ranks. 'We drew the final on St Patrick's Day, then we had the replay the following Wednesday which added to the sense of drama and atmosphere. It was certainly my first big final and we were playing a very well-matched team in Clongowes and were very close the whole way. It was like winning the World Cup. Fr Flavin was our manager and Brian Cotter and my Uncle Denis (who had played for Ireland in the late 1960s/early 1970s) were coaches. We were very happy to have won but they instilled in us a sense of modesty. We celebrated accordingly, but Fr Flavin's way was the kind cultivated within the school as a whole.'

He was taken many times to Lansdowne as a kid and the first Five Nations games he saw involved Doyler's 'flamboyants' in 1985. He took a shine to their speedy wingers Keith Crossan and Trevor Ringland and full-back Hugo MacNeill and also marvelled at their keeping-the-ball-in-hand beliefs. But he had to wait until after the France game (which Ireland drew 15–15) to see an Ireland win at Lansdowne Road.

He saw the France game as tough and uncompromising, which disappointed Denis as he liked the French attacking philosophy, their élan and elusiveness and sinuous running were belief systems that he would later embrace as a top international. Doyler's team, which had promised

Club is family: Denis Hickie, decked out in his beloved St Mary's College colours, steps on the gas against Lansdowne in the AIL, February 1997.

38

free expression all week, had to go fighting in the trenches against the French but then he saw plenty of the width and the 'give it a lash' evangelical preachings of Doyle on television in the wins away to Scotland and Wales before Ireland returned to Lansdowne for the Triple Crown win over England.

In his first year at UCD, Hickie played full-back but, when Leinster came calling, they believed his blistering pace might be better served on the wing. His speed could have marked him out as a potential Olympian because, at St Mary's, he also represented the college at All-Ireland athletics meets alongside class-mate John McWeeney. Indeed, as part of the rehab work after the Achilles injury he picked up against Argentina in the 2003 World Cup, Hickie went training with Irish athletes, all in a fitness race for the 2004 Olympics in Athens.

His Lansdowne debut as an Irish senior player came in February 1997 against England with the cheers that greeted his first Irish try in his first cap against Wales still ringing in his ears. Hickie, at only twenty, had returned from Cardiff on a high, his try having helped Ireland to a much needed 26–25 win. But up next were England and his illusions were quickly shattered in a forgettable 46–6 defeat. 'After my opening game, a win in the old Cardiff Arms Park, I thought all these international weekends were fantastic. Then we played a very, very good England team. Will Carling and Jeremy Guscott were in their pomp and I was opposite Tony Underwood. It was a heavy defeat. It was a tough time for Ireland as well. We were losing a lot more games than we were winning, no matter where we played, but it was great to play my first game for Ireland in Lansdowne Road, I enjoyed that aspect of it, but when the whistle went, there wasn't much to enjoy.'

Hickie's senior international career began in the Brian Ashton era. The English coach later made a name for himself under Clive Woodward as a backs coach of some renown, his ideas sparking the right responses in Woodward's England three-quarter line. But Ashton failed to ignite the Irish backs.

In 1997–1998 season, Ashton attempted but could not revitalise an Irish side low on confidence; instead, he grew flummoxed and frustrated as his ideas were reportedly not washing with many on the Ireland team which was still very much learning the coping mechanisms of professional rugby. After the visit of Scotland to Lansdowne in 1998, when Ireland lost 16–17, Ashton's patience finally ran out. With twenty minutes to go, Ireland led 16–11, but the team had neither the imagination nor the tactical nous to capitalise when opportunities arose out wide. At one stage, Ireland had six scrums on the Scottish line but could not fashion a try. Two Craig Chalmers penalties won the game for Scotland and pushed Ashton's nerve to the edge and prompted his famous line, 'I do not know whose game-plan that was, but it most certainly was not mine.'

Two weeks later, Ashton resigned citing an attack of shingles as the reason for his departure. 'You could say his methods were very different at the time and, yes, he was ahead of his time,' says Hickie. 'Looking back, his approach then would be pretty standard to what coaches are doing now, but I think, at the time, Ashton's ways were certainly different to what everyone else was doing. I think everyone enjoyed his coaching. But I think the reality was that we didn't have the type of players he wanted to implement the type of game he wanted to play. I think that is why he left. And there was plenty of frustration underlying it all. A lot of other stuff was said, and I'm sure there were other small reasons too. But if we'd had the type of players that he wanted us to have, the type of skills that he wanted us to have, he would have stayed.'

Three months before Ashton's resignation, Ireland had faced the All Blacks in November 1997. Ashton, impressed by what he had seen in the European Cup and in inter-provincial competition included five new caps in the Ireland team that afternoon – three from Hickie's club, St Mary's College, which included full-back Kevin Nowlan, wing John McWeeney and scrum-half Conor McGuinness while the other two new caps were London Irish duo Malcolm O'Kelly (lock) and Kieron Dawson (flanker). Opposite Hickie was Glen Osborne and opposite John McWeeney was Jeff Wilson.

The two All Blacks wingers scored two tries apiece in a 63–15 win. In the fifty-fourth minute, McWeeney was replaced by Kevin Maggs. 'There were a lot of new players playing that day but it was a different sort of time. There was a lot of chopping and changing on the Irish team in those days because results weren't great. Guys were getting played for one match and dropped for the next. It was a tough old time really. John was up against Jeff Wilson that day which wasn't an easy task. In that era, there used always be a kind of one-cap wonder team which people would pick on the bus – people who played one game and you'd never hear of them again. That is something that has changed a lot of the last few years, there's a lot more consistency in selection now; guys are given a chance to prove themselves and you usually award that kind of honesty. There was so much uncertainty with the new professional game coming in and the new coaches – some guys on professional contracts and some guys not being professional. It was probably bad timing for a lot of guys to get their first cap around then. John [McWeeney] certainly wouldn't have been the first or the last within a two to four year period around that time to have played one game and not played again.'

The All Blacks game whistled by very quickly in Hickie's eyes, and Ireland's attempts to keep the score respectable died a slow death as probably the most-talented All Blacks team of all time overpowered and overwhelmed an Irish team still grappling with the new professional era and getting to grips with Ashton's ways. It seemed the All Blacks were aeons ahead, though Hickie says there was one character in the Irish dressing room who was beating down the door of amateurism in Ireland and crying for everyone else to follow suit – Keith Wood, scorer of two tries in an afternoon of mostly forgettable memories. 'I don't think too many people get two tries against the All Blacks, certainly not in those days and certainly not playing for Ireland. Woodie at this stage was head and shoulders above anything Ireland had. In the 2003 World Cup, I feel he was in a team that suited him a bit more, surrounded by a lot more players that, you could say, complemented him. But he was so far ahead at that stage. So far ahead of everyone else even to the day he retired; he was a real world-class player and always will be regarded as a world-class player. Up to the time he finished, he could have got into any team in the world and that's the sign of a world-class player. Ireland don't have, and never have had, that many players at that level.'

Warren Gatland's arrival in 1998 saw Hickie retain his place for the remaining three games in the Six Nations against France, Wales and England. Ireland lost all three but Hickie's emergence as a genuine talent rekindled some hope for the future of Irish rugby. The St Mary's man ran in a memorable try in Paris – a game Ireland came desperately close to winning – and two against England in Twickenham. Ireland picked up the Wooden Spoon, but golden opportunities lost was the theme of that season.

Hickie was still waiting for his first try in Lansdowne. 'As a team, the confidence probably wasn't there that's probably there now. There were a lot of different reasons for that: a lot of uncertainty, a lot of changing in selection and many players were playing amateur rugby but trying to play the professional game – so there was a lot of different reasons.'

After the summer tour to South Africa, Hickie remained out of the picture for two years with loss of form an excuse cited by many selectors. But the Leinster man returned in style when Irish rugby took a turn for the better against Scotland in February 2000. 'It would have been our first Six Nations win in quite a while. I don't remember winning a Six Nations game really in between my first Six Nations game and that one. It was a bit of a change over really; Eddie [O'Sullivan] had come in as an assistant coach to Warren Gatland at that stage. Eddie had coached a lot of those guys at Under-21 level – Ronan [O'Gara], Peter [Stringer], Shane Horgan, myself – and after a defeat like the one at Twickenham (Ireland had lost their opening 2000 Six Nations game 50–18) sometimes you need to have a free hand to make those changes.'

Hickie, for one, never played through an era of slow handclapping or booing from the Lansdowne stands; instead his overall experiences of the Lansdowne crowd have been very positive. 'One thing I must say about Lansdowne Road – even in the games where we weren't winning – we always had massive support; like there was always a lot of noise. Because we hadn't won many games there, I'd always been impressed with the level of support whether we won or lost. It was amazing to see it increase even more when we started winning. You'd always depend on the crowd to give you a level of noise that's as good as anywhere. Even the bottom level of noise in Dublin is as good as you're going to get anywhere.'

His first international try at Lansdowne Road came against South Africa in November 2000, a game of scorching intensity but where a liberated Irish three-quarters conjured up a series of innovative moves that took even the visitors by surprise.

Though he admits Tyrone Howe's try was redolent of Ireland's new-found confidence, Hickie says his own try in the first half remains his all-time favourite. 'I haven't scored a massive number of tries at Lansdowne Road – a lot of my international tries have been away from there but one

Catch me if you can: Hickie evades the South African cover to set up Tyrone Howe for Ireland's second try in the 2000 autumn international. Hickie was man of the match.

of my favourites is in the match against South Africa, when I'd come back into the team after being out for a while. To get man of the match that day too was one of my best memories. It wasn't the most spectacular try I ever scored but, in terms of the day and who we were playing, I was thrilled with it. Rob Henderson chipped it through for me and I came up in the inside and beat him to it as he reminded me at the time. He insists he would have got there … but I wasn't so sure!'

Hickie was also at the centre of one the best tries ever scored at Lansdowne, a stirring move initiated by replacement out-half David Humphreys' first touch of the ball and moved through the hands of three players at such pace and with such alacrity it'd have done great, backline innovators the All Blacks proud. Humphreys, from halfway, passed a long ball to O'Driscoll. The centre then jinked pretending to go inside before flipping up a ball on his left to right-winger Hickie. Hickie had come around on the burst and the jet-heeled winger skipped out of Braam van Straaten's tackle before putting Howe over on the left. It was a wonderful try to level matters again, though the Springboks saw off Ireland on a 18–28 final scoreline. It was a thrilling game of rugby replete with invention from both sides. 'We went out and attacked from the start; we kind of caught them on the hop in that regard, I think. We probably didn't have the defensive organisation that we have now and that's what probably cost us the game. With ten minutes to go, we weren't sure we would win, even though we could have won – again it's a stage teams have to go through before they start winning.'

Hickie was part of the Ireland team that beat England in the 2001 Six Nations rescheduled because of the outbreak of foot-and-mouth that spring. Ireland did what Ireland do best at Lansdowne Road – they emerged breathing fire and played with incredible passion and took the shortest, most direct and simplest options. Humphreys, inconsistent from his place kicks, hammered England back with his kicking out of hand and, as Hickie recalls, the forwards loved him for it!

A neutral observer might have summed up that England allowed themselves to be sucked into a frantic harum-scarum game which suited the Irish. 'There had been two wins against England even before I was playing, two very famous ones [1993 and 1994] but there was never any consistency really before or after those wins. We got to a stage where we did well against South Africa, were going well against a few different teams but we never were able to drive the nail home. We needed to make that step. We got on top of the other Six Nations teams – Scotland and Italy – but we couldn't make the breakthrough against France and England. I think when we beat England in that rescheduled game in Lansdowne Road, it was a big confident step for everyone individually and collectively as a team.'

Hickie's best moments in the win over England were his defensive cameos, leaping confidently to fetch garryowens, calling for marks, which were all a throwback to his days as a full-back with St Mary's. Wood's try, Stringer's trip and Ireland's defensive heroics made the headlines the following morning, but Hickie likes to read the small print on days like that. No one stood taller, he said, than Eric Miller, a player who was striving to return to the form of 1997 which made him a British and Irish Lion. 'I think Eric had a really good game that day, a real stand-out player. He got a lot of flack over the years because he was injured a fair bit. But when Eric was fit and when he was at his best, he was probably the best Number 6 Ireland had produced in many years because he's a most natural footballer, extremely aggressive, great skills and when he gets playing, he's a match for anyone. You get a win like that and you go down through the team [ratings] and you find everyone has to play well. In the past, you had Woodie, world class, and he was too far in front of everyone. To beat a team like England, especially the team they were at the time, you needed everyone to play well.'

Buoyed by their heartening victory over the English, Ireland's new-found confidence found full expression against the touring All Blacks in the autumn internationals. A five o'clock kick-off under floodlights ensured a raucous din would reverberate around the old ground for this, the most glamorous of rugby fixtures. Hickie scored that day – a memorable cameo within a stirring November blockbuster. When the winger dived over two minutes after half-time to push Ireland 21–7 ahead, Lansdowne Road erupted and a first win over the All Blacks in fifteen attempts seemed entirely possible. But the All Blacks pumped up the volume and, in a devastating show of attack rugby, ran in four tries in the next twenty minutes. It finished 40–24.

Hickie agrees with Eddie O'Sullivan's view that Ireland had no defensive system in place to counter teams like the All Blacks. 'We didn't have the defensive organisation that we have now. We didn't have any real defensive organisation; [Mike] Ford wouldn't have been brought in at that stage. We were kind of defending on our wits, with a small bit of organisation but not what was required really. Certainly, against a team like that, we let in some soft tries that, two years later, we wouldn't have let in. It was an opportunity missed. Again, some guys had fantastic games. I remember Shane Horgan got a bad ankle injury before the game, or during the game, and managed to play up to the last six minutes and did a fantastic job on Jonah Lomu. Again, at the time, Shane would have been under a huge amount of pressure. I remember going into the game, there was a lot of noise that he wasn't going to make it as winger and I think he made the step up that day and the nation relaxed about him after that – he really proved himself against the best team in the world.'

Hickie's try two minutes into the second half pushed Ireland into a dream position and the build-up is still fresh in his mind today. 'Miller first went wide, Ireland recycled, Humps [David Humphreys] took it into the 22, Drico [Brian O'Driscoll] went close and fed me and dived over in the corner. We scored fairly early after the second half. Humps had a great say that day, made a great break for [Kevin] Maggs' try and made a break for my try as well. Backs and forwards involved – a very good team try.'

There was another changing of the guard when O'Sullivan replaced Gatland – Hickie's third coach since 1997 – but it didn't break the momentum Ireland had built up since the autumn and the winger was one of six try scorers against Wales in the 2002 Six Nations at Lansdowne Road. The game was well wrapped up by the time Hickie cantered over the line, but the move is worth retelling. Simon Easterby took the ball into the 22, O'Driscoll was involved but after being brought down, Humphreys took possession and fed Hickie for the easiest of run-ins.

A mixed Six Nations followed that win: a heavy loss in Twickenham, wins at home to Scotland and Italy before the defensive system, being embedded then by defence coach Mike Ford, was torn to shreds by the French in Paris.

World champions Australia arrived in Lansdowne in 2002 confident of turning over the Irish as they had done so often in the past. Hickie retired concussed before the break, at which stage Ireland had sailed into a 12–3 lead. 'I actually got knocked out and was taken off just before the end of the first half. I think I put my head on the wrong side of a tackle with Wendell Sailor, who is not a small guy, and got a knee in the side of the head. I can't even remember when they took me off. The next thing I do remember is the end of the game and celebrating with the rest of the lads. I don't remember any of the game to be honest.'

Hickie looked at a video and remembers it now for many reasons: Brian O'Driscoll's first game as captain, Ronan O'Gara's flawless kicking display landing all of Ireland's eighteen points and the re-emergence of Victor Costello on the international stage after a four-year absence.

'Woodie was injured at the time so Brian was brought in as a captain and talisman. We played in pretty horrific conditions. But Ronan O'Gara pretty much won that game for us – he got all our points in a masterful display. A lot of guys played well like Shane Byrne, throwing in not only torrential rain but unbelievable wind, but he hit the lineout every time. I believe we got a 100 per cent record in the lineout. Victor Costello too came in at Number 6 after being out in the wilderness for quite a while. He [Costello] was man of the match that day; himself and Anthony Foley worked very well at 6 and 8 and they'd never been tried at that and they swapped around positions having been on opposite teams and adversaries for so long. A lot of people didn't realise how well the swapping worked – and it worked well for us in the coming few games as well. That was a big step – our first southern hemisphere scalp.'

Ireland remained unbeaten until the Grand Slam decider against England in March 2003. 'We'd beaten England in 2001 and expectations were high but we were beaten by the side that effectively went on to win the World Cup. You'd guys like Dallaglio, Johnson and Hill in their prime, Leonard was on top of his game with Jonny Wilkinson there too, as well as Tindall. I remember everyone being disappointed after that game, but there was a sense that we could have no complaints; we were beaten by the better side and they proved that when they went on to win the World Cup.'

Injury at the 2003 World Cup against Argentina deprived Hickie of a chance to play in the 2004 Six Nations campaign – and a Triple Crown win. He did, however, return for the 2004 autumn internationals against South Africa and Argentina. 'The win over South Africa was another great scalp. Ronan [O'Gara] got all the points and the man of the match award. Again, it was a performance where everyone needed to play well, and did play well. Ireland had gone to South Africa that summer with full confidence. But our confidence might have been mis-interpreted. You go to a southern hemisphere team and, irrespective of what they say, they'll always expect to beat Ireland. For us to win a game out there, we have to go there believing we can win, so we have to go there saying we can win. If we don't think we're going to win, we're not going to win. They beat us 2–0 in the series. Then South Africa were making the noises of a Grand Slam tour in the autumn internationals – all that sort of stuff and we were keen to get one back on them.'

With Leinster, Hickie has also had his great moments in Lansdowne Road – great European Cup days against Bath in October 2004 when New Zealand out-half David Holwell gave a man of the match display and Hickie scored a gem of a try after twenty-five minutes dancing down the left wing to beat two men in a twenty-five-metre dash to the corner. That's tempered, he adds, by two gut-wrenching defeats there to Perpignan (2004) and Munster (2006).

The highlight of his Leinster career came in the inaugural Celtic League final against Munster in 2001 – a game that drew 30,000 spectators to Lansdowne Road and one where the Leinster coaching ticket of Matt Williams and Alan Gaffney saw their vision of total rugby

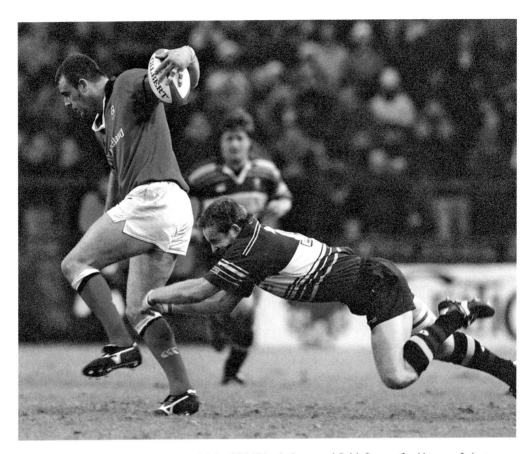

The fall of Munster: Hickie trips Munster's John O'Neill in the inaugural Celtic League final in 2001. Leinster won 30–24 in front of 30,000 enthralled spectators at Lansdowne Road.

realised. 'We had a great game in the Celtic League final in 2001. A great occasion, a lot of drama, we had a guy sent off early and were down to fourteen men. The Celtic League is not the European Cup but, in terms of important wins, it was huge to us at the time; it was the start of provincial rugby getting big. Having 30,000 there in Lansdowne Road where two Irish provinces were playing had never been done before up until that point. It was a great final. They [Gaffney and Williams] were trying to take us through a different level in our province and, at that time, it was as big a game as we played. Lansdowne can be the greatest ground in the world – I've good memories and heartbreaking ones as well, and that's what endears me to it more.'

The biggest heartbreak came against Munster in the 2006 European Cup semi-final when Leinster's backline was denied the freedom of the park by a superbly motivated Munster side. 'A lot has been made out between the two sets of backs. But Munster's backs played very well that day as well. I almost got in for a try at a stage when we really did need to get ahead, but we never got there. From our point of view, that's not what was needed.'

Hickie has scored twenty-five tries so far for Ireland and says the best feeling is running down the touchline with the crowd and those nearest leaning out over their seats, willing you towards the tryline. 'Nothing beats that feeling. Having everyone so close to the pitch, you can always see the whites of people's eyes. And, when you look up after grounding the ball, the people are smiling at you and they're only ten feet away. It's the only international ground in the world where that can happen and you could nearly go in and give someone a high-five. Not too many of the grounds are that close to the crowd. Lansdowne has had a pretty good innings; everyone is going to be glad to see it go, but I think there are enough memories in it – I don't think the old ground will be forgotten that quickly.'

Jack Kyle

Fly-Half

1948–1959

On international days at Lansdowne Road in the late 1940s and 1950s, there was no one with whom the gathered crowd wanted to identify more than with the slim Ulster fly-half named Jack Kyle. He was the consummate artist of his time, the poster boy of Ireland's golden generation between 1948 and 1951. In essence, he was 'the man', the *galactico* of his age. Those lucky enough to have seen Kyle play say he had an innate capacity to seduce a rugby audience with his elusiveness, fleet-footedness, soft hands and his judgement in punting. He was a line-breaker and a play-maker of the highest quality and, though slightly built, was a lightweight who packed a heavyweight tackle. Above all, records show that Kyle was the reason that Ireland were to the fore in world rugby during what are now termed, in reverence to the Belfast boy, the 'Jackie Kyle years'.

It's said Jackie mightn't do too much for an hour, but genius strikes at the most unexpected and opportune times in a match. He was the inspiration that brought wins to Ireland, but his most mesmerising knack was a patience to wait for the right moment to pounce. When you expected him to kick, he passed – and when you expected him to pass, he kicked. He also had, what Ronan O'Gara possesses today, a most astonishing diagonal kick.

Lansdowne Road was not home to his most striking cameo in test rugby – that was at Ravenhill against France in 1953 where he took off on a thirty-yard mazy dash for the tryline, leaving six French defenders in his wake to touch down almost apologetically. *The Times* rugby writer A.A. Thomson wrote: 'He has an extraordinary deceptive way of persuading opponents that he was about to do something wholly different from what in fact he did ... if you hesitated, he would dart by like a trout in a pool and either score a dazzling try on his own or put in a curling, puzzling cross kick which one of his wingers would eventually touch down.'

Jack Kyle, the pale-faced, freckled, flame-haired Queen's University medical student, made his debut at Lansdowne Road when Ireland played the first of its 'Victory Internationals' against England. On that day in 1946, nineteen-year-old Kyle introduced himself to the rugby world. Even the match programme that afternoon carried a biography of the teenager, stressing his strengths and burgeoning reputation: 'The discovery of the season, John Wilson Kyle was on the Ulster Schools XV two years ago and proved himself to be in the top class by his great display for Ulster against the Kiwi Servicemen in November, subsequently confirming that form against the army. A particularly straight strong runner, he looks to have a brilliant future.'

Kyle remembers travelling to Dublin with the Ulster Schools team for an inter-provincial against Leinster in 1943. Not only was he chirpy about the prospect of visiting the Irish capital, but relished the chance of running out at Lansdowne Road. 'My earliest memory of Lansdowne Road is being picked to at out-half to play for Ulster schoolboys against Leinster in 1943. It's hard to believe it now with the world of travel, but I had never been outside Ireland. I was about seventeen at the time. I think, as a child, I had been to Dublin with my mother and father at some stage when I was old enough to appreciate a major city. I remember getting brochures and reading all about what I should see in Dublin – Trinity College, *The Book of Kells* – but the excitement of being picked on an Ulster schoolboys side to play at Lansdowne Road topped it all. One of the perks of representative rugby was that when your school team [Belfast Royal Academy] photograph was taken, you wore your Ulster jersey so you stood out from the rest of the side.

'We travelled by train and we went to the hotel of Freddie Moran's father Pa Moran, up from Amiens Street [now Connolly] Station, and had a lunch there. Freddie Moran, who was a sprinter, played for Ireland many times before the outbreak of the Second World War. We played the game and won 16–3. My old headmaster at Belfast Royal Academy, Alex Foster, had played and captained Ireland in 1910, 1911 and 1912 – he had also gone with the Lions in South Africa in 1910 and had introduced rugby to the Royal Academy. Alex was a wonderful man and a great influence on many of us. I always think of those of us, who are old like this now, knew guys who had played for Ireland nearly a hundred years ago.'

The match programme may have introduced Kyle as the player to look out for in the match against England in 1946 – the year of unofficial internationals when no caps were awarded – but Kyle picked up a serious foot injury that day and didn't play again for the rest of the season. Although he hoped to make a quick comeback, his return was halted by a doctor in Queen's who had attended the match and was aware of his injury. In hindsight, Kyle is thankful for his medical intervention. 'When I look back, I give thanks to that man who got hold of me. He was head of the fracture clinic and had been at the game and told somebody in the anatomy department that he wanted to see me.'

Kyle arrived at the clinic in the hope of getting the plaster off. But the doctor had other ideas. '"What are you here for?" he said to me. I replied that I was here to get my plaster off. "How long is it on?" "Four weeks," I said. "I think the plaster needs strengthening! And come back then in four weeks' time!" Looking back, it was the best

The Jackie Kyle Show: Ireland greatest ever out-half clears to touch during a record 22–0 win over England in the 1947 Five Nations Championship.

51

thing that ever happened to me because a lateral ligament tear can be worse than a fracture of the outside bone of the leg there. I strapped it up for a season or two and never had really any trouble with it.

'I remember that day in Lansdowne – and the injury – well. It was my right foot. It was another player on the Irish side, we were both going for the ball at the same time and he took a dive and hit me in the ankle. I couldn't run at out-half and you often didn't go off in those days but I went onto the wing, and hobbled. It was only time I ever played wing.'

Kyle was back in Lansdowne in 1947 when Ireland defeated England 22–0. 'It was a windy day. I think that was our biggest victory ever against them beating them by twenty-two clear points. That was a great old boost for us. Con Murphy of Lansdowne, who had played with Ireland before the war, was captain of that side and I think he was dropped after the game. We couldn't understand it – we won twenty-two points to nil after all! It was quite a good England side with Dickie Guest and Jack Heaton. They weren't hammered and may have won some of their other games. We beat England, then Scotland and were then going for the Triple Crown in 1947 but we lost 6–0 to Wales in Swansea.'

Kyle could be quite a laid-back character and apocryphal tales abound of him arriving at training sessions with only one boot or of being fast asleep on the bus as it pulled up outside the old Lansdowne Pavilion before internationals.

'We got the train down on the Friday morning, got to the Shelbourne, got our lunch, had a run out in Trinity College or Bective. We'd come back and usually have a team meeting. But the practice itself was always a casual affair. You didn't do too much because the match was the next day. The team meetings were quite informal gatherings. You'd have the captain sitting on a table and everyone gathered around him. Usually, it was a case of, "Anyone have any ideas for tomorrow?" Compared with what the guys go with today...'

Despite the openness and democratic nature of team meetings, the players were tied to a very strict amateur code. Even the jerseys they wore for internationals had to be returned after games. Kyle remembers a time when the players turned up in their club socks, Barbarian-like. There would be Jim Nelson in Malone's complete red socks, whilst Kyle wore the black, blue and green of Queen's. 'Later, the union decided they could afford to give us socks, but players still had to bring their own shorts and boots. The jersey had to be returned after a match. Dear old Billy Jeffers would be in the pavilion after the game saying, "Jersey, jersey!" But after the last game of the season, we were allowed to keep the jersey. The late Robin Thompson told me this story. In the first game, we usually played France. He exchanged his jersey with a French guy and went into the pavilion and Jeffers was there saying, "Where's your jersey, pal?" "I exchanged it," said Robin. "Well, get it back. Quick." Robin says he was very keen to have it and said he would give him the cheque for it. "No," Jeffers went on, "that was meant to be the jersey for your position during the season." Robert had to go to this French guy and ask him for the jersey back. The French guy wasn't at all pleased because he probably got a jersey every game.'

The players would be weighed before internationals, and there were other rituals to be fulfilled too. 'We'd be called out before the game to have a photograph. There would be different photographers around and then we would get back into the pavilion again. Then a few words of encouragement from the captain before we ran out onto the ground to play the match. The one thing I liked about Lansdowne Road was I felt the turf had a certain spring about it compared with some other grounds which were heavy. Take the Mardyke, in Cork, for example, which could be flooded at times. Lansdowne, I think, drained very well.'

In 1947, fourteen new caps were introduced for the first official post-war international against France. There was a vibrancy to the Irish play, something, says Kyle, not too dissimilar to the jauntiness of the New Ireland that rang in the new millennium in February 2000 against Scotland.

Going into 1948, confidence was high in the Irish camp despite the Triple Crown loss to Wales the previous season. The season started with an international against the visiting Australians in December 1947 when more changes were made with eight new caps introduced. They lost heavily to the Aussies – 16–3 – but then began a run of four matches that concluded with Ireland's only Grand Slam to date against Wales in Ravenhill.

At the centre of this team, steadfast, steady and unwavering was Jackie Kyle. As a stand-off, he was described as the ultimate improviser, the orchestrator-in-chief, who, with a shimmy of those hips, could create something out of nothing. 'What we reckoned was that the game of rugby was a game of spontaneity. When the chance is there, you had to take your opportunity. And as I mentioned to you, there was no game-plan – if you saw the gap, you went for it. Some days, you went out and you just couldn't see them. We'd have those days where you'd look, having to pass the ball out or kick the ball, you were well covered so you depended a lot on your scrum-half to give you a good pass that you ran into, a pass that you could pick out of the air and keep going. The 9 and 10 combination was important. Like Johnny O'Meara who I played with for years. Because we didn't see each other very frequently, we would work out uncomplicated signals. When I met him, I'd say, "Nothing too complicated, Johnny. If I'm going to the right, I will tap my right leg and if I'm going left, I'll tap my left leg."'

Kyle distinguished himself against France in Stade Colombes in 1948, scored a try against England in Twickenham and notched another against Scotland at Lansdowne Road – and as it turned out the only score – in a 3–0 win. 'I remember running towards the old Lansdowne Road Pavilion where we togged out. I got one of those lovely passes outside the 25, one of those wee beauties that fall into your hands. Then that gap appeared in front of me and I was able to get through it. The timing was everything. If you take a three-quarter who can run a hundred yards in thirteen seconds – which isn't great – but if you get half a second, you've got four yards on your marker. Also that good pass that you're running into makes all the difference between scoring a try and your marker being upon you and catching you.'

The Grand Slam match was taken to Ravenhill and Ireland triumphed 6–3 – Barney Mullan and John Christopher Daly getting the tries but the legend of Kyle was growing by the day. Indeed, many went as far as to say that Kyle carried the Irish backline, which was reputed to be only able to defend well. 'That wasn't exactly true. You had Bertie O'Hanlon scoring tries, you had Barney Mullan scoring tries, Paddy Reid scoring tries. I wouldn't agree with that at all.'

The 1948 survivors have been wined and dined many a time since and there's the old story of the two guys from the 1948 team coming out of Lansdowne Road after Ireland were going for another Grand Slam and one says, 'That was a close shave – Ireland nearly won!'

He saw 1970 and 1972 as lost opportunities to attain a Grand Slam and quotes French philosopher Rousseau who said, 'Nature gives the ability and Chance calls it into play.' 'You have to be born with certain genes to do certain things but you've got to have the opportunity and many the unfortunate person hasn't the opportunity to show their potential. There was such potential in that side, they were a great side – should have had Grand Slams but didn't get the opportunities.'

Kyle again inspired Ireland to a Triple Crown in 1949. There were no coaches in those days and teams often hit the park with no thought-out strategy. 'Except once, against Wales in 1949 (we won that game 5–0 at Swansea), when we were going for another Triple Crown and I remember Karl Mullen saying, "Look, we're fitter than the Welsh guys and we don't want to be getting ourselves involved in mauls and battling it out. I want you to put the ball in the left side of the field and in the right side of the field." And we ran these guys all over the park and they were unable to get any ball. And that was where Karl was a very good captain – he was cute enough to see that things like that would work. I think that was the only time I remember us taking any kind of a game-plan into a test. Nobody ever said that I want you to do this or I want you to do that. Except when I heard Des O'Brien saying to me before a game at Lansdowne, "You haven't done very much recently, Jackie – you better do something today!"'

54

The Irish team having lemons at half-time – Kyle is wearing the Number 10 – during their international match against England on 10 February 1951 in Lansdowne Road.

While Ravenhill had its own unique charms for a Belfast boy done good, nothing stirred Kyle more then running out at Lansdowne Road and into the roar and approval of the crowd. He even admits to taking great pride in lining up for 'Amhrán na bhFiann'. 'We lined up for national anthems and we turned around and we faced the flag. There was never any problem doing that. We felt like guests of the country, if you like, though we were playing for Ireland. There was never the slightest bit of trouble – it was just an acknowledgement that here we were in Dublin. There was nothing mentioned about the politics of the time at all. I think it has been a great thing for Irish rugby and very fortunate for us from Ulster to play on an Irish side. We were able to play unlike the soccer that split. And what a thrill it is to play for your whole country rather than say Northern Ireland – it would have been hard to get a side together if we'd had to.'

Ireland won another championship in 1951 and, two years later, Kyle took over as captain of Ireland, a position with which he was never comfortable. 'It should never have been me – I wasn't a captain at all. I think there are certain players who shouldn't be made captain. I think I got it because of my length of service to the team.'

Kyle had been star of the British and Irish Lions tour of New Zealand in 1950, and re-acquainted himself with the touring All Blacks at Lansdowne in January 1954. He says in hindsight his decision to play against the wind in the first half impinged on a historic result for the Irish against New Zealand. 'When we played New Zealand that year, I had a choice – there was a wind blowing, which there nearly always is in Lansdowne Road – and we won the toss. I thought if we could hold these guys in the first half against the wind, maybe then with the wind we could do something in the second half when we were fresh. But it didn't work out – we lost 14–3. It's very easy to be wise after the event. Nobody today would play against the wind if they won the toss, they'd probably say take your advantage – you don't know what the wind is going to do for a start. Maybe it wasn't a good decision. I thought it was the right one. I liked playing with disadvantage in the first half and maybe advantage in the second half. I think maybe it was far better to leave me alone and not have me thinking for the rest of the side.'

While All Black Bob Scott was effusive in his praise of Kyle during the Lions tour four years earlier, Kyle believes he has never seen anyone like the New Zealand full-back before. Poetry in motion is an oft-used phrase to describe a wonderful athlete, but, Kyle says Scott 'had it all'.

'When I was in Auckland in 2005 for the Lions tour, I phoned him up and spoke to him. And we were reminiscing. I remembering saying, "In our last game in Auckland (which we lost 11–8), you kicked a penalty, you dropped a goal and converted a New Zealand try. If it hadn't been for you, we would have probably won." We drew the first and lost the other two fairly narrowly. Even in Lansdowne Road that day, Bob had a wonderful balance. You'd be running towards him and he'd move to the side. He was a very good kicker – he used to practise kicking in his bare feet. I don't how he did it with the old leather ball. He was one of the great full-backs of all time. He always had plenty of time to do things, no matter what the pressure was on him, you always felt he was going to get out of this. He had wonderful hands and was a terrific kicker. Ollie [Campbell] is in touch with him still and says he was very influenced by Bob Scott.'

A player Kyle remembers with great affection is Marney Cunningham, a blindside flanker who made his debut against France in 1955, but played his last game the following season against Wales at Lansdowne Road. 'They were going for the Triple Crown – Marney, our wing-forward, scored a try that day and, the next day, the paper said he was entering the priesthood much to everybody's surprise. Marney was the sort of guy you wouldn't have thought would have entered the priesthood – the real life is what goes on in here [pointing to head] rather than what you show off to the outside world. It turned out to be his farewell to international rugby.'

Much was written at the time about the fact that, in over forty internationals, Kyle hadn't scored a drop goal for his country. 'The only drop goal I ever dropped in international rugby was at Lansdowne Road and that was against Wales in 1956 when Wales were going for the Triple Crown. Marney got the try, Cecil Pedlow kicked a penalty. I see Cecil and he reminds me of that

The hunted: Kyle's popularity is all too apparent as autograph hunters surround him after Ireland's 3–0 win over England in 1951.

56

game occasionally. The last time I was sitting beside George Hook at a function, he told me that he was out in Barbados and there was a fellow out there who says he was responsible for my dropping that goal at Lansdowne! The Welsh full-back kicked the ball towards the East Stand and I got it about the ten-metre line. I looked about frustrated and didn't know what to do and thoughts of the last time I ran across the field and gave a stray pass entered my mind. Apparently, this fellow said, "Have a wee shot, Jack?" Why not indeed, so I gave it a shot.'

Kyle remembers it sailing high from forty-five yards, bisecting the posts and the crowd going into a frenzy. He had now done just about everything he could in a green jersey – but not quite. More glory was to follow with a win over Australia in January 1958.

'It was hard old game. The Aussies were expected to beat us and it was their first defeat at Lansdowne Road. Nick Shehadie hit Noel Murphy with a clout. It was Noel's debut. Afterwards, I heard Nick became Lord Mayor of Sydney. I remember Noel Henderson's try too. The ball came out along the backline, I think David Hewitt got it, gave it to Noel and Noel set off. Tony O'Reilly was outside him but Noel turned in.'

Everywhere he goes, Jack Kyle is treated with unwavering reverence. He was perhaps Ireland's first superstar. Today, he gets his two international tickets for the Upper West Stand and usually goes with his son, Caleb – he has to pay for the tickets of course.

He is proud of today's generation, but adds that they'll find it hard now to win a Grand Slam given the level of competition around. He looks at today's incumbent at Number 10, Ronan O'Gara, and sees a player blessed with all the out-half's skills, but says people see him in the pivotal position and then place all their hope on him winning games. 'You could play brilliantly and lose a game. In the long run, that's the thing that counts. O'Gara seems to win games. He has been very successful and that counts for a tremendous lot. Because, in many ways, the out-half has to direct the play. They used to say to us in the old days, "There's nothing a centre wants less than the ball at the same time as the opposite centre hits him." Also an out-half has got to see where he should kick and what he should do with his own kicking abilities, drop goals and so on.'

Kyle did it all with poetic class – definitely deserving of the name genius.

57

Lansdowne FC

Founded 1872

Henry William Dunlop is the founder of Lansdowne FC and is credited with the early development of Lansdowne Road, a stadium which evolved from a multi-purpose stadium to rugby national headquarters. After being banned from holding athletic championships at Trinity by the board, Dunlop was forced to look for another plot of land. He took a sixty-nine-year lease on the Lansdowne Road site, though comprising only part of the present premises, stretching from the railway to about sixty yards from the Dodder river. He wrote about this process later in his diary: 'I will not say much about the difficulties and struggles in connection with the Ground and its enclosing and preparation (of which I could say much) further than to record the following facts: I laid down a cinder running path of a quarter of a mile, laid down the present Lansdowne Tennis Club with my own theodolite, started a Lansdowne Tennis Club, a Lansdowne Archery Club, a Lansdowne Cricket Club, a Lansdowne Croquet Club and, but not least, the Lansdowne Rugby Football Club – colours red, black and yellow.'

In the winter of 1872–3, Lansdowne FC played their first game at Lansdowne Road and, in time, the ground was carefully cultivated and a permanent pavilion was erected. A grandstand to facilitate 400 people had been erected with sloping seats for 600 more, while a dressing room was also fitted under the railway arch on the ground. Lansdowne's ground ran along Havelock Square, but it suffered drainage problems early on. Dunlop wrote: 'It lay so low that, one winter, I paddled a canoe in about eighteen inches of water through the two goals, while a few sheep stood on a little island in the middle. With proceeds, I raised the ground by taking 300 cart loads of soil from a trench along the railway and raising the playing ground two feet. It was excellently drained and levelled and became one of the best grounds in Ireland.'

The story of Lansdowne's pavilion is quite extraordinary. The first pavilion was burned down, the second was in the northeast corner (between the East Stand and Havelock Square End) and the third (on the site of the original) was also burned. Today, the Lansdowne Pavilion lies behind the new East Stand, but it will move again when redevelopment begins. The Lansdowne Tea Pavilion still stands and has hosted press conferences for the Republic of Ireland soccer team.

The lease to the ground was originally passed to the IRFU by Dunlop, who remained President of Lansdowne FC from its foundation 1872 until 1904 and, amazingly, over a hundred years later, his son Eric is still involved with the club as an Honorary Life Member. Lansdowne's contribution to the national team is also a huge source of pride to the club. To date, ninety-nine of their players have won international caps, including many well-known names in Irish rugby – Moss Keane, Eugene Davy, Ernie Crawford, Ned Lightfoot, Mick Dunne, Jack Arigho, Morgan Crowe, Robin Roe, Mick English, Pat Casey, Sean MacHale, Gordon Wood, Alan 'Dixie' Duggan, Barry McGann, Mick Quinn, Noel Manion, Eric Elwood, Philip Danaher, Michael Kiernan, Conor O'Shea, Donal and Dick Spring (former Tánaiste), Michael Gibson, Des Fitzgerald and, of course, the great Con Murphy. Murphy is the only player to represent Ireland both before and after the Second World War and was captain of the famous Irish team that defeated England 22–0 in the first official post-war international in 1947.

The Lansdowne Club has also supplied nine British and Irish Lions, including two members of the 2005 New Zealand squad, Shane Horgan and Gordon D'Arcy. More recently, Felipe Contepomi became the club's ninety-ninth overall and first overseas international. Today Horgan, D'Arcy and Contepomi are also vital cogs in Leinster's exciting three-quarter line.

On two occasions in 1931, Lansdowne supplied the entire Irish three-quarter line – Jack Arigho, Eugene Davy, Morgan Crowe and Ned Lightfoot – one of only three clubs ever to have done so at international level worldwide.

Lansdowne have won the Leinster Senior Cup a record twenty-four times, as well as winning the most Leinster Senior League titles (at nine). Since the club's first Senior Cup victory in 1891, Lansdowne has won a total of 104 Leinster branch trophies as well as six national titles.

Donal Lenihan

Lock

1981–1992

He was fourteen when he and a few school friends first travelled by train to Lansdowne Road to watch Ireland play an Overseas XV in September 1974. Donal Lenihan was giddy with the prospect of watching Irish players – Willie John McBride, Fergus Slattery, Mike Gibson and Tom Grace – who had morphed into legends after the most successful Lions tours ever in 1971 and 1974.

These were the names that fascinated him most as a schoolboy while training at Lansdowne, Christian Brothers College training ground in Cork. Little did the teenage Donal realise that he would one day line out alongside some of these luminaries.

The South Terrace was his vantage point that afternoon when Ireland drew 18–18, but the day is locked forever in his treasure chest of Lansdowne memories. And, in an era when pitch invasions were the norm, Lenihan couldn't resist the opportunity of squeezing his way through the throng and onto the hallowed turf. The young Lenihan was developing into a second-row of some renown at CBC, so he could really only identify with and be drawn to one man. 'I remember Willie John going off the field and I managed to run over and give him a tap on the back. That was the first time I ever got on the pitch at Lansdowne Road.'

Lenihan worked his way through the Ireland system and was capped at Schools, U23 and B levels before going on to earn his first cap at senior level against Australia in the autumn of 1981. He had become good friends with Trevor Ringland, who also won his first cap that day, through their University Colours games; Lenihan lining out for UCC and Ringland for Queen's.

He wasn't without other friends on the team that faced Australia when Brendan Foley stepped in for the injured Moss Keane to partner him in the second-row. It was a partnership that had helped beat Australia five days earlier when the duo lined out for Munster. 'It's funny but, in those days, it was almost sacrosanct that you didn't play the Saturday before your first cap,' says Lenihan. 'I played for Munster against Australia on the Tuesday before my first cap [against Australia]. We beat Australia in Musgrave Park and a few days after I was playing the same opposition. So, in some ways it was nearly an anti-climax that you played Australia and beat them on a Tuesday, then you're playing them in your first international game on a Saturday. But in those days – and again it'll tell how things have changed – it was felt that Australia was a good game to get a taste of international rugby before the Five Nations came around in January.' Instead, it turned out to be a good game for Australia who won 16–12.

Lenihan's second cap came the following January against Wales in the Five Nations at Lansdowne Road. Moss Finn was also making his debut at a time when only few Corkmen got on the Irish team. 'Moss got famously concussed that afternoon but scored two tries in the game, David Irwin broke his leg and Michael Kiernan another Corkman came on for his first cap. The three of us would have been great buddies, so for all that to happen in the one game, it was phenomenal. Ringland also scored that day, so it was a memorable game from that point of view.'

It was an extraordinary day for the Irish who beat a much-vaunted Wales team, 20–12, but Lenihan's memories of the crowd's contribution to the occasion lived with him long afterwards. As a columnist with the *Irish Examiner*, he wrote after the Munster–Leinster European Cup semi-final at Lansdowne Road in 2006 that, while Leinster fans came to be entertained, Munster fans came to participate. That's how it was in Lansdowne Road twenty-five years earlier. The large Wales following, blessed with so much success, waited for the fireworks; the Irish fans instead played the veritable sixteenth man and, allied with a mammoth input from the forwards, the occasion was momentous for a lad like Lenihan new on the Irish scene. 'Try scoring wasn't as prevalent as it is now. So for Ireland to score three tries against Wales was special and the crowd really got behind the team.'

Lenihan roomed with Moss Keane and, before his first cap, he remembers waking up in the Shelbourne Hotel to the sight of Keane eating three raw eggs. He says their room was like an alternative medicine centre but Moss doctored him brilliantly through his first cap. 'I had played with him for Munster for a year beforehand. We went on to play on the Irish team together for

First cap, first steal: Corkman Donal Lenihan starts his international career in spectacular fashion stealing an Australian throw in autumn 1981. Other Irish players in shot are Phil Orr, Robbie McGrath and Willie Duggan.

three years, and we always roomed together. I have always said that if you survived the Thursday and Friday with Moss before the match, the game was a piece of cake! Moss would have around six raw eggs wrapped up in newspaper. He was ahead of his time in terms of nutrition! After missing the Australia game, Moss came back for the championship and I had held on to my place. Moss was coming to the end of his career so he allowed me to dictate the lineout on the premise that I would pick up their best man on their throw. So it worked in his favour as well! Moss would be thinking "leave the younger fellow off" but we had a great relationship. He is eleven years older than me. He used get great fun out of the pack called Dad's Army because I had just turned twenty-two.'

John O'Driscoll was twenty-eight but the rest of the pack was all over thirty. 'But, as Moss Keane used to say, Ollie Campbell and Robbie McGrath were half-backs and when everyone was talking about Dad's Army, he used to tell everyone that the average age of the second-row was less than the average age of the half-backs.'

Away from the madding crowd and the buzz of match days, masochistic mornings were spent on the two pitches behind the East Stand at Lansdowne in preparation for the Five Nations. The memory of those sessions on the back pitch puts a shiver up Lenihan's spine even now, but he was thankful in the end for the thorough preparation. 'Lansdowne Road for everybody is the pitch. For us who trained there every Sunday morning in squad sessions before internationals, we've horrific memories of being slaved to death on the back pitch. Half of the sessions were physical ones where you were run to death. While the glory part of the Five Nations is out on the main pitch, they say there are other parts where fellows would have a lot of shocking memories of endless training sessions!'

Training sessions were mostly just the team and a whipping wind in arctic conditions, but Triple Crown hype in 1982 and 1985 swelled attendances on the Sunday mornings before the deciders. 'You might have 1,000 people who would turn up on a Sunday morning to watch you training. We trained in Merrion Road before we played Scotland for the Triple Crown in 1982 and Tommy Kiernan was running the legs off us the Sunday before Saturday's game. I always remember Willie Duggan going up to him saying, "Tommy, unless you want me to sick in front of 1,000 people you better stop doing this training fairly quickly."'

Scrummaging in those days was 'live' and unmerciful. The absence of machines meant the daunting prospect of eight against eight in full combat. To the players, it resembled the closest definition of sadism, with onlookers seemingly taking pleasure in the combatants' pain. Lenihan recalls a morning when 500 people gathered in a circle watching Ireland going backwards or forwards in the scrum. These sessions would be ultra-competitive. Players would do anything to get ahead of another for a place in the pack on match day.

'Players would be getting pent-up, they'd be playing for their places. I remember one famous incident in 1982 before Ireland won the Triple Crown. Ginger McLoughlin was the only forward who got dropped and Mick Fitzpatrick from Leinster came in at tight head. But we had one of those full-on scrummaging training sessions. Ginger was at loose head for the opposition against Fitzpatrick; Brendan Foley was in the second-row behind Ginger and Colm Tucker was wing-forward. Fitzpatrick twisted in the scrum. The boys saw their opportunity and just drove right through it. Fitzpatrick destroyed his groin, Ginger got back into the team, held his place and we won the Triple Crown.'

Lenihan believes there is no stadium in the world where fans are as close to the players as they are at Lansdowne Road. As a youngster, he said he could literally see the steam rising from the packs and smell the Wintergreen rub. In recent years, he feels the 'Lansdowne Roar' has diminished into a squeal. The advent of the Celtic Tiger crowd and the accompanying corporate sideshow has resulted in a lowering of noise levels.

There was no better demonstration of this than Ireland's first Six Nations game against Italy in 2006. It was a one thirty kick-off and, when the players arrived out on the field seven minutes before kick-off, the East Stand was half empty and Lenihan, working for RTÉ Radio, empathised with the players who were greeted by hollow clapping and the sight of too many empty bucket seats.

'As a player you're so pumped up and then you come out on the field and all of a sudden you're looking at an empty stand. That would never have happened in the old days – people would be in their seats forty-five minutes before the game started.

'I think the crowds have changed in the last twenty-five years, the corporate element has come into it. "Cockles and Mussels" was the song most synonymous with Lansdowne Road. I'll always remember the 1982 game against Scotland, we were playing for the Triple Crown and there was so much hype because Ireland hadn't won it in thirty-nine years. With ten to fifteen minutes to go it was obvious Ireland were going to win the game, and there was a constant strain of "Cockles and Mussels" for ten minutes. I remember a 22 dropout for Ireland. The noise was so intense at that stage, an almost celebration that you were going to win something that hadn't been achieved for so long. Fergus Slattery had been on the team for twelve years at that stage and I remember just looking across – I was only a young fellow, my first year, my fifth cap – and catching Slattery's eye, he smiled as if to say, "Don't worry, lad, we have it won."'

There were many leaders in the Ireland dressing room, none more so than Willie Duggan, Slattery and Ciaran Fitzgerald whom Lenihan describes as 'real men'. He remembers going to the toilet ten minutes before kick off and seeing a trail of smoke snake over the top of one of the cubicles. It was Willie Duggan having the obligatory pre-match cigarette. 'That was sacrosanct, that was part of Willie's preparation.'

In 1985, Lenihan won his second Triple Crown and the build-up to Michael Kiernan's match-winning drop goal has gone down in folklore as a 'Cork' score. 'We were 10–10 with about four minutes to go. Michael Bradley, myself and Kiernan were involved. However Brian Spillane, a Kerryman, won the ball in the lineout but he was based in Cork at the time. I took it up the middle, Bradley fed Kiernan and Kiernan would have been shot if he didn't land the drop goal because we had a three to one overlap! I was in an unusual position, I was under on the sticks on my back. My son pointed me out in 2004 (the score was on the news over and over again for about three days prior to that year's Triple Crown match) on the ground as the ball was going over the bar with my hands up in the air. It looked a bit embarrassing.'

The crowd invasions deprived the team of enjoying a lap of honour and that is one of Lenihan's greatest regrets. Their moment of glory was over before it even started, although one or two grabbed plenty of limelight by strategically placing themselves enough distance from the players' tunnel so as to merit being shouldered off.

'Hugo MacNeill was a great man to land himself in the far corner, so he always got shouldered off, whereas all the dopey fellows ran off quickly! That's why he is in all the photographs up on people's shoulders. He didn't have the pace like the rest of us to get out of there! At least players today have an opportunity to savour a victory.'

Mick Doyle's idea for the 1985 Five Nations was to play a fast running game with Paul Dean, at out-half, chosen to execute a game-plan alien to the Irish rugby public. Doyler's free-spiritedness carried plenty of scepticism in the press and mockery across the water. When Will Greenwood's father said that 'the nation would need a brain transplant for Ireland to play running rugby', the Irish players needed little more motivation for the England game which was first in their Five Nations itinerary. The anger had to be stored up though when the game was cancelled due to a snowed over Lansdowne and the fixture pushed to the tail of the championship. But after wins over Wales and Scotland, it set up an intriguing Triple Crown face-off for the final game. 'Certainly, in 1985 when we won the Triple Crown, we played superb rugby right up to that England game. It lashed rain about an hour before kick-off and we had to change tactics in everything we did. In fairness to Doyle, that Irish backline was every bit as skilful as the backline that is there now. Dean was a gem at 10, he wasn't a great kicking out-half, but he had fantastic vision, superb hands.'

One of the Lenihan's proudest moments as captain was when Ireland beat England 17–0 in 1987. 'We destroyed them up front. It was a wet day, the pack were superb that day. You don't often beat England 17–0.'

Lenihan continued to soar to great heights during years of transition, and the glory years of 1982 and 1985 seemed a distant memory heading into the tumultuous 1990s. Before the 1991 World Cup, Lenihan knew that there wasn't much time left in his career. As he says himself, 'There were bits and pieces falling off me at that stage.'

Ireland played Australia in the quarter-final at Lansdowne Road and, as Lenihan recalls, the noise level was quite phenomenal. The Wallabies were favourites for the World Cup but Ireland were closing in on a shock win as Gordon Hamilton scored a try with a few minutes to go. The impossible seemed possible. Lenihan says he will never forget the silence that enveloped the old stadium when Michael Lynagh scored the winning try late in the game or the contrast in attitudes in the Ireland dressing room afterwards. 'My sister was at the game. She said afterwards that she just saw me coming off the field and never saw me so crestfallen. Some of the younger guys were saying, "Didn't we play great" whereas I knew we were within minutes of a home semi-final against the All Blacks who weren't going great – Australia hammered them the following week.

'I nearly had to be held back in the dressing room because one of the new younger players wanted to swap his tracksuit with one of the Australians. I was at the other end of the experience spectrum to the younger fellows who had played Australia for the first time. I had played against them seven or eight times at that stage. Beat them in a Munster jersey, was close a few times with Ireland but never beat them in an Irish jersey. Australia were an outstanding side in 1991 and they went on to win the World Cup.

'On a lighter note, I remember that day too that Nick Farr-Jones' wife had just arrived from Australia. They had a young baby and they were in before the game under the stand looking for the crèche facilities. I had to laugh. As players, we barely had showers!'

Lenihan was manager of Ireland when a new era of Irish rugby was ushered in for the Six Nations game against Scotland in Lansdowne Road in 2000. The game came hot on the heels of a thumping at Twickenham and, after ten minutes against the Scots, Ireland were trailing 10–0. Then everything changed with new caps Peter Stringer, Ronan O'Gara, Shane Horgan, John Hayes and Simon Easterby, helping Young Ireland to a 44–22 scoreline. 'Before the Scotland game, Warren [Gatland] had said that he was going to step down if we lost. Young fellows have no inhibitions, that's why if they're good enough, they have to be given the opportunity whereas a fellow who has been on the team for seven or eight years, he becomes so cute, he sees all the problems before they arise where as the young fellows have no inhibitions.'

Lenihan retains one hope when the great stadium does come tumbling down – that the new arena will retain that intimacy which made it so unique in world rugby. 'When comparing the old Lansdowne Road to the new Lansdowne Road – there is an intimidatory factor there in the old one which you tend to lose in new stadia, let's hope they'll be able to retain in the design. Because it's different to everywhere else, even the visiting teams like it from that point of view. They do find it intimidating when an Irish crowd gets behind a team … but the one thing that puts the visitors off even more than Ireland are the wind conditions, particularly for kickers. In our time, your main attribute was to get into teams, play with your heart and soul type of thing, and the conditions probably suited us. In latter years, with the improved quality in Irish play the conditions are a hindrance to them.'

Possession game: Donal Lenihan holds the ball close during the 1991 World Cup quarter-final against Australia at Lansdowne. Afterwards, he said he never felt so despondent. 'My sister was at the game … and said she'd never seen me so crestfallen.'

Syd Millar

Prop

1958–1970

Those who attended the final Irish training session twenty-four hours before the arrival of a glittering France team to Lansdowne Road in 1959 might have suspected something big was going down. Not a revolution, but a statement of sorts from the Irish forwards. For thirty relentless minutes, Syd Millar, the Ballymena tight-head prop, and his forwards executed moves similar to those that had given France all her success to date.

At this time, the French were a delight to watch, and had earned a reputation throughout the 1950s as the most exciting team in world rugby. Quite simply, they just loved to run the ball, with sleight of hand and adventurism the key components in their attacking armoury. They brought a flamboyance and romance to the game when most teams seemed happy to just kick to the corners and work off set-pieces. They invented what became known as the Lucien Mias peel (or as the French called it *percussion*). This move involved throwing a ball to the back of a lineout and flicking it down to a forward before driving at an opposing defender. It was most devastating on a five-yard lineout.

For that half hour during training at Anglesea Road, Ireland felt they could do the same, and Millar felt he was being transported to a more daring rugby world as captain Ronnie Dawson directed a series of drills and tactical manoeuvres that he hoped would ambush the French in Lansdowne Road.

Millar remembers drills consisting of quick, short passing moves and the flick backs from a lineout to another forward – the winds of change were blowing and it looked like Ireland were aiming to beat *les Bleus* at their own game.

Dawson's manoeuvres could be termed avant-garde, but whether it was his temerity or wisdom that made him adopt such a brave choice of tactics, they lifted the spirit of the squad. And Ireland's hopes of toppling the champions and the prospect of avoiding the Wooden Spoon that season grew as kick-off approached. 'There was a spring in our step going into that; after Ronnie [Dawson] drilled us in the finer arts of French forward play, some of us thought we were bloody invincible. But it was good to see so much confidence in the squad.'

On Saturday, 18 April 1959, Ireland was at its best for years, devising a fearless victory based upon the brilliance of the front eight led superbly by Ronnie Dawson and Number 8 Tony O'Sullivan. Quite simply, they mastered the French pack.

There was no stopping Ireland in a famous 9–5 win over a French team that could not get to grips with the pace of the Irish forwards, and what surprised *les Bleus* even more was the ability of Syd Millar and his front-row colleagues Dawson and Gordon Wood to cancel out their supposed superiority in this area. France, aiming for the Grand Slam, bottomed out and, though showing signs of a recovery late in the second half, found the bold, bright, adventurous Irish too good.

'1959 was exceptional year,' says Millar, 'because France were playing football differently and they had created a lot more in the forwards where they did the roll around the back of a lineout, and where they used their back-row in scrums. We didn't play that way – nobody played that way. Everybody said that was the game of the year and it probably was – we just shaded it. Our forwards were good; we got on top that day and we had a quick pack of forwards. We proved we were the team people said we were but we lost to Wales earlier in the championship on a dreadfully muddy, mucky Cardiff Arms Park.'

Millar has high praise for the half-backs who controlled matters against the French and who added their own sense of individualism to an occasion where teamwork was the mantra. He recalls Mick English playing 'hide-and-seek' with the French flankers and the amazing sight of the Limerick out-half slaloming by a few tackles and coming within inches of scoring a try. But the decisive score came after an inspired cameo from young Wanderers centre Kevin Flynn who set up Noel Brophy to score the try with a delightful pass.

In the other games of the 1959 championship, Ireland lost narrowly to England 0–3, beat Scotland 8–3, and were defeated by Wales in the mud at the Arms Park 8–6. Against England, Ireland wasted numerous opportunities to put points on the board and dominated the English for long patches.

It was incessant, relentless stuff as Ireland stormed the English line from kick-off but there was no breakthrough. England survived and managed to conjure up the only score during this period of Ireland dominance. 'He was only twenty-one at the time, but Beverly Risman beat us that day,' says Millar. 'We were hammering away at their line for the first twenty minutes but could not get a try or win a penalty. They were very disciplined under all that pressure. Still, I found they had a tough, abrasive pack. We were always accused of falling asleep in the last twenty minutes – that wasn't necessarily so. Teams would think, 'Ireland teams always go hammer and tongs for the first twenty minutes – if we hold out for that, they'll tire and make it easier for us.' But that team wasn't like that at all. It was a very good side. Especially Ronnie Dawson as hooker. He took about 50 per cent of their ball against the head. I remember Mick English, who I think got better as the tournament progressed, struck what we thought was a nice drop goal late in the first half. Most of the crowd thought it went over but the referee adjudged it to have gone wide.'

Millar knew he was in a game when South Africa came to Dublin in December 1960 – the battle up front was the ultimate battle of brawn. But Springbok teams of the 1960s were exciting and adventurous and those amongst the 40,000 at Lansdowne Road got the perfect opportunity to see some of the great players of South African rugby. One of the most noted was the centre John Gainsford. The Western Province player brought physical presence to midfield, a trait which modern Springbok teams possess to this day, and was regarded as a first-class crash tackler. Dave Hewitt was faced with the task of negating the influence of the Springbok centre, who won thirty-three caps for his country.

Captain for the Springboks was Avril Malan, the lock-forward who was regarded as one of the great leaders of South African rugby, but Millar's preoccupation centred on their feared props – loose-head Fanie Kuhn and tight-head Piet 'Spiere' du Toit. 'South Africa came and beat us but only just and that team was only beaten once on their tour by the Barbarians at Cardiff Arms Park – Wood, Dawson and myself were the front-row. They had outmuscled everyone in the scrum. We held them and took four against the head. But we thought very carefully about our scrum. They had a certain way of scrummaging – they went in very low and that could be troublesome. In those days, the tight-head could catch your jersey turn in and drive you down. Piet du Toit, for example, was a very strong guy, would take people down. We could have won that game. They scored a pushover try at the end.

'I still have a tape recording of that game. Samuel Walker did the commentary and he was saying at the end, "How are these packs still running?" It was a five-yard scrum and we got down a bit late. They managed to move and made it a two to three-yard scrum, then they moved us across the line and scored a try. I walked back into the dressing room exhausted – we all were, especially the front-row. The scrummaging was brutal. The difference between South Africa or New Zealand was the body contact against the South Africans.'

The 1961 Five Nations started at home with a first win over England in ten years, a match that owed more to Ireland's defence than attack; an attack where Tony O'Reilly was left cold on the wings. It grew increasingly tense in the second half as a talented England side launched a series of furious attacks on the Irish line and, though their rugby was open and attractive and they brought the margin down to three points, they were foiled by stoic Irish defence.

Millar remembers the danger came from England's out-half Richard Sharp. In possession, he knew the Number 10, alongside Dickie Jeeps, was capable of conjuring up the unexpected. England probed and asked questions of the Irish defence but the home side had all the answers.

Five minutes after the break, Ronnie Kavanagh's try and Jonathan Moffett's conversion made it 11–0, though Sharp and Rogers got tries to bring the margin down to three. The *Cork Examiner* pointed out that Millar 'with even more than his usual power did a towering job in the scrums and rucks'. Millar praised the Irish defence but he pointed to the coolness of scrum-half Jonathan Moffett who scored eight of his side's points – two penalties and conversion into a difficult breeze – it was so strong that Ronnie Dawson had to steady the ball for all three kicks.

'I had told Ronnie Dawson before the game that this guy can knock them over from well out. I remember a cup final in Ravenhill, when the kick was ten yards inside our half and Jonny hit it over. Now that was a heavy ball in those days. So we got the penalty and Ronnie says, "What do you think?" and I said, "Give it to the lad," and Jonny whacked it over. The two touchline kicks and were far out as well. Jonny went to New Zealand subsequently and still is there (a very big fruit farmer). But he was a hard man. But he got just two caps, the other was against Scotland.'

Millar remembers Tommy Kiernan's part in setting up Kavanagh for the try early in the second half. Kiernan, a member of a Cork rugby family with a long tradition in the game, came into the Irish team against England at full-back in the match at Twickenham in 1960. Overall, he played fifty-four matches for Ireland with his international career ending in Murrayfield in 1973. 'Tommy was a very skilled footballer,' says Millar, 'and in later years got a reputation as a classic full-back. He was a guy who could run and who changed the course of a game. Tommy always blamed me for dropping him when I was coach and I used to joke, "No, Kiernan – I kept you too long!" England is the one game we wanted to win more than any other. Lansdowne Road was our home and you could see people in the crowd that you knew. It held over 50,000 then, so you always felt you had a responsibility to these people, like you owed them something, something like what Munster have today. To win in Lansdowne Road in front of your own supporters was huge because you're doing something for them, never mind yourself. And beating England is special. I used to say, as coach when we played in Twickenham, "When you win here, every Paddy in England is standing tall for a year."'

Syd Millar learned that he was surplus to requirements at the end of the 1964 season when the Irish selectors dropped him; even Ulster dispensed with his services. The selectors considered him too old to continue propping their scrums, but Millar didn't curl up and fade away and knew props in the northern hemisphere got better in their thirties, often reaching the apogee of their career.

A dedicated player, the Ballymena tight-head aimed to become even stronger and fitter by undergoing a strict training and dieting regime. And he did. At thirty-three, he made his return to the Ireland team, this time on the other side of the scrum, in January 1968 at the very same venue where he won his first cap – the Stade Colombes. The result also went along similar lines as his first cap – a 6–16 defeat, but the season picked up with a draw in Twickenham and wins at home to Scotland and a star-studded Welsh side.

For the third time in three seasons, Ireland beat Australia in October 1968. This wasn't a bad Wallaby XV – earlier in the year they had already beaten the French and lost by only a point to New Zealand – so to see Ireland again triumphing on a scoreline of 10–8 brought into sharp focus the depth of talent on this Ireland side; in many people's estimation this was a group potentially on the cusp of greatness.

Ireland dominated the forward exchanges but displayed little imagination in the three-quarters. The game was won most impressively by Millar and the enormous contribution of Willie John McBride, Mick Molloy, Mick Hipwell and Ken Goodall. 'That quartet was masterful in every aspect of their game. We won an enormous amount of ball and perhaps should have scored more than ten points that day.'

Mike Gibson had one of his rare off days, his handling circumspect, he was unable to break the gain line and he couldn't inject any fizz into the Irish attack. The only sparkle came from winger Johnny Moroney.

Australia gave the excuse afterwards that they were tired after all their travelling, but this didn't cut any ice with the Irish – the Aussies had been out-muscled up front and, besides, the contributions of their half-backs, John Ballesty and John Hipwell, and the tireless foraging of flanker Greg Davis, could have lost by more than a mere two points.

The crowd had little to get excited about, too, and even Millar and McBride were reminded of their duty to entertain coming back to the pitch after half-time. 'I remember walking out with Willie John McBride after half-time and one or two of our committee members weren't too happy with the game, "Do you want us to win our not?" Willie said back.'

The match narrative should revolve around the best moments, which were the three tries. Ireland's first arrived after only seven minutes. Gibson's chip in behind the Australian defence was inch perfect, new cap Jimmy Tydings kicked it towards the line, Barry Bresnihan followed up and touched down, Kiernan added the extras.

Australia got on the score sheet close to the half-hour mark. A garryowen was sent into the Irish 25 and Taylor combined with Ballesty for the out-half to score. The conversion was missed.

Ireland completely dominated affairs in the second half, but their only reward was a try on sixty-five minutes. Millar remembers the sequence, 'Willie John's strength and quick thinking saw him break from the lineout, cut through the Wallaby defence and put Mick Doyle into space to run for the line. Doyle was halted but Goodall was in support, took the pass and scored.' Moroney, who was handed the kicking duties after Kiernan discovered it wasn't his day when he missed a few chances, converted to hand Ireland their third successive victory over the Wallabies.

Though the performance was imperfect, confidence soared going into the 1969 Five Nations. Another great Lansdowne memory was made against the reigning Grand Slam champions France in the opening game, and England fell in the next home game. Their win in Murrayfield put Ireland on course for a Grand Slam showdown in Cardiff but the bubble burst and the dream died a slow death. Their chance of immortality was gone.

Millar was part of the Irish team that played South Africa at Lansdowne Road in January 1970. 'We drew 8–8 and they didn't like it. They didn't play as well as we did and they blamed the referee for playing extra minutes.'

There were massive protests surrounding this fixture with the anti-apartheid movement staging a rally and march to Lansdowne the day of the game. Millar remembers the scale of the anger even when he and the team left the Shelbourne Hotel for the bus trip to the ground. 'As we walked down the street, they threw fruit at us but rugby players want to be apolitical – they're just interested in playing. We're better playing than trying to shift things along, I think. When we went to South Africa, we said we wanted to play against mixed teams, which we did, and we wanted a mixed crowd, which we didn't quite get. The Dublin match in 1970, whether it was right or whether it was wrong I'll never know. We were getting loads of stick but, once the game starts, you try to put it to the back of your mind.'

The spectre of politics surrounded this fixture against South Africa, but Millar never had any problems coming to play in Lansdowne and face the Tricolour for the national anthems. 'I took great pride in playing in Dublin. As far as we're concerned, in rugby football we're one country. To wear the green jersey that's a source of great pride. I'd never any trouble facing the Irish flag. I felt comfortable with that. In later years, some of the Paisley faction would have comments about playing there. It doesn't matter what a man's religion or politics are – that's his own business.'

Syd Millar played his last game for Ireland in 1970 in Lansdowne Road – a revenge result from 1969, a thumping 14–0 victory over Wales. He has the unique distinction of playing for his country in three different decades.

Four years after stepping down as a player, Millar was the architect and brains behind Ireland's 1974 Five Nations championship triumph in his capacity as coach. Ireland probably should have had a few Grand Slams by then; in 1972 Wales and Scotland refused to travel to Lansdowne after receiving death threats from the IRA. The following season saw John Pullin's England side travel and receive an emotional welcome and standing ovation. 'The Scots let us down first of all. Ronnie Dawson had developed a very good side before – I tweaked it a bit more. I just felt sorry for him – he didn't get what he deserved and that was a Grand Slam winning team.'

When Millar took over as coach in 1974, he masterminded a victory for one of the greatest ever Irish teams, peopled by such legends as Mike Gibson and Willie John McBride. It was a monumental achievement by Millar – coaching wasn't really in vogue then, with Ronnie Dawson only coming in as Ireland's first coach in 1969. Millar's emergence as a top-class coach drew praise from Dawson who described him as one 'who had a fine rugby brain, was a good communicator and tactician'.

'We won the championship in 1974, Ireland's first success since 1951. That year also signalled the arrival of Moss Keane against France,' says Millar. 'We lost in France and beat England in Twickenham as well; Gibson scored two tries that day. Then we beat Scotland in Lansdowne to take the championship. As coach, I always started with attitude and pride in the performance and pride for the team. We were proud to be Irishmen that day. I used to do quite a bit of analysis on a board, and show it to the boys. I would ask them as well to analyse a red team and another group analyse a blue team. They do these swat tests now, squad analysis. We looked at the key factors like quality possession, giving quick ruck ball to the backs. The forwards know that the best ruck and mauls are the ones that kept the ball alive, which the French were very good at. We carried that philosophy through to South Africa in 1974 [where Millar coached the Lions and won twenty-two games from twenty-two including the three tests]. We wanted to keep the ball, we wanted to change the target of attack.' That they did and more, and Lansdowne Road witnessed one of its greatest ever occasions when Scotland were defeated 9–6. The championship was Ireland's.

Munster Supreme

The European Cup, 2006
Paul O'Connell & Declan Kidney

It might as well have been Thomond Park for two glorious spring days in April 2006. It sounded the same.

Anthony Foley didn't need to put in a request to Munster fans prior to their European Cup quarter-final against Perpignan to transform Lansdowne. No, the Munster captain knows better than anyone else the telepathy that exists between team and supporters and, on 1 April 2006, Munster's travelling horde helped in no small way to transform the old stadium into the most compelling theatre for European club rugby. The architecture of Lansdowne might differ to Thomond but the sound created inside by the red multitude was just as guttural as the renowned Thomond Roar. The estimated 47,500 Munster fans in attendance were going to give their boys the perfect backing track to the rock 'n' roll of their rugby. And, whether preordained or not, they were determined to distil an atmosphere more raucous and more intimidating than the bear pit that is Perpignan's Stade Aimé Giral in the Catalan region of southern France.

Head coach Declan Kidney – master motivator and tactician of Munster's success.

In the build up to their first Lansdowne date, Declan Kidney had been talking up Perpignan's strengths and ignoring their apparent weaknesses, arriving at a press conference in Thomond in midweek armed with a book of statistics, eulogising the French side's mean defence, their refusal to be intimidated by Munster and their huge fan base. Indeed, Perpignan's record in the qualifying stages in Pool 2 made for impressive reading and Kidney accentuated this point: fifty-two points and five tries conceded in six matches. That's some record, he was saying. Yet Munster boasted the second-best record from the pool stages – conceding eighty-seven points and just six tries. Kidney's ability to play down Munster's chances and play up the opposition's is part cute Corkonian, part psychology. One bookmaker had Munster five to one on to win and, when the information was relayed to the top table, Kidney just deflected the attention away from his side and again onto Perpignan, and you felt that the province rested more easily that night with this man in charge. 'Thankfully, we didn't pay any attention to them [the bookies],' Kidney reflects, 'because they [Perpignan] had the best defensive record in the European Cup and we hadn't played together for over two months. A lot of guys were coping with things that were happening off the pitch too.'

Indeed, the weeks around the tie had become difficult ones off the field for the players still coming to terms with the tragic death of their friend, Conrad O'Sullivan, the Cork Constitution three-quarter who had worn the Munster jersey with distinction at various levels in previous seasons. A minute's silence was respectfully kept when both teams lined up in front of the West Stand, but the poignancy of the moment, wrapped into the biggest game in world club rugby that weekend, was too much to bear for some players. Especially Conrad's good friend and Munster out-half Ronan O'Gara, who allowed tears to stream down his cheeks.

Emotions were high and it spurred some players to greater performances. They had spoken about it and vowed to give a performance that would do Conrad proud. Paul O'Connell's friendship with Conrad went all the way back to schools level. 'A lot of guys played with him, a lot of guys knew him growing up,' O'Connell says. 'It was very emotional. We were discussing all week what things we could do to remember him. It became a big motivating factor for us that week. He was a great guy. His career was destined towards Munster and maybe it had taken a turn in the last few years. I think he would have come back into the fold. I think if you look at the minute's silence a lot of guys there got very emotional. If you look at the funeral and the number of guys, many UCC guys, so many guys from Cork and the rugby scene in Cork, you could see how popular he was. I played with him with Munster schools. They played the video of him at half-time on the big screen and we were all aware of that happening. It was mentioned several times. It did his memory proud.'

With a home venue and the vocal power of the sixteenth man, Munster were expected to win but there were mitigating factors going into their eighth consecutive European Cup quarter-final. The last time they had lined out with a full complement was for their captivating win over Sale Sharks in Thomond Park on 21 January. Nine of the side that defeated Sale had just come off a successful Six Nations, capturing the Triple Crown in Twickenham on St Patrick's weekend but there was a fear that lack of playing time together as a whole Munster unit might tear their season apart. Then, seven days before facing Perpignan, Munster's preparations were thrown into disarray: their Celtic League game against Llanelli Scarlets had to be cancelled due to a flooded Stradey Park. Perpignan, on the other hand, looked in fine fettle in their preparations scoring an amazing three-point victory away to Bourgoin in the French championship in front of 30,000 delirious home supporters the weekend before the quarter-final. Over the previous six weeks, they had played each of the Heineken Cup contenders, Biarritz and Toulouse, as well as other French heavyweights Stade Français and Clermont Auvergne. 'We came off the Six Nations and had no game as a team for two or three months. That was a big issue,' says O'Connell. 'No matter how big you are, no matter how good a team you are, if you don't play together week in, week out, you don't get the consistency you need, not to mention not playing together for three or four months. So that was a big thing for us. But, essentially, we were at home, we were in a very good frame of mind and a very focused frame of mind at that time. I think guys were in very good shape after the Six Nations. We didn't play well against Perpignan but I don't think we were ever going to lose to them.'

Kidney hadn't been in charge the last time Munster played a knockout tie in the European Cup at Lansdowne Road. In 2004, on a balmy afternoon of high expectations amidst a heart-warming kaleidoscope of colour, Warren Gatland's Wasps came and spoiled what was otherwise a magical Lansdowne day in the semi-final. Kidney, as a spectator, saw battle-hardened men like Lawrence Dallaglio and Joe Worsley unfazed by the red tsunami on the stands and terraces and knew, deep down, that Perpignan were of the same ilk – tough men who would come to fight and not be intimidated. And he knew, too, that Perpignan had the added advantage of having won a semi-final against Leinster in Lansdowne in 2004. 'There's a little bit of a belief that if you get a home quarter-final against a French team you're OK but that's very far from the truth – that's like saying we can't win in France. The last time Munster had played a European Cup match in Lansdowne Road, we'd lost and the last time Perpignan played a European Cup match in Lansdowne Road, they'd won – so thankfully we didn't feed into that. The game was exactly as we thought. There were a lot of things going on leading into the 2006 quarter-final – the television was on in the hotel, for the first half of the Leinster match so, the draw had been made and it was quite apparent that the winners of our game would be playing Leinster.'

Without match practice on the Celtic League stage, Munster practised on the back pitch of Thomond and confronted any apparent flaws head on – literally. Utility forward Mick O'Driscoll had spent two years in Perpignan and understood the Catalans' psyche and that they possessed one of the most abrasive packs in French or European rugby. Not that Munster were shrinking violets in the forward exchanges. Munster's reputation had been forged on their forwards, but this would be a different kind of battle and preparation was key – O'Driscoll and Foley brainstormed and came up with a key training drill. 'Micko came in on the Tuesday,' says O'Connell, 'and said, "This is what they'll give us – they'll hit hard. They're going to be offside in a ruck, so they're going to be offside in a maul and you have to deal with it, you'll have to hit them hard in rucks, you'll have to protect your rucks, get numbers to the rucks." We kind of trained like that during the week, struggled with it at the start until we realised what level we had to get to, to defend the way they play. That training was excellent.'

'It was a real squad effort to win,' says Kidney. 'Because the players were without any match practice we had a ten to fifteen-minute training session on the Tuesday before and they flaked into one another. The fellows who took the pitch on the Saturday were well used to what was going to come against them, which was just as well.'

The game against Perpignan fell on Saturday, 1 April and a story hit the front page of the *Irish Examiner* that Ronan O'Gara might miss the game because of a hamstring injury picked up at training the previous day. Despite rumblings from supporters that this story was written in bad taste, O'Gara's injury was no hoax. 'Yes, he was struggling badly with a hamstring injury,' says O'Connell, 'and he said that was the closest he ever came to pulling out of a game. We didn't know ourselves up until the last minute whether ROG was going to be playing or not. Thanks be to God he made the field.'

Kidney adds, 'It was touch and go as to whether he would be comfortable enough to take the pitch and to be able to take it under those circumstances with everything that was going on. Then there is that case where you're 10 goes out, you get the best medical care, you weigh up the situations, but you don't put the player out unless he's comfortable – that's putting a huge onus on the player. You don't put anyone out who is unnecessarily in danger. When you have an injury like that and you're the place-kicker, you're a pivot for the team, it takes a lot of courage to go out and do what he did that day.'

As predicted, the Catalans came out in bullish form. After the friendly fire posted by both camps in the pre-match build-up, it was down to an old-fashioned shootout in the oldest stadium in the world. From the off, the game took on the spectre of a war of attrition and Mick O'Driscoll's 'boot camp' cameo had its uses. 'I remember the start of the game,' says Paul O'Connell, 'where we took the ball into contact once or twice, literally in the first few seconds and got blown off it, and it was a real wake up call for us.'

'There are many, many ways in playing the game of rugby – some are more television friendly than others, but I respect all the types of rugby games,' says Kidney. 'They were playing to their strengths; they were incredibly quick on the counter-attack but, thankfully, we didn't give them the space to show that. We managed to close them down and not give them too many loose balls to come at us – I mean that's where they got their try in the first half.'

For the opening fifteen minutes, Munster engaged in an all-out attack, but the Perpignan defence remained unyielding and steadfast. If nails were being whittled to the quick amongst the red hordes, Kidney revealed afterwards it was a game of patience, even when it seemed a stalemate was ensuing. 'We were on the attack for the first ten or fifteen minutes, we didn't score, we kept the ball in hand, we were against the breeze, so you can lose games in the first fifteen minutes, but you don't actually win them. So it was a bit like the final. It was 10–10 after twenty-one minutes in Cardiff. In the Perpignan game to be 0–0 wasn't the worst place to be after fifteen minutes and we were against the wind. The conditions weren't great; there was a bit of a wind, moisture around. It was a tough, tough game. If you asked any of the players, they'd tell you if it wasn't the most physical match that they played in 2006 it was right up there with it. We won a couple of penalties but opted to kick to touch instead of taking a pot at goal. Against the breeze, they weren't kickable options and they were around the halfway line. If that was against the breeze and they fell short that would have given them easy ball, if O'Gara felt it was outside his range. Better to kick to touch, retain the ball and play the game like that. At that level, you need to play two or three different type of games in an eighty-minute period.'

Eventually, the breakthrough came via O'Connell on nineteen minutes – the lock's form had reached extraordinarily high levels and some commentators were drawing colourful comparisons between his deeds and Superman's. He crashed over the low tackle of Christophe Manas to score in the very same corner of his first Ireland try which came against Wales in 2002. 'We kept trying and trying to play for eighty minutes non-stop,' recalls O'Connell. 'Very often when you're hammering at a team's line, you may not score. But you're sapping them and you're taking the energy out of their legs. We were just working so hard to get over, we had a few pick and gos, a few one-off runners like Flanns [Jerry Flannery] running at their backs, and then Strings popped it to me on the blind side. I probably could have passed it to Axel [Anthony Foley], but I think I flopped over the winger. We were on the way then.'

Kidney says that, because they were playing against the wind and because they had to keep ball in hand, the champagne rugby and new-found optimism in the backline served up away to Castres and at home to Sale earlier in the competition had suddenly morphed into something less attractive. In the end, winning was all that mattered. 'It really was just battering, wasn't it?' he says. 'We just stayed at it and stayed at it. It might be unattractive but to be able to do that against a team of their record is commendable. It is tough, tough rugby. The men that were out there on both sides would have to be respected and I think you see it when the final whistle goes, they all shake hands – I think sometimes that's neglected.'

Superman arrives: Munster lock, Paul O'Connell breaks the deadlock on nineteen minutes against Perpignan crashing over in the exact spot (the East Stand corner) of his first Ireland try against Wales in 2002.

On twenty-eight minutes, twenty-one-year-old Mathieu Bourret scampered through a hole in the Munster defence and Lansdowne fell silent. Some say Bourret eyed up the inexperienced Tomás O'Leary – nominally a scrum-half – but the Cork lad was asked to fill a position vacated by the injured Barry Murphy. 'We left a loose ball and they picked it up and counter-attacked,' says Kidney, 'and if you like we had a system error that wasn't actually Tomás's fault – Tomás was the easiest fellow to pick on because he was new to the position. We would never name names, there was a system error between us, and it wasn't his error in any shape or form.'

'There was a half mistake made and no little skill from them as well. It did us no harm,' recalls O'Connell. 'It put the guys on their toes. When we played Leinster, we defended outstandingly well against one of the best backlines in club rugby.'

The positioning of O'Leary at centre was a risk but as they say in soccer parlance 'the boy did good'. Barry Murphy's absence, after picking up an ankle injury against Ulster in the Celtic League on 3 March, left Kidney with the task of reinventing their whole backline. 'Any time a team plays, you try and play to your strengths so you see who you have. I've had many discussions with a good friend of mine, Tim Crowe in St Clements, as to whether you pick the best players or the best team. It's just different approaches to games. It was really a case of horses for courses on the day given everything that was happening in the lead up to it – like not having played as a full squad for two months; the Llanelli game being called off the week before; dealing with other real-life issues; O'Gara getting a hamstring strain, and, most important of all, Conrad's death – we all knew him so it's a real-life event.'

The collisions at the breakdowns were colossal and fiercely competitive but Perpignan's indiscipline in this area proved costly and they suffered two sinbinnings. And, just on half-time, they got a little tetchy by the touchline under the West Stand. Coming to pick a fight in what was Munster's backyard for an afternoon was a silly tactic by Perpignan. 'They were full of aggression and you have to meet that aggression every time and let guys know you won't be going backwards,' says O'Connell. 'They'd a few tough guys in their pack like [Marius] Tincu and [Rimas] Alvarez and there were little schmozzles. You try not to throw a punch or whatever, but you let them know that we're not to be messed with. That's an old-fashioned French thing and it doesn't really work anymore against Irish teams, and you just have to make sure they know that.'

Perpignan's indiscipline allowed Munster to turn a 10–7 half-time deficit into a 13–10 lead by the forty-eighth minute. Munster, sensing the finishing line, defended Perpignan's mauls expertly with O'Connell at the centre of them driving the French left and right and never allowing them to build up any forward momentum. The French team's frustrations multiplied and, by the sixty-ninth minute, O'Gara had scored three more penalties making it 19–10. There was pain etched across the out-half's face when he struck his last penalty. 'Obviously, the leg would have been tight,' says Kidney. 'When you kick, you extend your body to a limit. Knowing that you have to go through that to get to the point where you can't hold back from the kick. But that's the nature of the game; it's the nature of all top-class sport that you push yourself to the limit.'

Still Perpignan came hunting and carved open some opportunities, but Bourret missed three eminently kickable penalties in the last fifteen minutes while their attempted drop goals, a feature of their game in the French Top 14, failed to hit the target. 'They took a drop goal from the ten-metre line, and it went wide,' recalls Kidney. 'Then we took a long 22 and then he [Bourret] tried another one from his own ten-metre line and he wasn't too far off it – drop goals were in their game-plan.'

'We needed to close the game off,' says O'Connell. 'We just kind of squeezed the life out of them. We weren't as fluid as we would have liked to have been. We hadn't played in three or four months. It became a game of patience; it was about winning the game. And that's what we did.'

It wasn't until the seventy-seventh minute that 'The Fields of Athenry' once again began to reverberate around Lansdowne and the Munster fans could rest a little easier. 'Anytime the Perpignan fans starting shouting, that's when the Munster fans dug in,' remembers Kidney. 'They weren't found wanting. At half-time, everybody would have been getting a bit nervous, but you have to play through that – the Munster fans are knowledgeable and they know when you're trying and that's the only thing they ever crib about – if we aren't.'

Boks of class: Perpignan's Ovidiu Tonita and Rimas Alvarez struggle to dispossess South African Trevor Halstead.
Halstead left a magnificent imprint during Munster's 2006 European Cup odyssey.

Perpignan went home thinking they could have won this game. 'I wouldn't argue with that,' continues Kidney. 'That game could have gone either way. And that's why it was such a great win because, if you can come through days like that, they're good wins. Like the game against Dragons earlier on in the year when people didn't give them credit for being the team that they are.'

Hours before Munster toppled Perpignan, Leinster had travelled to southern France to take on Toulouse, the reigning European champions, in Le Stadium in front of 37,000, including 6,000 of their own. It proved to be an extraordinary day for Leinster, producing one of the greatest performances in the European club competition. Munster's win later that afternoon set up the mother of all meetings in the semi-final – a local feud that would capture the imagination of everyone in Ireland. An All-Ireland final, the culchies against the city slickers, a clash of rugby cultures or, as Matt Williams, former coach of Leinster, wrote in *The Irish Times*, 'Munster reminds me of an anaconda. They attack in a vicious and brutal way, pin you down and then squeeze the life out of you. You suffocate under the pressure. Leinster reminds me of a cheetah, so quick to strike you almost don't see it coming.'

The subplots, the head to heads, the strengths and weaknesses were dissected and trisected in the build-up to the Battle of Ireland: Ronan O'Gara versus Felipe Contepomi; Paul O'Connell versus Malcolm O'Kelly; David Wallace and Keith Gleeson – and was Declan Kidney about to mastermind the downfall of a Leinster side he managed the previous season? Munster and Leinster had met 121 times but, in a packed ground on a scorching hot day, Lansdowne reverberated like never before.

Eight years earlier, just 1,000 souls had bothered to turn up for a Munster–Leinster inter-provincial match, ties which historically always had their fair share of needle and niggle and battle for local bragging rights. 'In 1998, we'd a cracking 9–6 match!' Kidney jokes. 'I think there might have been 1,000 to 1,500 at the game. The following year we were in Dooradoyle – we'd a big crowd that day – 2,000! And we managed to lose that one and then, around 2001, we managed to half fill Lansdowne Road between us for the Celtic League final. Munster were hugely disappointed that time.' These old inter-pros would usually see Munster arrive with a perceived sense of injustice wondering why so few of their players, and so many of Leinster's, were making the Ireland team. It was also easy to be over-simplistic when figuring out their playing styles. Munster would bring the pack of forwards, Leinster the backs and the comments prior to the 2006 clash were no different – Munster forward power versus Leinster's swashbuckling three-quarter play.

Ever since their defeat to Northampton in the 2000 final, the European Cup had turned into a crusade for Munster, and for their supporters. Each new season brought new hope, incredible highs and the pain of defeat in the latter stages of the competition. Many Munster fans were living their lives through this Munster team – 22,000 tickets were available to divide between the provinces for the 2006 semi-final, but there wasn't enough to satisfy the red hordes. On match day inside the stadium, Munster's resourcefulness was yet again evident, as they outnumbered the Leinster support by three to one. On the team bus from the Radisson Hotel, the players passed through Ballsbridge and Shelbourne Road, but all they saw was a tide of red shirts. If ever a team had found the formula for province-hood, it was Munster. 'There's a huge honour to try to represent the people who come along to these matches,' says Kidney. 'Whether people actually get tickets or not, it's all the one to us. We are a representative side. We accept the responsibility that goes with that but also the honour that goes with being able to do it.'

The hysteria surrounding 'Seismic Sunday' reached epidemic levels but these were golden days for Irish rugby. The streets of Limerick and Cork were battlegrounds for those players brave enough to walk down O'Connell Street or Patrick Street. 'There was a massive build-up to it, but that's part and parcel of it,' says O'Connell. 'You can't hide away – you have to deal with it and get on with it. We've all played in big games, big games in Ireland and in Munster and, sure, this was maybe a little bit higher again but you just get on with it and deal with it. That's what we did – we dealt with it quite well. You don't try and pretend it's nothing. It is big and you acknowledge it and say, "God this is massive," but you just try and get on with your job. The money supporters spend is incredible. That's something we always try to get across to the supporters that we appreciate. It's not cheap to go to the south of France; it's not easy to go to Wales, England all the time. They've just been remarkable – the money they spend and the emotion they invest in supporting us, it's incredible and it has been brilliant for us.'

O'Connell says the red tsunami in the South Terrace and on the East Stand proved a huge motivating spur during the pre-match warm-up, and the bond between team and supporters seemed stronger than ever. 'You use any bit of motivation you get for every game, the supporters are something we feed off all the time.' Clichés regarding the importance of the sixteenth man had never become more pertinent, not that Leinster's supporters – who proudly chanted '*Allez les Bleus*' – shirked their responsibilities in cheering their men in the blue end of Lansdowne.

In one sense, it was strange and surreal watching best friends warm up in different corners in different colours, friends who'd spent so much time in Ireland camp, hotels from Auckland to Sydney to Cape Town, who once played boules on the manicured lawns of their hotel in Paris in the springtime. Only on St Patrick's weekend had they being celebrating into the late hours in central London a Triple Crown victory and suddenly … they were opposites for eighty minutes. 'Strange? It is – but it's actually just a game,' says O'Connell. 'There's no real mouthing going on in the game; there was no bitching at each other – just two teams going at it as hard as they could. And that's all it was.'

Injuries to key players has deprived Munster of certain victory in previous European campaigns and, this time, Peter Stringer's participation was in doubt right up to kick off. The progress report read good that morning, the scrum-half looked waspish in the gardens around the Radisson and, six hours later, looked lean and hungry in the warm-up. Kidney, his mentor since their days in PBC, gave Stringer every chance to prove his fitness. He remembered the moment Strings received a lash in the back four days before the game at training in Musgrave Park. 'He got an awful clatter in the back which was reverberating right down through his leg like sciatic pain. But the power of positive thinking is amazing. Peter said, "No, I'll be fine." I had brought in two extra scrum-halves and that probably made him get better even faster. He was taking all the treatment, getting acupuncture. From his point of view, they couldn't put enough needles into him! He took all that, got himself ready and played the match and, through experience, managed his way through the game.' Even O'Connell paid tribute to the big heart of the little fellow. 'He's a born winner. He has a refusal-to-lose attitude in every game he plays – it was a brilliant sight to see him take the jersey and say, "I'll play."'

Munster returned to the 'home' dressing room which they'd chosen after a flip of a coin. 'This was no different to when we tossed for the dressing room in Bordeaux in 2000,' says Kidney, 'or for warm-up in the South Terrace where the fans were in situ – all that is pre-decided before the game – tosses for dressing room, tosses for which supporters go to which end of the ground, or whichever end your supporters were in you had to warm up in – that's all preordained.'

Former Munster full-back, Dominic Crotty dropped into the dressing room in advance to say

87

Red tsunami: Supporters celebrate Munster's second try during the European Cup semi-final against Leinster. 'They've just been remarkable,' says Paul O'Connell. 'The money they spend and the emotion they invest in supporting us has been brilliant for us.'

a few words, John Kelly's pre-match words brought the importance of playing for Munster out in each player and messages from former players were read out. The tools of motivation were working wonders and the adrenaline was pumping. 'It all helps,' says O'Connell. 'You use everything and anything you get your hands on. The whole fraternity of Munster that week came together.'

Kidney has been in these big matches in the past. He knows the score, the players know the score and he left them to their own devices during those six minutes after the end of the warm up, when they return to the dressing room before taking the field again. Kelly spoke passionately, as did Foley, who'd seen and experienced it all. 'The six minutes before they leave the dressing room again − that's their time. They don't really want a whole lot more time in there. It's about the players ownership of what they're doing and Munster are very lucky that they have men to do that. The idea of the warm-up is that they're all but ready to go. You don't want to be cooling down too much. It's an interesting thing, the Premiership has fifteen minutes at half-time − I'd say some of the players might not be too keen on that. If Claw was around, I could imagine him not being overly happy with having fifteen. It's bad enough having ten minutes sitting around the place − after fifteen you start getting stiff and the bones have to get going again.'

Both teams walked out to the deafening din side by side, although Munster had kept Leinster waiting under the West Stand for a few minutes. Few players looked across at each other although Rob Henderson winked at Emmett Byrne. When they walked up the steps and onto the field, the noise level peaked.

Munster got the best possible start from the kick-off. Malcolm O'Kelly dropped the ball, Donncha O'Callaghan gathered and Munster banged over a penalty but Kidney looked sympathetically on O'Kelly pointing to the Lansdowne Road factor. 'You're playing in Lansdowne Road remember. It's very easy to be critical from the stands − all of a sudden you get that little whip of wind. You're under the ball one minute, then a little breeze comes in off Sandymount and it's two yards away from you. That's the nature of Lansdowne. You don't have to worry about that in your indoor stadia; you don't have to worry about that in a lot of other stadia. But if you get the nature of stands the way they're built there − two open-end terraces, just away from Sandymount Strand − you never know what way the breeze is going to go. Everybody would talk about the likes of Girvan Dempsey, Hugo MacNeill or Tommy Kiernan − that they were all safe pairs of hands. You'd want to be one hell of a full-back to be safe in Lansdowne Road. Nobody had any idea how good those players were to be able to cope with that side of Lansdowne. Any full-back who can manage Lansdowne there's a lot of credit due to him.'

O'Connell was a force of energy from start to finish and, on eight minutes, his lineout steal earned Munster a penalty forty-five metres from goal. Foley and O'Gara had a quick chat, and seemed to be putting down a statement that they were going for touch and going for a try. O'Gara, in the form of his life, placed it beautifully in the corner and, from the lineout, O'Connell brought the ball down one-handed and the ensuing wedge to the line saw Denis

Leamy power over. 'The maul was a bit of a messy one,' remembers O'Connell. 'I think good players have a very good nose for the line; you see it with Axel all the time. There was a lot of work there to do that for Leamy. He got the job done and got over the line. I think we'd done enough to get over and he just had a good little nose for the line.'

On thirteen minutes, John Kelly took a 'stinger' on his left shoulder and walked off disconsolately and in his place came Rob Henderson. 'Rob hadn't a lot of time to warm up,' says Kidney, 'and he hadn't a lot of game time this season either because of different injures and bangs and knocks. O'Gara showed his experience from a lineout off the top and moved the ball to Hendo to give him a quick first touch. That's experience for you. I think Paul said at the end of the game that he didn't know who the backline was but he didn't care because he knew that whoever came in would do a job.'

The fury of Munster's challenge, allied to workmanlike recycling and smooth offloading and the sheer power of the forwards was relentless and unending. Inside the Leinster half, Munster pounded the blue *résistance* but, to the Leinster forwards' credit, they didn't wilt or leak another try until the eightieth minute. But the greatest tribute that could be paid to Munster was their

89

Old friends are best: Ireland's three locks grapple at a maul during the European Cup semi-final. On the left is Malcolm O'Kelly (Leinster), middle of picture Donncha O'Callaghan and Paul O'Connell.

ability to deny the Leinster three-quarters possession during almost the entire first half. Felipe Contepomi, who did so much to bring Leinster to this stage of the competition, couldn't settle and looked ruffled and cranky with the red shirts in his face. Only once in the first half did Michael Cheika's side manage to give legs to their backline. Keith Gleeson – Leinster's best player – turned over Munster ball, Contepomi swept wide to Shane Horgan who found Denis Hickie and the winger switched into fifth gear.

From these positions, Leinster could carve open opposition, and what was probably the try of the tournament – when Hickie scorched over for a glorious second-half try against Toulouse in the quarter-final – had come from a similar position. Horgan's pass sent Hickie winging down the touchline and then … well, Superman flew cross-field doing enough to put the flying winger off kilter. 'I may have pushed him a bit wider,' says O'Connell, 'but Shaun Payne was the one who essentially got across and made the tackle and got him into touch. It was outstanding work by Shauny – he is one of these guys who does his job week in week out at the highest level without us having to worry about him at all. He's an outstanding athlete, a great pro and he had been brilliant for Munster.'

Kidney, who had coached the Leinster *galacticos* the previous season, knew their instincts and abilities and their eye to ruthlessly expose defences. According to Kidney, stopping Hickie was a huge turning point in the game. 'Well, he [Denis Hickie] didn't really get past Paul – Paul pushed him enough to the touchline, then Shaun was coming across. The pitch in Lansdowne is four inches narrower than the pitch in Toulouse because Denis did the exact same thing against Toulouse – he wasn't pushed as much to the touchline but I think it was the way Paul pushed him that extra six inches closer, then Shaun came across and all of a sudden there's a toe in touch. So, instead of the score being 10–7, Munster were 13–0 up. That's a huge advantage. That moment was pivotal.'

You could say Munster monopolised possession in that half; they'd a vice-like grip of the ball and wouldn't share it. It sucked the life out of the Leinster attack. In the upper tier of the West Stand, Leinster backs coach David Knox was animated and urged his team to run with the ball. But with the little ball they had, they were swallowed up by a tide of red shirts. Leinster, in need of oxygen, flatlined. 'I think Leinster won the toss and went against the breeze, so we had to try,' says Kidney. 'Leinster are the sort of side that you don't give up the ball to easily. They are capable of running in a lot of points in minutes – you look at their game against Bath, the previous season, they were dead and buried and, three minutes later, they won the match because they scored fourteen points in three minutes. It wasn't down to me – that, in 2005, was purely the players.'

Munster led 13–6 at half-time and continued to bombard the Leinster line after the interval. Leinster impressively withstood three quick tap penalty attempts by Munster close to the line, and then started playing a bit of rugby themselves, generating quick ruck ball and moving it wide. In the midst of all this counter-attacking stood O'Connell, putting in hit after big hit. Munster had lost the full-time services of their defence coach, Graham Steadman, after flooring Sale in January, and in his place came Australian Tony McGahan. The changing of the guard was smooth and the results refreshing, according to O'Connell. 'Defence is all about working hard and communicating and doing all the basic little things well. Graham Steadman leaving was a big loss to us but Tony McGahan came in with new ideas and refreshed us a bit which was great. It kicked us on and, essentially, a lot of the newer stuff we were doing was very helpful in defending a team like Leinster. They love to offload so much; they look for one-on-ones and switches and, very often, we work on our system with Mike Ford and Graham Steadman, but with Tony McGahan it was defending the individual a lot and doing little bits like that. We were under pressure in the game but that happens in every game. 'Every team has its purple patch and I think if you can react and defend well when a team has its purple patch, keep your head, not give away penalties just trust your defence which we did, you go a long way to winning a game. We came out of our line three times in the whole game but we managed to close up the gaps.'

'Thankfully we didn't panic,' recalls Kidney of that period when blue kept red from scoring a try time after time. 'Because we didn't get over at that stage, it was a case of fair play to them, they stopped us – we're in a hole but there's no need for us to dig further by forcing it too much. Then Felipe had a penalty in the second half that seemed to be going quite central, but Lansdowne Road and all its mysteries took over and it hit the left-hand post. That would have brought it to 13–9. So with Denis's chance in the first half and that penalty in the second half; now all of a sudden the game is turned on its head.'

Seven minutes from time, Freddie Pucciariello got sinbinned. The game was still in the balance – 16–6 – and the thought of Leinster running in two tries in five minutes must have crossed Kidney's mind. The sinbinning was something no Munster man needed. But panic stations in the red corner? You must be kidding. 'Freddie got sinbinned which was a bit of a worry,' says O'Connell, 'but, essentially, we stayed very patient, trusted our defence and kept going at them and weathered the storm and finished back up on the attack as well.'

At the next scrum, Kidney withdrew his skipper and spiritual leader, Anthony Foley. Foley, who is surely destined to one day be the province's head coach, admitted afterwards that if he were in Kidney's position, he would have made the same decision.

'The sinbinning was something we could have done without,' says Kidney. 'There were ten points in the game, they were worrying moments. Because you had put in a huge effort for seventy-odd minutes, you're hoping something like that won't cost you the game. But the other fourteen certainly dug in at that stage. You have to pick somebody to come off; there's nobody going to volunteer. Anthony is such a professional he will do … just like he did in the final in Cardiff … whatever it takes. That's the epitome of the man, that's why he'd been vital for us in the whole year with his leadership. Munster have been blessed with good leaders over the years – Mick Galwey, Pat Murray, Tom Kiernan – you look down through it and there have been good men there.'

When O'Gara capped off his best-ever performance in a Munster jersey or in any colour – whether with Ireland or the Lions – with a smartly taken try, the game was up for Leinster. Flashing a smile as wide as Patrick Street, O'Gara jumped the hording behind the goal and embraced the few fans who spilled down to the field from the terraces to embrace the golden boy of Irish rugby. 'The eightieth minute wasn't it?' says Kidney. 'We had defended well for the previous six or seven minutes and we had got the ball, Ronan went for something and he got through. The nature of the game at that stage, you had fourteen against fifteen in defence so, anyone who made a line break was gone. The line break could just as easily have gone the other way but, fortunately, it went for Munster.'

O'Connell felt he couldn't afford to breathe a little easier, even after O'Gara's try. He couldn't say they had tamed the Leinster Lions yet. 'O'Gara's try was brilliant, but I don't think we had the game 100 per cent won at that stage. You never know with injury-time; you never know what is going to happen. Those guys are capable of pulling fourteen points out of anywhere, so I don't think the game was won but, at the time, there was a sense that we might have it. We just re-gathered at the halfway line, put our heads back on and that is something that we did really well. You hear all sorts of horror stories; we just wanted to make sure.'

And they did make sure with a Halstead intercept try from inside halfway adding gloss to Munster's taming of Leinster, though Kidney admits the final score – 30–6 – wasn't a fair reflection of the overall pattern of the game. 'I think the last score or two were maybe a reflection of how things went for us on the day. In the same way, maybe, as the Celtic League final the previous time [2001], a few things might have gone against Munster, but that's the nature of rugby.'

'It was probably not a true reflection of the day,' says O'Connell, 'that's the way it happens sometimes. It didn't matter whether it was twenty-four points or one point, it's all about who got the win – I think we deserved to win.

Afterwards, O'Gara spoke of the stomach sickness during the week, the antibiotics he took and why he wore small boots to get a better 'feel' for the pitch.

O'Connell said there was no name written on the cup. 'You're never going to say this is our year. You might look back at little incidents throughout the year and say, "Yeah, it was our year, the bounce of the ball went our way, once or twice we got a few lucky breaks." At the time, you keep your feet on the ground and you keep working. Destiny had nothing to do with it – it's all about the preparation you put in, the players you have, the staff, the passion they have for it. After the game, we were just keeping our heads screwed on.'

For the record, Munster went on to win the European Cup, beating Biarritz 23–19 in the final at the Millennium Stadium in Cardiff.

As for the Lansdowne experience that day, O'Connell never felt so good in such a theatre. 'It is very loud but it's a great thing that the crowd is so close to you and you hope you won't lose that within your ground. I know it's an old rickety ground, but it really is a fabulous place – the

We are family: Munster player Ronan O'Gara is hugged by a fan after scoring a try to clinch the win against Leinster during the second half. Munster defeated Leinster 30–6.

atmosphere for those two games was just incredible and couldn't really be replicated in grounds with that capacity. There's terracing on the sidelines which doesn't happen very often now. I think Newlands in Cape Town had it. It just adds to massive kind of atmosphere and those few days in Lansdowne Road rank right up there as the happiest in the old ground – hopefully there's more to come in the new.'

Noel Murphy

Flanker

1957–1969

When Noel Murphy ran out in an Ireland shirt for the first time at Lansdowne Road against Australia in January 1958, he was following in the footsteps of his father, Noel Snr, who played for Ireland in the 1930s.

While a student at CBC in Cork, Noel Jnr lined out at scrum-half, a position he temporarily filled for Ireland in 1958, after John O'Meara went down injured against Wales in the Five Nations. But it was to the flanker's position that he was born; comfortable on both open and blind sides. Syd Millar, who played alongside him on countless occasions with both Ireland and the Lions, offered this assessment, 'Noel was very quick. He never flinched and never drew back. He was very strong mentally, a huge tackler and good footballer too.'

Nick Shehadie, a future Lord Mayor of Sydney, landed the debutant with a haymaker in the second half of the match, but Murphy survived to tell the tale of Ireland's first-ever win over a touring side. 'We were all delighted to see Jackie Kyle bookend a remarkable career with a win over a touring side,' says Noel. 'I played flanker but you would not like to be a flanker on a team facing Jackie – he was so quick, he'd dodge a bullet. There were six new caps that day and the selectors seemed to have got it right. I suppose it was a great day and the selectors didn't realise it but three of us would go on to captain Ireland – Bill Mulcahy, Ronnie Dawson and myself.' (The other three new caps were Dave Hewitt, J. Stevenson and J. Donaldson.)

Murphy, Dawson and Hewitt made the Lions tour to New Zealand in 1959 – regarded as one of the greatest ever trips to the Land of the Long White Cloud. Hewitt was making all the right moves and noises during 1957–1958 and a made a grand entrance onto the international stage against Australia, creating the opening for Dawson's try.

Lansdowne Road witnessed a thriller in the last game of the 1959 Five Nations when 'world champions' France came to Dublin. It will be remembered as a match where Galway man Tony O'Sullivan gave his most complete performance in an Irish shirt. 'Covering, displaying great ball control and tackling almost everything in sight,' says Murphy. France came with quite a reputation, especially their captain, Lucien Mias. But he was quiet by his usual high standards and the Number 8 was never afforded too much room to exert his influence on proceedings. Murphy depicts it as a classy Irish performance and there were plenty of reasons to support his view. There were flick backs to fellow forwards, short passing, quick and solid blinding at ruck time, and a succession of neat heels to the scrum-half. It all came as quite a shock to the French, who, without monopolising possession, produced vignettes of their best which impressed Murphy. 'They were as physical then as they are now. They were introducing a different type of game to what the other four nations were playing. They had beautiful hands, great pace; they began to introduce back-row moves, peeling off the lineout – these were all the new things that they brought to the game of rugby.'

In some ways Ireland – led superbly by Ronnie Dawson and O'Sullivan in the pack and by the brilliant half-back pairing of Andy Mulligan and Mick English – tried to imitate their Gallic counterparts, at least for an afternoon. Murphy points especially to the contribution of a young Wanderers three-quarter, Kevin Flynn, who turned the game in Ireland's favour that afternoon. 'Kevin was the star of that victory, a wonderful footballer and should have got more caps for the Lions. That game for me was Kevin Flynn's.'

In order for Flynn to get his hands on the ball, Ireland needed to force turnovers and there was no one better at scavenging than Noel Murphy, a foil to any semblance of continuity the French tried to bring to their play. The try started with Murphy getting stuck into the French. From their scrum, the Ireland flanker eyed up their out-half, Montoulan, grabbed him and when the ball spilled, Flynn scooped up the ball and initiated the move to put Ireland 6–0 up. Mick English had already landed a fourth-minute penalty. Flynn engineered Brophy's try, picking up a loose ball, darting away from the opposing forwards and then drawing the French defence. Then, he dispatched this clinical overhead pass to Niall Brophy.

Despite a late comeback by France, Ireland proved worthy 9–5 winners. Even French newspaper

Le Journal du Dimanche applauded Ireland's heroics the following morning, attributing their success to a superb all-round game. 'Ireland unlucky in its other matches of the five-nation tournament was intent in avoiding last place in the final classification,' said *Le Journal*. 'Victorious Ireland saved its honour. The Irish forwards were stronger than the French. Mulligan and English dominated the French backs. O'Reilly, Brophy, Hewitt and Flynn were faster than their French counterparts.'

Murphy adds, 'It was a great victory because they came as champions and came with the reputation of being fast, highly skilled and difficult to defend against. How did we manage to contain such a team? Well, we spent a lot of time at the practice on the Friday dealing with how we were going to stop their back-row movement, their peeling, their counter-attacking, their fluent passing and the running off the ball. Physically, it was a hard game – it was probably the hardest game of all. And mentally you had to be strong as well. You were always thinking, thinking. It was a great victory because it surprised a lot of people, came out of the blue. It was one of the great wins but, then again, Kevin Flynn's try that day was talked about for years and years after. He was so unlucky because had the Lions team being picked after that match Kevin Flynn, the nineteen year old, would have made it.'

The win also marked Noel Henderson's final game in an Ireland jersey. 'He was one of these wonderful characters who played for Ireland and graced Lansdowne Road. He was an unbelievable captain, a very enthusiastic player. He was very good to me when I came on the scene. He looked after the younger members.'

After a whitewash in the 1960 Five Nations and a narrow loss to the Springboks that December, little was expected of the Irish when the 1961 championship campaign opened against England at Lansdowne Road. When the final whistle blew and the home side won 11–8, there was a tangible sense of relief around the old ground. It was Ireland's first international win in nearly two years and first over the 'old enemy' in ten. Regarded by many as the best international Ireland featured in since the win over France in 1959, it saw the emergence of a new exciting scrum-half in Jonathan Moffett, who notched two penalties and a conversion into what Murphy describes as 'the capricious Lansdowne wind'.

Still no one stood taller than Murphy's cousin Tom Kiernan in his second full season at senior level and while still a student at UCC. 'Ronnie Kavanagh got the try but it was brilliantly set up by Tom,' recalls Murphy. Indeed, Kiernan's run bore all the hallmarks of what great full-back play is all about. Firstly, he gathered a kick ahead by Dickie Jeeps, the England scrum-half and captain, on the halfway line, hit fifth gear to bypass the English pack, then dropped a shoulder to glide by England out-half Ricky Sharp, and swerved left to draw John Wilcox to send Kavanagh over untouched.

Jeeps, considered to be England's greatest attacking threat, was snuffed out by the Ireland back-row with Murphy again prominent repeatedly taking him in possession. Murphy, despite

97

picking up a facial injury late in the first half, was inspirational as England probed and searched for that all-important try near the finish – but Ireland's defence stood firm. The sight of white shirts bouncing off Murphy and company in those frantic closing moments brought everyone in Lansdowne to their feet and, at the end, a massive roar went up. 'All I remember is us managing to throw back wave after wave of Englishmen. We put in tackle after tackle and the crowd was loving it. There was a pitch invasion and I was being carried off. I suppose everybody liked to beat England. I always felt it was a compliment to beat England because they were the people everybody wanted to beat. I wouldn't say they were the enemy. A lot of us toured the Lions with a lot of English players and made great friends. But, to this day, you can see what a win over England – especially at Lansdowne Road – means to everybody. But, as I say, it's a huge compliment to beat them because they felt they were the country that invented the game.'

Murphy broke his collarbone against England in Twickenham in 1962 that kept him sidelined until the visit of the All Blacks to Lansdowne Road in November 1963. 'We should have won that game. In fact, we scored a try that was disallowed for offside and I'm convinced to this day that it wasn't. Johnny Fortune scored a try on his debut but the All Blacks were unbelievable. They were unbeatable at the time. Munster should have beaten them as well, but I will always remember their forwards like Colin and Stan Meads, Wilson Whineray and Kelvin Tremain – Kel Tremin scored their try that day. Sadly, he is no longer with us, he passed away in 1992, but I will always remember him that day as being a real leader who had a great ability to score tries. Unfortunately, it came against us. And, of course, I thought the contribution of Donald Clarke from full-back was truly stupendous. He is one of the greatest ever All Blacks.'

This heroic Irish performance seemed the perfect prelude to the 1964 Five Nations. Things started so promisingly in Twickenham where Murphy scored a try and this should have propelled Ireland to greater things and the Triple Crown, but they contrived to lose to both Wales and Scotland at home, failing to capitalise on the excellence of their showings against New Zealand and England.

The following season offered more in the way of victories with a draw against France and a win over England at Lansdowne Road. The win over Scotland in Murrayfield set up the prospect of a Triple Crown against Wales in Cardiff. The upsurge in form and performance coincided with the appointment of Ray McLoughlin as captain, the prop who brought his own methods to training and who prepared his charges thoroughly for the campaign ahead. His preparations and scientific approach to the game won approval with Murphy, though it was said that McLoughlin's methods were too inflexible in theory and not workable by the players at his disposal.

'Ray McLoughlin technically was as good a prop forward as there was in that period of time. He was a deep thinker of the game. He is basically a very intelligent person, spent a lot of time preparing for matches. We prepared well before Ray McLoughlin but he added a little bit more to it. He was probably stricter in the routine of preparing – he used tell us not to read the papers or to get more rest and get plenty of sleep before big matches. He was captain of sides that should have won Triple Crowns and didn't because we were beaten by Wales, but they had world-class players. It is mischievous if it was said that players didn't like his methods. There's a responsibility coming with lining out for Ireland and it was his responsibility to prepare us as best as possible for the matches.'

McLoughlin's influence was written all over Ireland's victory over South Africa in April 1965 at Lansdowne, less than a month after the agony of losing in Cardiff. It proved to be Ireland's first victory over the Springboks. 'It was strange to have a game played in the middle of April and the wet conditions weren't ideal. As usual, we had to contend with a wind and there were sporadic rain bursts during the game which made handling difficult. Still, they came into the game as favourites and they'd world-class players. They'd beaten the All Blacks and beaten the Lions. I will remember it for different reasons. I broke a little bone in my back and spent five weeks in plaster down to my toe. I was falling to the ground and somebody double-tackled me. I went to the hospital, got my back x-rayed and they put me in plaster there.'

With the wind to their backs in the first half, South Africa conceded the opening try. Scrum-half Roger was the creator chipping a ball over the line for winger Pat McGrath who managed to get the touchdown despite the efforts of the covering Springboks. South Africa hit back with a penalty, piled on the pressure before the break but a stoical Ireland held them to 3–3 at the break. It looked ominous for Ireland when W.J. Mans scored a try after half-time but the sides were level soon after when Tom Kiernan notched a penalty. When Mike Gibson went over for a try, it was disallowed because of an outfield infringement. The stadium then exploded into life when Tom Kiernan scored a penalty which proved to be the winner and give Ireland a wholly unlikely victory.

On 21 January 1967, Noel Murphy captained Ireland to another 15–8 victory over Australia at Lansdowne. 'We had a good record against Australia and we beat them well I thought. We were very unlucky not to win a Triple Crown that season after beating Scotland and Wales, losing to England because of a last-minute try in a game where we did everything but score. We were attacking on the 22 when a crash tackle by one of the English forwards, Danny Herm ended the move and the ball was turned over. Danny had connections with Munster. In fact, he got a final trial with Munster two years previously but we didn't pick him and then he played for England. His tackle denied us a Triple Crown.'

Murphy missed the entire 1967–1968 season through injury, but returned in January 1969 for the win over France at Lansdowne. He scored a try against England in a 17–15 victory in Dublin, one that will stay with him for a long time. It came eighteen minutes into the second half and, with Tom Kiernan converting, it gave Ireland a 17–12 advantage. It proved to be the winning try. Mike Gibson made the initial dash for the line but was bottled up. From a loose ruck, Murphy emerged with the ball taking the opposition unawares and sauntered over the line. He could be

'Go boy!' says Noel Murphy, as he passes to scrum-half Colin Grimshaw during the 1969 Five Nations tie against England.

seen smiling as he walked back after scoring the try because he'd realised how easy the English had made his run.

Murphy was seen as the experienced hand in the pack and never stopped working from the first whistle. 'We came from behind to equalise on four occasions. I thought everyone put their shoulder to the wheel in the last twenty minutes. Some papers wrote that it was Munster's win because all the points came from Munster players. Barry Bresnihan and myself got the tries, Tom Kiernan got two penalties and conversion while Barry McGann scored a drop goal. We went on then to beat Scotland in Murrayfield scoring four tries but lost then in Cardiff. That one really hurt.' It hurt because it came on the day Noel Murphy played his last game for Ireland. A bad day got worse when, ten minutes in, Murphy received a punch from Brian Price.

Noel Murphy took up the position of Ireland coach from 1977 to 1980 and part of his legacy will point to his role in the Ollie Campbell–Tony Ward debate. Murphy handed Ward his first cap against Scotland in 1978 in Lansdowne Road but, on the two test-winning tours of Australia in 1979, the coach opted to play Campbell at out-half.

'Nothing compares to playing for your country. It's hard to explain. We were different coaches in the 1970s and the 1980s. We were more the category of organisers and motivators and worked very close to the captain. I was lucky I had Fergus Slattery, a great forward and a very good captain in my view, a dedicated player. We had a certain amount of success. My years as coach will be remembered for the dropping of Tony Ward. Much is written about it and much is written wrongly about it. Ollie Campbell would do the job we wanted done to play against Australia, and I think I was proved right. Ollie, as we know, was picked by several other Irish selectors and sometimes people forget that Ollie Campbell contributed hugely to the success in Australia. If it wasn't a success, it would probably have been the end of Noel Murphy. Tony Ward brought an excitement to Irish rugby. Tony and myself are very good friends now, we meet regularly and he's a dedicated individual. He is well able to write and has got a lovely attitude when he's coaching the younger lads. Most internationals get dropped at some stage in their lives – I don't know how many times I was dropped.'

Lansdowne holds many dear memories for Murphy. Naturally, he will be sad to see it go. 'It still means an awful lot to people. Ex-players love matches at Lansdowne Road, and no matter what people say about how rundown it is, there are a lot of people in world rugby have happy memories of it.'

Brian Price (Wales, left) punches Noel Murphy (Ireland) to the floor during the 1969 Five Nations match. It proved to be Murphy's last outing in an Irish shirt.

Bertie O'Hanlon
& Jimmy McCarthy
Winger & Flanker
1947–1950 & 1948–1955

Scoring two tries on your debut in the home of Irish rugby is usually the stuff of fantasy, and to supporters the stuff of legend. Bertie O'Hanlon lived that dream when Ireland produced a utopian performance against England and recorded its biggest ever win (22–0) over its closest rival on a bitterly cold February in 1947. Dolphin's Bertie O'Hanlon arrived up from Cork, a rebel with a cause and something of an unknown quantity but the darting debutant was the name on everyone's lips by full-time that day. Lansdowne's magical rhythms and sounds, sweeping down from the stands and terraces, didn't unnerve the twenty-three-year-old three-quarter; instead the pulse of the ground inspired him, and the memories today are locked warmly inside his heart: the cacophony of unbroken cheering amongst an Irish support who had little time to draw breath; the roar when he twice crossed the whitewash; and the sorcery of the enchanting Jack Kyle.

Bertie O'Hanlon, winning his first cap, seen here fending off David Swarbrick (England) and heading for his second try in the 1947 Five Nations.

O'Hanlon remembers his heavy-duty boots were not made for the hard surface on which he ran that afternoon, but it might be unreasonable to suggest that he should have worn the spikes in which he trained at the Mardyke in Cork. The great freeze that winter left many grounds around Great Britain and Ireland unplayable, but the speed and fire of the Irish XV seemed the perfect antidote that thawed the frozen surface. O'Hanlon remembers straw scattered around the field and a scything diagonal wind, but would it matter to the Cork athlete who could run the 100 yards in 10.1 seconds? Not a jot – it's said the jet-heeled winger's feet never touched the ground.

The first Five Nations campaign since 1939 had kicked off a fortnight earlier, and Ireland, with fourteen new caps, in their first championship game since the end of the war, came agonisingly close to beating France at Lansdowne Road. It ended 8–12 with Jack Kyle marking his debut replete with the magical cameos and the precocity that would suffuse his impressive career. When England came to town in 1947, nobody expected Ireland to score such an emphatic victory, but the visitors' giant pack was pulverised by an inspired Irish effort. This was a young Irish side that would evolve as the championship progressed and which was polished and modified a year later for the 1948 Grand Slam journey.

O'Hanlon's emergence as a finisher of real quality and a robust tackler may have been one of the main talking points, but the Dolphin man says the advent of a half-back pairing of Ernie Strathdee and Jackie Kyle signalled the start of a beautiful relationship in Irish rugby. 'There is something similar in their arrival on the scene in that time to that of Peter Stringer and Ronan O'Gara at the beginning of the new millennium. Jack and Ernie was a match made in rugby heaven; they were almost telepathic. There was an easiness between the pair that is hard to describe and Jack always seemed to receive the perfect pass.' In O'Hanlon's eyes, this era was all about Jack Kyle.

M.F. Landers, writing in the *Examiner*, lavished praise on the two wingers in a superior Ireland three-quarters where O'Hanlon and Barney Mullan shared a try apiece. 'It is no exaggeration to say that O'Hanlon's wonderful pace saved the situation on several occasions. His crashing tackles on Swarbrick, the English wingman, stopped all English hopes in that direction, while his two tries were the highlight of the game.'

O'Hanlon's skills to execute his two tries were honed in his rugby alma mater, Rockwell College in County Tipperary. The dribble was a skill practised by most rugby players in those days, but O'Hanlon was coolness personified as he demonstrated his neat footwork when rounding both Swarbrick and Gray for his first try. It came on twenty-nine minutes when the ball arrived at his feet after Barney Mullan's attempted drop goal backfired. Swarbrick fumbled Mullan's effort before the Dolphin flyer utilised his soccer-like dribbling skills to stunning effect and punished an English mistake. 'In my day, you dribbled. I learned that in Rockwell too. Today, it's all handling. I dribbled the whole way to the line; there were two Englishmen there and, with the ball about a yard from the line, I managed to dive over with it. That was the first try.'

He truly delighted the packed ground when he scored his second in the sixty-fifth minute. He picked up inside his own half then swerved and slalomed his way to the line past Swarbrick, Gray and finally White, who had come cross field to try to prevent the try. The double thrill of scoring in Lansdowne and the lulling rhythms, which flowed down from stands and terraces, still moves O'Hanlon to this day. 'I gathered that ball on my own 25. I slipped the winger, the full-back and the wing-forward and touched down behind the posts. Sheer pace, do you know! Lym Hall was the English out-half, but when he kicked for the corner flag, I gathered it and put it under my arm. In those days, we learned how to side-step. And when I was in Rockwell, I learned how to kick with both feet, learned how to swerve and side-step. You never see that at all now. We went for the corner flag, now it's a case of blowing the guy in front of you out of the way. It's rugby league now.'

It wasn't O'Hanlon's first game in Lansdowne; he had to cut a path to the Irish team via the obstacle courses that were the Irish trials. 'I was exactly twenty-three when I got a call up to play for Ireland. The first trials were inter-pros, then you had a Combined Universities versus Rest of Ireland. I was on the Rest of Ireland because I was with Dolphin. Jack Kyle for example was with Combined Universities, which drew players from UCD, UCG, Trinity and Queen's. Then you had the final trial – Possibles versus Probables. I remember playing in the Possibles and got picked thereafter. What was very strong at the time was Ravenhill – you had the split and, in those days, you had more Ulster men on the team than Leinster, Connacht and Munster. You had players from Instonians, North of Ireland, Malone, Queen's – which had very strong senior sides.'

With England taken care of, hopes of a first Triple Crown since 1899 were kept on track with a 3–0 win away in Murrayfield but the wheels then came off the wagon against Wales at St Helen's. Even the genius of Jack Kyle couldn't conjure up anything as Ireland fell 6–0 to the principality.

In December, Australia came as the Third Wallabies to Lansdowne Road. In fact, it was only the second fully representative side from Australia, for the Second Wallabies came and went in 1939 without playing a match. O'Hanlon would have loved to have played southern hemisphere opposition but fate dealt him a cruel blow. 'I was injured for the Australia game. I sprained my ankle after an inter-pro match and had to cry off. Kevin O'Flanagan came into my place. He was a soccer international, a champion athlete and later a golfer and brother of Michael, who also played soccer and rugby for Ireland. That time, Australia beat us 14–6. In those days, you got no caps for those games – they were only touring sides. The caps were given against the home countries.'

Ireland hadn't won the Five Nations since 1935 and, on 1 January 1948, played France in Stade Colombes. O'Hanlon was joined on the team by his Dolphin team-mate Jimmy McCarthy to compete in the toughest and most volatile stage of all. France were viewed with a degree of suspicion – for the eight seasons leading up to the Second World War, they had been excluded due to allegations of professionalism within their clubs. 'Jimmy had boundless energy,' says O'Hanlon, 'and he was tremendously fit, he trained and trained and trained. There was only a pound or two between the two of us. Jim was about five-foot ten inches and I was only half an inch taller then him. I was twelve stone five pounds and he was twelve stone three pounds or twelve stone six – but he was playing wing-forward and he was like a terrier in the pack. He timed his run to perfection. He'd arrive with the ball and hit the opposing out-half at the same time; a great defensive player; a great man to handle the ball and a great dribbler.'

Alongside Bill McKay and, later, Des O'Brien, McCarthy was part of the greatest back-row in Irish rugby. Bill McKay, known as 'the enforcer,' was an Ulster boxing champion and packed a heavy weight tackle but possessed great stamina as evidenced by his prowess as a 400-yard runner. McCarthy was Kyle's real collaborator, who caused enough fuss in the opposition cover that allowed Kyle the latitude to breach a defence. And, for the England game in Twickenham – which Ireland won 11–10 – Des O'Brien completed the great back-row line-up. O'Brien was an international squash and hockey player but his greatest deeds lay on the rugby field. O'Brien recalled in Peter O'Reilly's *The Full Bag of Chips – Ireland and the Triple Crown*: 'In those years, when we played for Ireland, none of us had a wife, let alone a motor car. We either walked or cycled. It gave us a natural fitness which players don't have today.'

Ireland's greatest ever back-row: From left Bill McKay, Des O'Brien and Jimmy McCarthy.

In Munster in the late 1940s, Dolphin was regarded as the best club side in the province accumulating silverware like modern-day Shannon. In 1948, they did the clean sweep – Munster Senior Cup, Munster Senior League and the Cork Charity Cup. O'Hanlon and McCarthy were at the centre of their success.

When they lined out together at Lansdowne on the third leg of their successful Grand Slam journey in 1948, the duo worked as much as possible in unison when the first whistle blew. When not scavenging for possession, McCarthy was on O'Hanlon's shoulder, a willing proxy to any opening that may occur near the tryline. On one occasion in the first half, a combination play between the Dolphin pair nearly produced a try. 'It was hard and it was tough against Scotland but not dirty,' says McCarthy. 'I remember reading afterwards that the real heroes on the day were the sixteen forwards. There were some ferocious battles around the fringes – these were as tough as Munster club games – but I felt we had the edge. I think our scrummaging was far superior. Karl [Mullen] won three out of every five scrums against the head.'

'I didn't get over for a try but Jack Kyle was magnificent,' recalls O'Hanlon. 'Barney Mullan got the first try after a magnificent overhead pass from Des McKee but, in the last ten minutes, I remember we had to put in some last-ditch and desperate tackles. Then, with about five minutes to go, Jack Kyle cut through the Scottish defence and scored near the post. We had the championship wrapped up before attaining the Grand Slam against Wales. Against Scotland, I thought Kyle was absolutely outstanding, brilliant in my eyes, in all our eyes; he was the brains behind the Irish team. He had a superb swerve, and he was great to read a game. Kyle could make one break or two. He was great to knock the ball over behind a defence onto the wing so I could run on to it.'

McCarthy says, 'My job would be to protect Jack and he'd always slip the ball in to me. Jack was the best. A lot of people compare O'Gara with Humphreys but they don't compare him with Jack. When Jack was playing for Ireland, there was a guy called Johnny Hewitt, a fabulous player. He could have played for Scotland, England or Wales and, in the end, they gave him a charity cap at out-half.'

Ireland went on to win the Grand Slam in Ravenhill on 13 March, beating Wales 6–3 with tries from Barney Mullan and Christopher Daly. O'Hanlon puts his try famine in Grand Slam year down to the presence of two Olympians on the England and Wales sides. 'The Olympic Games were in Wembley that year and Great Britain had two entrants, Ken Jones of Wales and Owens of England who were on their respective rugby teams. No way could I round those fellows – they were sprint champions.'

Ireland's hopes of retaining the Grand Slam went up in smoke in their first outing against France in the 1949 Five Nations, but their Triple Crown ambitions were kept alive in the next month with a resounding win over England. McCarthy and his back-row colleague McKay upped the ante from what McCarthy describes as a 'sluggish' forward display against the French. 'We were in England's faces from the beginning, breaking quicker than we did against France from rucks and scrums and making life hell for their half backs Rimmer and Hall.'

Before the match, Hall would have been regarded as England's most lethal weapon, but McCarthy met fire with fire from the off, taking the out-half in possession at every available opportunity. Despite McCarthy's efficiency as flanker, he says the reasons for their success again lay at the dancing feet of Kyle. 'Kyle was again outstanding. There was a lot of messing the year before as to who should partner Kyle at half-back, but I thought Ernie was on his wavelength.'

O'Hanlon agrees, 'Kyle's running in attack that day was outstanding and, before the game, I discussed with him that he should use the kick ahead as often as possible and allow myself and Mick Lane run on to them. But he was great in other ways too – the way he'd be in the right place at the right time to gather a loose ball or when another Irish player got into difficulty there would be our Jackie.'

O'Hanlon was once again a thorn in the English defence for the second time in three years. The creator, again, was Kyle who feinted past Rimmer and Hall, laid off to McKee and the centre took a more direct line to goal crashing through a few English defenders and finally setting up O'Hanlon who scuttled up near the touchline and over in the corner. Before he went over, he has a sneaking suspicion that he might have put a foot in touch. 'Des McKee broke on the blindside

108

and I was playing on the left. Bill flashed the ball to me, a couple of yards from the line. A *Sunday Press* photographer took a photo and it showed my foot on the line scoring for Ireland; but the touch judge was from Connacht! There was a picture I think of the dog getting in the way of the touch judge and I often thought afterwards – if only the dog could tell tales.'

The Triple Crown was attained at St Helen's with Jimmy McCarthy getting the try in a 5–0 win. The following season was O'Hanlon's last for Ireland as a succession of injuries took its toll on a short but remarkable career. 'I played against France in Stades Colombes, then Louis Crowe came on instead of me. Louis was better than me – and I was a travelling sub for all the remaining matches. If a guy cried off long before the match, a sub would get in but if it was during the match, no way. Once a team goes out onto the pitch you could lose two or three players, you could be playing with twelve or thirteen for a while. We've had a fabulous innings – ever since we've been wined and dined.'

'Bertie was around for about five years and he only got eleven caps, but if he was around today I'm sure he would have got double that,' says McCarthy. 'If you play for Ireland over one year, you can earn sixteen caps. You start playing in the autumn and play until the end of the World Cup the following autumn and, assuming Ireland get to the quarter-finals, you get sixteen caps, maybe more.'

In 1950, O'Hanlon departed the international stage and McCarthy missed all five games through injury, as he says himself 'a burst knee'. 'I cried off three times with an internal lateral ligament in an Irish trial at Lansdowne Road. It happened down in the Lansdowne End as I was going over to score a try, beside the post. But Des McKibbin hit me. I never forgave him because it nearly cost me a place on the Lions tour, and certainly cost me three caps.'

McCarthy returned in 1951 when Ireland won the championship – a 3–3 draw in Swansea denying them a second Grand Slam – but that win brought an era of unprecedented success to a close. Between 1948 and 1951, Ireland played seventeen games, won eleven, drew two and lost just four – a phenomenal record. It was a side that didn't know the meaning of the word failure, a special group with a winning mentality. 'Our best year, funnily enough, was 1951 when we won the championship,' says McCarthy. 'We threw away a game in Wales. Nobody could even manage three points from in front of the posts. That was an absolute tragedy. We were a winning team. The Munster team today seem to be the same. Losing? We didn't talk about losing, only about how we were going to win. That's the way New Zealand think and that's why they're winners.'

Jimmy McCarthy is regarded as one of the greatest flank-forwards ever to play for Ireland and he was one who lived and breathed down the opposition on the offside line. This was the era of the foot-rush. Defending backlines weren't required to stand ten yards behind the lineout, while the offside line was in the middle of the scrum. Kyle's ability to evade the attention of opposition flankers was indeed an astounding feat, while McCarthy appeared to be in a perpetual state of offside. 'Bill McKay, Des O'Brien and myself played twenty times together as back-row for Ireland: I played at Number 7 but McKay and I used play left and right. At that time, you could break from a scrum faster than you can now. They changed the rules because of me living on the offside line, I think. Bloody McCarthyism!'

Before mastering the art of open-side flanker and becoming the greatest pest to opposing out-halves, McCarthy learned his trade under Gussie McSweeny, a Sunday's Well man, at one of Munster's finest rugby academies, Christian Brothers College in Cork where, in 1943, he won a Munster Schools Senior Cup medal. He loved his first trip to Lansdowne when he travelled with his father to the last game before the outbreak of the Second World War, when Ireland beat Scotland 12–3.

McCarthy earned his first cap against Scotland in 1948 and went on to play twenty-eight times for Ireland captaining the side four times in 1954 and 1955 and scoring eight international tries. 'When you're a kid in Ireland in a rugby school, you think you'll play for Ireland some day in Lansdowne Road. Lansdowne Road is a kind of heaven for you – it's where you're trying to get to. You don't appreciate it until years afterwards – it would dawn on you and it's so funny at the time. I was always mad keen on rugby and I was determined to get an Irish jersey. You really feel that you've achieved your aim, it's always a thrill playing for Ireland anyway no matter where it is – but at Lansdowne Road, it's extra special because the family are there. Lansdowne Road is full of tradition and we were very conscious of that.'

McCarthy remembers a custom that is now long gone but prevalent in the days of trials. 'We weighed ourselves before the trial. Of course, some fellows would be putting weights on themselves. A guy called Bodie O'Neill was thirteen stone something and he was a prop forward but Bodie was trying to get his cap. He used say, "If I could get over the fourteen stone mark, I'll get on the team." And he was right. So he got a set of "special" insoles made and put them inside his socks and he got up on the scales. He was fourteen stone two pounds. He got picked the next day.'

It was an era when those who presided over Ireland teams ruled and a player had to keep in their good books. Always. As McCarthy told Peter O'Reilly in *The Full Bag of Chips*, 'Back then, a selector was God and a player kissed every ass he had to. It didn't occur to you to question why they travelled first class when you were in third. You had guys like Ernie Crawford, who did everything – he'd do touch judge and give the team talk beforehand. I was told to stay in his good books and I'd be well set. Some of them were good as selectors, some were awful but they were all nice gentlemen. They'd have two from Ulster, two from Leinster and one Munster and one from Connacht. They used to say then that it was harder to get off the Irish team than to get on it. There wasn't a huge selection, nothing like the number of players who play now.'

The week before a big international, McCarthy's preparations would begin on the Wednesday where he'd meet up with Dolphin club-mate O'Hanlon and UCC's Mick Lane at the Mardyke for running and fitness drills. McCarthy also put aside time to pray for divine intervention on match day. 'I would say I was the fittest man in Ireland. I would run six miles every day. I was always training. I used go to seven o'clock mass every morning so Jesus would help me play well every Saturday. Your preparation would start on the Wednesday – you'd do a certain amount of running, then the next day some passing and sprinting. We always wore spikes and, when you do, you must always get up on your toes. When you put your boots on, you automatically got up on your toes. It made you faster. I always say to be fast, you've got to train fast.'

A special Lansdowne memory for McCarthy is when Ireland beat France 9–8 in 1951, and extra special because of the arrival on the team of another Corkman, John O'Meara from UCC. 'There were four new caps that day but O'Meara had a spectacular outing. O'Meara was a marvellous passer of the ball and I'll always remember the heading on the *Sunday Independent* the morning after the match, it had "O-O-O'Meara" right across the page.'

McCarthy captained Ireland in the middle of the 1954 Five Nations and played his last game – one he skippered – against England in 1955 – a 6–6 draw. Afterwards, the selectors never capped him again for his country. It ripped him up inside. 'This with two games to go in the championship – you'd think the selectors would leave me on. No. I never, ever forgave them. It tore the heart out of me. When you have the guts and heart you want to keep going for ever. I was going to chuck it in that season because I was getting married and we were having a baby! The real reason behind me being dropped was age: I was thirty. In our time, they threw you off the team when you hit thirty or when you got married. It was a real anti-climax. I was at mass at Clarendon Street church the morning before the team announcement for the Scotland game and, halfway through the mass, I turned to my wife Pat and said, "I've just been dropped." I just knew that I was gone then.'

Still both McCarthy and O'Hanlon look back fondly on those magical days in Irish rugby's golden age. Proud Corkmen delighted to have shone in the Dublin 4 venue.

111

Nick Popplewell

Prop
1989–1998

113

The opening lines of his book *Time to Ruck and Roll* best capture Nick Popplewell's emotions on winning his first cap; a moment he'd looked forward to all his life. 'On a Saturday afternoon back in November 1989, I raced as fast as my short legs would take me onto the international rugby stage for the first time. The place was Lansdowne Road. The team at the opposite end of the ground, sharing the billing with Ireland, was the All Blacks.'

He'd arrived in his kind of rugby utopia; 50,000 spectators and a madding Lansdowne crowd and a couple of hundred thousand watching on television. Could life get any better for the twenty-five-year-old prop from Gorey, County Wexford? 'It appeared to be the perfect start,' he says, 'Lansdowne Road, the All Blacks, and yours truly in the green Number 1.'

He was so consumed in the moment and the enthusiasm to live every minute, that he remembers the exact moment he cracked two ribs in a scrum. 'Eighteen and half minutes later, my international rugby career came to a grinding halt. I was slowly led back to the sideline and into the Irish dressing room. It was a huge baptism of fire. It was unfortunate. I cracked three or four ribs and, when you're scrummaging, it's like standing on a nail – you can't walk after it, so off you go.'

Not many players get the opportunity to pull on the green against the All Blacks and run onto Lansdowne Road. It is the ultimate dream debut and, though Poppy's first cap ended with a whimper, it was still a moment to savour and to roar about loudly in the pubs afterwards. 'It was a great, fantastic, totally enjoyable eighteen and half minutes, and I can definitely understand how players who have only played for Ireland once still feel that they have experienced just about everything in their career,' he wrote later.

The prelude to the match was entertainment in itself. Willie Anderson's famous tête-à-tête with the New Zealand Haka set Lansdowne ablaze and the Irish players' adrenalin pumping. Led by Anderson in the centre, Ireland – linked arm to arm – crossed the halfway line shouting and roaring at the New Zealand Haka. Popplewell admits that Ireland's response to the Haka wasn't premeditated, but the new kid on the block ended up about three inches from Wayne Shelford's teeth. Scary stuff for a new fella, but confronting the Haka had the desired psychological effect as a pumped-up Ireland put up a good fight – though, ultimately, never came close to the then reigning world champions and lost 23–6. 'Was I intimidated by the Haka? No. I think if you are worried about it, all you have to do is look at the new cap – who is hope-fully white – and follow him. And it's quite funny because he's totally out of sync. It's a bit like learning to dance. I think looking on at the Haka, you respect it for it is; it's part of the occasion, part of the folklore. It's just a sequence of events. You could say our action was disrespectful but it was also a spontaneous action.'

A quick examination of the ribcage and a few painkillers later, Poppy watched the rest of the game from the sideline. 'I delayed going to the hospital until the Sunday afternoon. I didn't want to go on the Saturday night. I drank a few pints. To be honest, I drank more than a few pints before the night was over. Ribs or no ribs, I collapsed into bed in the end and slept my head off.'

Whether his was the perfect or imperfect start to an international career, Popplewell's injury cost him the best part of two years in the international wilderness. 'The first time I heard I was dropped was on the radio, things were quite casual. Just as well I had a radio, I suppose! They dropped me for a year, then they brought me back to play Argentina, then they dropped me again for another game. And then they couldn't get rid of me for seven years after that!'

In the 1990s, Irish rugby entered its darkest period, and Poppy, though dropped for close to two years, went on to suffer plenty of heartbreak. 'Since I've retired, it seems they haven't lost a match and, when I was playing we hardly won one – so you kind of wonder what the common denominator is. It was tough. There was a huge amount of change. We were coming off the back of Fitzy's Triple Crown win, and that squad was held together for a long period of time. A huge feat was accomplished and then there was a huge transition. We went through as many coaches and players. Every f***ing year, it was a different coach. That was desperately unsettling.'

As he says himself, the whole country was pulling its hair out for three years – 1990, 1991 and 1992 – watching the Irish rugby team fall from defeat to chaos to complete capitulation. 'A lot of people were mad as hell with what they saw.'

In October 1991, Popplewell played against Australia in the World Cup quarter-final – one peak amidst all the troughs in a transitional and forgettable period for the game in Ireland. The Aussies won an epic clash but only just. 'I got concussed from the start after a belt from Willie Ofahengaue. I was totally concussed for the rest of the game, and everyone says after it, "You made that tackle there, you got there, you got that man … geez, Popps is there again!" Maybe I should have got a few more slaps before other matches! We should have had it in the bag but experience cost us and they were bloody clinical.'

Fitzy did his best to try and lift players afterwards. 'He never stopped trying to build us up individually and collectively. He was brilliant in the dressing room and deserved better on the field.'

Popplewell made his debut in the Five Nations Championship in the middle of a ten-game losing sequence crossing Jimmy Davison's, Ciaran Fitzgerald's and Gerry Murphy's reigns as Irish coaches. The game was against what he considered an inept Welsh team at Lansdowne Road in January 1992. Ireland lost 16–15. Cue more disillusionment among Irish supporters. 'The whole ground seemed to be quiet and depressed by the end of the afternoon, even though there was only one point in it, and even though the fantastic World Cup game against Australia was still in everybody's system. People expected so much that day … that one-point defeat was like fifty points and it ruined the entire championship.'

The team went from heroes to zeroes within three months of the World Cup quarter-final. Some players got it worse than others; and no one more than out-half Ralph Keyes. A darling of the 1991 World Cup, Keyes got jeered against Scotland in the 1992 Five Nations every time he kicked the ball. Irish supporters expected more fireworks after the World Cup; expectations were high but the team couldn't deliver. 'The Irish public had had enough and the Irish players did not know which way to turn. We honestly didn't. There was not much fun left in playing for our country. Confidence was almost at nil.'

The mood in Lansdowne Road had altered considerably from that giddy October day when the Wallabies almost fell to Irish heart and passion; now the singing was replaced by jeering, booing and slow handclapping as Ireland lost to Scotland for the fifth successive time. 'When we played Scotland, they were without Finlay Calder and John Jeffrey who had both retired after the World Cup. We had them in Lansdowne Road. We lost 18–10 … it was during that match that Molly Malone and all her friends left Lansdowne Road and all we could hear was booing every time the ball went near Ralph Keyes. It was a sad day for Irish rugby.'

If the players thought the season couldn't get any worse, next up were trips to Parc des Princes

The brightest star in Ireland's darkest times – Nick Popplewell stays on his feet here, but the legs were taken from under countless Irish teams during the 1990s.

to face France and a summer tour to New Zealand. Defeat followed defeat. And then Australia arrived for the autumn internationals, a day to rekindle old scores a year on from that epic World Cup quarter-final.

Popplewell's good buddy John 'Spud' Murphy finally realised a life-long dream and won his first cap at hooker that afternoon. 'Nobody in the team was up for it. We were all wishy-washy, apart from Spud, of course. John was very talented and he would have been one of the most talented rugby players I ever played with – he could play wing-forward and hooker equally well. I felt very sorry for him. Johnny came in very late to play, and that was the Willie Anderson era where we had 150 lineout calls, an absolute ridiculous number, and Spud had to learn those before his first match for his country. For your first test, you have enough things on your mind, but to have to learn these lineout calls and every one of them had different names. Years ago, you got to the halfway line and you knew what the lineout was going to be: either over the top or middle going backwards.

'And with the noise of the crowd as well, I felt sorry for Spud. He was made a scapegoat. It was unfortunate, but I think he had an extremely good game around the park that day; it was just the lineouts were a disaster, but through no fault of his own. Somebody should just have said, "Let's bring it down to basics with three lineout calls and revert to easier calls."'

Management looked for scapegoats in a further fall from grace for Irish rugby and they cast Spud Murphy aside after the defeat against the world champions. Later, Popplewell wrote fondly of an old mate, who answered Ireland's call and more. 'At the end of his career, Spud has one Irish cap and that is one cap more than 99 per cent of the rugby players in this country. It's proper that he won that one cap at least. People talk about "one-cap wonders" and try to feel sorry for those players, but why be sympathetic? Spud played for Ireland, and that's something.'

Ireland seemed to have turned some make of a corner in Cardiff Arms Park in the 1993 Five

116

Nations. That 19–14 win over Wales in Cardiff will be remembered for Popplewell's tears as he borrowed a handkerchief from a cameraman and wept openly. Could anyone blame him? After playing seventeen times for Ireland, he had finally won a game in the championship.

Next up were England at Lansdowne Road, and they needed a good win to clinch the championship. Popplewell and Ireland, however, had other ideas. 'We had just beaten Wales in Cardiff and then we had England in Lansdowne. Everyone builds themselves up to play England. It's a major bloody scalp to get. Eric [Elwood] kicked the ball to start off the match but, before anybody got a touch on it, Paddy Johns took one of their lot completely out of it. Paddy could be an old briar at times, he'd surprise you. If you annoyed him long enough, he'd swing. He wouldn't go in with the fist but, if you're playing against him, there'd always be a knee and an elbow or something.' Paddy's action triggered the rest of the team into a berserk mode of playing. '"Big Paddy is getting annoyed, Jesus Christ something must be up!" I said to one of the players. Paddy would lead by example and always got his ball in front of the lineout and make the hard yards. He'd be very honest.'

Ireland blazed to a wholly unexpected but deserved 17–3 over Will Carling's England. Corner turned? Maybe. Monkey off the back? You bet. Not since Donal Lenihan led Ireland to a wholly unexpected 17–0 win in 1987 had Ireland scored a victory over the auld enemy. On the morning of the 1985 Triple Crown match against England, Popplewell had played his first senior game with Greystones and watched Fitzy's men win in Jim Doyle's pub in Bray.

'In the 1993 game, we didn't need a last-minute kick to win it. We knew we had the game won long before the end. The amazing and funny thing was that we won the game in the lineout more than anywhere else. On paper, that should not have been possible. They had Bayfield and Rodber. Galwey was at Number 4, and I was looking after them, shunting them up, as well as disrupting the opposition. There were quite a few digs going in from both sides, I have to admit.'

He remembers big hits and tackles and personal duels happening all over the ground. He says Pat O'Hara was phenomenal 'the hardest tackler I have ever witnessed up close', but it was Elwood and McBride, together, who totally creased Rory Underwood early on and, along with John's indiscretion, set the tone for the rest of the day.

He remembers Claw [Peter Clohessy], Terry Kingston and himself putting in the hard tackles too. The front five were producing the goods in the loose and Poppy had a good feeling about the outcome. Elwood put Ireland 3–0 up converting beautifully into the wind from an angle. Then another bout of fisticuffs ensued after Stuart Barnes launched a garryowen and, after the ball returned from the heavens, a slap landed on an Englishman and Jonathan Webb added the resultant penalty.

It stood 3–3 at the break and, after the interval, Elwood's precision from placed kicks pushed Ireland 12–3 in front with three penalties. Popplewell was at the other end of the field when Galwey scored the try that really clinched it. 'Near the end of the game, I suppose we were shouting our mouths off a fair bit, especially in the scrums. I never said anything to [Jeff] Probyn. I would

After the famine the feast – 20 March 1993, Ireland 17 England 3: Scenes reminiscent of the 1985 Triple Crown win saw a huge outpouring of emotion when the green masses descended onto the Lansdowne Road pitch to celebrate a historic victory over Ireland's nearest rival. Ireland's hero, Eric Elwood, can't conceal his joy and is held aloft by delighted fans. The Connacht out-half played his greatest ever game in green, kicking two drop goals and two penalty goals, while Mick Galwey followed in the footsteps of his neighbours from home, Mick Doyle and Moss Keane, by scoring in Currow Corner. Ireland played out of their skins to beat Will Carling's England in what was the first win over the 'auld enemy' since Donal Lenihan led Ireland to a 17–0 win in 1987. 'In the 1993 win, we didn't need a last-minute kick to win it,' explains another hero of the hour Nick Popplewell. 'We knew we had the game won long before the end. The amazing and funny thing was that we won the game in the lineout more then anywhere else. On paper, that should not have been possible. They had Bayfield and Rodber. Galwey was at 4, and I was looking after them, shunting them up, as well as disrupting the opposition. There were quite a few digs going in from both sides during the game, I have to admit.'

respect him far too much to start down that road with him, but I enjoyed myself with Brian Moore, "Come on, Brian" that sort of stuff, "Good boy, Brian … No, Brian, that's no good." Claw and myself had several good chats in the scrum. "What do you think, Claw? Will we push them back a bit?" It's OK doing that in Moore's face, because he would be the very one who would be rabbiting on and laughing at us normally. It's not often we have England on the rack. They were in pain and we were dead right to smile at them. Things went very sweet that day. Certainly, a lot of the problems over the years is that, although, yes, we're a fifteen-man team, you always seemed to be carrying four or five people. There were certain days where everything clicked like the Australia match [1991] or the English [1993] where everyone was on full cylinder and covering everyone else and you just seemed to be doing no wrong. If Dean Richards was playing, you were Donald Ducked because he was able to dictate the whole game and he wasn't playing that day with England. With Probyn, you'd never get much change out of him – he was always a difficult opponent, he was a light prop, only about fifteen-and-a-half stone, he had a huge work ethic around the pitch. We were able to psyche them out a little bit.'

In the early hours of the morning after the England match, a Dublin taxi driver refused to take his fare from Poppy and his wife, Rachel. 'He told us we had paid enough having watched Ireland that afternoon.'

The Lions team to face New Zealand was picked early that night – Clohessy and Probyn (England) were overlooked and they brought over Paul Burnell who didn't really cut it during the tour. 'Probyn should have been brought out there as well as Clohessy.'

Between 1994 and 1998, the heavy losses were sometimes tempered by an odd heroic win to lift spirits, but it always seemed a struggle. Through it all, Poppy soldiered on despite the criticism and pessimism and the jeering. 'There were loads of games where they booed and slow hand-clapped. That's why we used wear bandages around our ears, you see!'

Even in the dark days, there was a support mechanism in Noel Murphy, to lift players with bruised egos and shattered spirits. 'He helped the team enormously. He was most human and good fun, and certainly kept me going in the latter years. He had a terrible job to do, and was asked to do in his spare time when the national team manager really should be a full-time position. He came into the manager's job at a time when the Irish players were on the point of revolt, but Noisy was like a father to us from the word go. I toured New Zealand with Noel, and Eddie O'Sullivan was on it starting off on a long coaching career. When you tour a country, they pay your expenses but they only pay so much for thirty players and eight management. Eddie wasn't part of that eight, but Noel gave Eddie his daily allowance – and these were the times when every bloody pound was precious.'

Popplewell was also part of those Irish teams who like to forget those defeats to Italy at Lansdowne Road. Losses like that only added fuel to the critics' fire and they didn't hold back. 'I think I lost to Italy twice in Lansdowne Road and once away. If you had a bad referee against

Italy and you didn't sort it out yourselves, you were dined and ducked. They were offside all day long, the way we used to play. But they were always offside, pulling people's jerseys, and, if you weren't able to null that out and the referee wasn't doing anything either, what chance did you have? It was open season for them.'

Popplewell made his last full Lansdowne appearance against Canada on 30 November 1997 (his last at the old ground was against Scotland on 7 February 1998 in a 16–17 loss, when he came on as a temporary replacement for Paul Wallace). He captained Ireland for only the second time against the Canadians and led them out under the newly installed floodlights. Poppy made way for an up-and-comer from Greystones named

Poppy the human JCB: Irish duo Nick Popplewell and David Corkery lift Jeremy Davidson to win possession in a lineout against Australia on 25 November 1996. The match saw Keith Wood captain Ireland for the first time and Paul Burke kick four penalties – but the Wallabies, aided by a David Knox try, triumphed 12–22.

Reggie Corrigan. 'I was captain against Canada and Japan in the 1995 World Cup. We won both. I can proudly claim I have a 100 per cent record as captain! Reggie was coming through and it was time to vacate. I would have coached him in school and that depressed me even further and told you how old I was.

'I remember going to Lansdowne Road when I was nine or ten with my dad to watch internationals. We were very posh; up in the West Upper! My first taste of playing on the pitch itself and coming up against Des Fitzgerald of Lansdowne FC and I got throttled that day too, so it was a bit like the All Blacks one. Dessie was the main man at the time, and I wasn't going to get in his way. I learned a lot that day – I learned what not to do. Now I'm bringing my kids there. It has come full circle.'

Fergus Slattery
Flanker

1970–1984

Fergus Slattery's first cap for Ireland on 10 January 1970, should have been a celebratory event for the Dublin man, but, instead, he found himself embroiled in the controversy surrounding the visit of the Springboks. He even ended up in debate at UCD with the vice-chairman of the anti-apartheid movement, Kader Asmal – the motion being: Should the fixture go ahead or not?

Slattery remembers a week of mixed emotions, pitted first against Asmal on the intellectual front and then in a physical confrontation against fiercesome Springbok openside, Jan Ellis.

'It would have been typical of a university debate. The actual venue was in the medical part of Belfield, but it wasn't a radical meeting by any means; I found it to be a very tame affair. And it wasn't used as a demonstration by the anti-apartheid movement either. It was Kader Asmal calling a motion against the game going ahead and there was myself as someone who was playing in favour of fulfilling the fixture. There was a vote taken about whether or not the game should go ahead, but there was a show of hands and I don't know who actually won it. Outside of this debate, I think the trade-union elements and the anti-apartheid movement was probably more demonstrative than anything else. It was a controversial time, yes, but I don't believe it was as controversial as when we went on the 1981 tour to South Africa. I think there was more controversy then than in 1970. The one thing about the anti-apartheid movement was that they were very good at making up numbers. I remember they marched by the Shelbourne, we counted the numbers and we also went out and asked the guards what their interpretation of the numbers were. And, of course, the numbers that appeared in the newspapers the next day were a complete exaggeration – though that didn't bother me.'

A barbed-wire fence surrounding the pitch made it impossible for anyone to get onto the pitch on match day and attack any of the players, and the ring of steel was further reinforced by the large numbers of gardaí around the perimeter of the field. While managing to preserve the peace inside the ground, the guards also had to keep a close eye on any attempts by protestors to climb the walls of the stadium. One photograph taken on an emotive day captures one demonstrator scaling a Lansdowne wall as two gardaí try to undo his efforts.

Only 30,000 turned up that cold January afternoon. The terraces were completely empty. The weather had been so bad that week that straw was liberally spread around the pitch and, according to Slattery, it was like running into a barn. The match didn't entirely pass without incident. Hooker Ken Kennedy suffered an injury when a bottle was hurled from underneath the East Stand hitting him on the back.

It was said that Ireland was lucky to escape with an 8–8 draw as the Springboks failed to convert a far greater proportion of possession into scores. They complained afterwards that the Scottish referee played far too much injury-time, which allowed Tom Kiernan to snatch a draw with a penalty goal.

Slattery had shown his intentions as a fearless flanker, a tag he carried throughout his sixty-one caps for his country. 'I think it was Paul McWeeney who wrote in *The Irish Times* afterwards that I wrecked their out-half Lawless' confidence. They had a massive pack, which could move a bit too. We gave away a bit in weight and, sometimes, it was unbearable for the forwards in there.'

Still there was no complete capitulation from the Irish pack. And Slattery has fond memories of playing alongside Ronnie Lamont and Ken Goodall in that match. He recalls Goodall might have been frustrated in his efforts to attack the gain-line more, but the Number 8 saved Ireland's bacon in the sixty-seventh minute by running cross field and tackling Andy van der Watt into touch in goal when the Springboks' left wing seemed destined to score a try. 'When people mention the name Ken Goodall, I just have one word – brilliant. He was very, very quick, great pace and very, very athletic. Jesus, he was massive but such a huge loss to Irish rugby. That tackle was just one facet of his game. I was so, so upset when he left for league [at the end of the 1969–1970 season]. He came up to me when I played for the Barbarians against Fiji at the back end of 1970. We played it up in

Newcastle and he came across from Lancashire to see the game, but he made his way to meet me – I was moved by that. We really missed him and it was a shame to lose him. A big loss to Ireland; a serious loss.'

There were still plenty of characters left who both humbled and inspired Slatts. He sometimes felt blinded almost by the sight of so many luminaries in the one dressing room. 'Syd Millar came in to the side in 1958, Willie John [McBride] came in to the side in 1962 and [Ken] Kennedy in 1965, Mick Molloy a year after that, Goodall and Lamont were both Lions in 1966 and 1968 – it was just really a fantastic pack. Then you'd players like Gibson, Kiernan, Roger Young, Alan Duggan around for five, six or seven years. It was a cracking Irish side.'

The genius of Gibson didn't pass him by that January afternoon. He just watched with awe as Gibson picked up a bouncing ball on halfway, skipped through the Springbok line and laid off to Alan Duggan who sprinted under the posts from forty-five yards for Ireland's one and only try.

Ireland led at the break but a converted try by South Africa in the second half put them in the driving seat as the game entered injury-time. Seven minutes more was played, the Springboks seemingly bewildered by all the extra time and, when Duggan intercepted Tonie Roux's pass to van der Watt, the Irish winger ran and chipped over the full-back's head and forced the South Africans to concede a penalty which Tom Kiernan converted.

Slattery is loath to make comparisons with other 'momentous' victories at Lansdowne but beating Triple Crown-chasing Wales in 1970 – the team of 'All Stars' – is not easily forgotten. 'Beating Wales was a huge win. People look back now and when they see 14–0, it just doesn't sound like a great game; it sounds simply like two tries by today's standards – 14–0 was a hiding in those days. We scored two tries [three points for a try], a penalty, drop goal and a conversion. They were hammered. We just got in amongst them, broke up their rhythm and the Barry John–Gareth Edwards half-back axis. God, Goodall had a great game. One of the tries was a kick and run by him, he chipped the Wales defence, ran through from thirty yards out and scored what was very much an individual try. I thought it was a super try. It just showed his whole array of talents. And Alan [Duggan], at the time, was one of the most prolific try scorers. That was his talent – give him the ball, anywhere near the line and he'd score. Don't know how he managed it, but he just had an instinct. He just had total confidence. The closer he was to the line, the closer he was to scoring.'

By 1972, Slattery was part of a team capable of achieving something tangible. Slattery says because of the political situation in the North, and because Wales and Scotland would not travel to Lansdowne that year, a Grand Slam eluded that Ireland side. The circumstances surrounding that campaign hurt Slattery to the core, but the pain was all-pervasive on the Irish team of all talents. 'It was the biggest tragedy of my career. I always thought I had loads of time. I was just so young but I felt really, really sorry for the likes Tom Kiernan and Mike Gibson and Willie John. Those chances are not going to come around too often. You go to Twickenham, you go to Paris and you win your

Even before the Springboks touched down at Dublin Airport just before three o'clock on Wednesday, 7 January 1970, there was strong resistance to their arrival from many quarters, including the anti-apartheid movement, high-profile politicians, the trade union movement and many individual citizens.

As the match neared, the nationwide protest was gathering serious momentum. Most protests were peaceful but others offered a more menacing vista on match day. The IRA had issued a statement saying it would 'take action' against the president and committee members of the IRFU if Irish citizens in protest were injured at Lansdowne Road. Meanwhile, a counter-demonstration was planned by the Derry Ulster Volunteer Force. In a letter to the Belfast Telegraph, *they said an armed service unit was being sent to Dublin on Saturday 'to take care of the Papists who would attempt to make a British game of sport impossible'.*

The anti-apartheid movement held its demonstration outside Lansdowne Road. Vice-Chairman, Kader Asmal, said in a statement that they were using only legal and non-violent means to demonstrate against 'the evils of racism and against the action of the IRFU in so shamelessly condoning the degradation of human dignity that is apartheid through its invitation to a racially selected all-white team to tour Ireland'. But emphasising that the movement 'repudiates the use of force as a means of propagating opposition to apartheid in Ireland'.

CIÉ cancelled a special train due to bring rugby supporters from Cork and Limerick to Dublin on the day of the match. A service that usually was booked out for an international match had taken only ten bookings for the Springbok match.

The match went ahead under heavy security inside and outside the Lansdowne Road and the game was drawn 8–8.

Flank and fearless: Slattery seen here in action against Wales in the 1971 Five Nations. Regarded as Ireland's greatest open-side flanker, Slatts felt Ireland could have won a Grand Slam had Wales and Scotland travelled to Ireland for the 1972 Five Nations.

128

two hard games, and today they're still regarded as the two hard games. And we hammered Scotland and Wales two years earlier. We'd have hammered them if we got them that year – there's no doubt about it. They would have had no chance and I can say that, but you can't prove it. I just know it as much as I knew we'd beat Scotland in 1982 for the Triple Crown, they'd absolutely no chance.'

France did travel to Dublin in 1972 to fulfill an extra fixture on the rugby calendar, but by then, the season was dead. 'We played them twice. The poor old French came over and we kicked the bejaysus out of them! They didn't deserve it but I think they got it from us. We beat them fairly easily. However, the whole championship was a bloody nonsense but it happened and there's nothing we could do about it.'

Slattery thought the team could have at least achieved immortality if they had defeated the visiting All Blacks in January 1973. Ireland managed to draw 10–10 and denied Ian Kirkpatrick and his All Blacks the accolade of becoming the first team from New Zealand to beat all four home countries on a single tour since the Originals in 1905. 'In a lot of ways, we mightn't have deserved to win. I think that would have been fair comment. Based on one or two other matches we had against them, we might have been unlucky.'

All that afternoon, he tried to keep his eye on New Zealand scrum-half 'Super Sid' Going, whom he describes as one of the best in his position at the time in world rugby. While Slattery was regarded as decisive and aggressive in his play, Going was a plucky character with a penchant for doing the unorthodox. Slatts, who had made mincemeat of Gareth Edwards two years earlier, had met his match in Super Sid, once described as 'a bundle of barbed wire, cast iron and rubber, [he] runs like a slippery eel making for the water'. Slattery found Going fast and elusive and difficult to tackle.

The enduring memory of that game for many people is Slattery's intervention in the build-up to the Irish try that leveled matters. They said the ground shook a tad after Slattery brought their Number 8 Alan Sutherland to the ground with a thunderous tackle after a lineout. Scrum-half J.J. Moloney gathered possession, stole away from the ruck and delivered a sweet pass inside to Tom Grace. 'Grace did brilliantly – the old chip over the top, chase and follow. The ball ran over the tryline and Grace took off in a race with their out-half Bob Burgess. The ball was crawling over the dead-ball line but Tom got there and beat Burgess. Still there are about twenty people on the Irish team who claim they got a hand on the ball that led to that try!'

Barry McGann stepped up to take the difficult conversion, but the phantom Lansdowne wind again cast its malevolent spell over the ground taking the ball wide of the posts. 'I knew a lot of the All Blacks because of the 1971 Lions tour. And they had a nucleus of that New Zealand side still together. They were really hurt after that Lions tour and they wanted victory at any price. But that Irish side was good enough to play anybody, and they were capable of beating anybody. And that's why I say we were just robbed in the 1972 Five Nations. That was a Grand Slam on a plate. We don't win many Grand Slams and that year we had it on a plate.'

While regarded as one of the finest open-sides to have ever played for Ireland, Slattery was gaining notoriety on the airwaves as well. He was playing for Leinster against the touring Fijians in 1974 when a radio show he had recorded in London was broadcast at the same time as the match. Those who brought radios to the game were getting a little confused but acknowledging the fact that Slattery could cover all areas of the field at various stages in a match, they thought he'd mastered the art of bi-location as well.

'I did a BBC radio programme called *Man of Action*. The sort of people they had on were lords of the realm, prime ministers, stately types. The producer got this idea that they wanted a sports person on so they first asked Cliff Morgan of Wales. But Cliff suggested me. I went over to the BBC and did this programme which was one hell of a challenge because I wasn't up with serious music, classical music and the like. I think it was a two-and-a-half-hour programme. But it was broadcast at the same time Leinster played Fiji – and, when I came off the pitch, this rather grand-looking member of the old empire came over to me, completely bemused by the fact that I was playing on the pitch and he was listening to me on the radio. I didn't know it was going out at the same time as the game.'

By 1975, he noticed that the wheels were beginning to come off this fine chariot of an Irish side. 'The old brigade like McBride and Kennedy were starting to burn a bit of diesel in the pack. I think someone termed us "Grandad's Army". Later, of course, the 1982 side were christened "Dad's Army".'

Slattery took the captaincy for a period but it didn't suit him, but the leadership qualities and fearlessness on the field necessary for the role never deserted him. And, in 1982, he and Dad's Army landed a Triple Crown at Lansdowne Road. 'The Dad's Army label didn't annoy me. This was second time round now with labels. I had heard all that in 1975 with [Ray] McLoughlin, Kennedy and Molloy. I was used to it. The 1982 side was mature – that's the word I would use. That 1982 side came out of the 1979 tour to Australia, slowly but surely. That tour to Australia was a big help. And the tour to South Africa in 1981 produced players like Paul Dean, Michael Kiernan, Keith Crossan. Players, like that, just popped out of the woodwork and, all of it was really a result of that tour to South Africa. I think we found five or six players and a lot of them made it into two Triple Crown sides.'

He acknowledges the contribution of Ollie Campbell to this win. 'We wouldn't have won anything if it wasn't for Ollie. It's a bit like Martin Johnson – how important was Martin Johnson for England winning the World Cup in 2003? Ollie was our man. It might be unfair on others to say it but that's the reality of it. He was just such a massive player for us. And the great thing about the pack was it was earthy and there was good representation from all four provinces. We'd a bit of people from everywhere in there.'

Farewell to a legend: Slattery gives it welly in his last appearance in a green shirt against France in the 1984 Five Nations.

He regards the 1982 Triple Crown win over Scotland as the most important game in his career. Most of all, it gave an Irish people and an Irish society – up to their eyes with unemployment – a huge lift. 'It was like Jack Charlton's two World Cups. It was so important to the dignity of Irish people. We see that Gaelic Games and Munster winning the European Cup have had an enormous effect on people. But winning that in Lansdowne Road was so important for Irish rugby. It was a bit like the 1971 Lions tour to New Zealand, it was just so important to everybody. It broke the duck and it made the next thing possible and we won another Triple Crown three years later.'

However, Slattery wasn't about to bow out of Lansdowne Road quietly and notched a try against England in 1983 – a year Ireland earned a share of the championship. In the game, Campbell was the architect of England's downfall, scoring twenty-one points. It was Slatts' sixtieth international and his third try at this level. In the immediate aftermath, an emotional Slattery quipped, 'I've been over the line more times than I care to remember. This time I managed to ground the ball!'

He recalls that it was down in the Lansdowne Road corner, 'one of those messy old fumbles, and a pick it up and drive over the line type of tries. I actually drove through Clive Woodward. He was the man between me and destiny! I think it was Moss [Keane] who gave me a pass – you wouldn't get a pass from a back, I'll tell you that. You'd have to have been playing for Ireland for ten years before you'd get a pass from a back!'

Peter Stringer

Scrum-Half

2000–

Bill McLaren once said that the ideal scrum-half has to be very brave. Brave because he's in the frontline, brave because he has to deal with a big opponent coming around the corner. Peter Stringer – a Lilliputian in a forest of Gullivers – has often earned the tag as Munster and Ireland's Braveheart and, figuratively speaking, we have seen him knock down a few pinetrees over the years. Sometimes, we close our eyes and fear that he might never get up again, but he always rises, dusts himself down and gets on to the next big hit.

But to focus merely on his five-foot seven-inch frame diminishes the other facets of his game. The pass is his weapon, his forté – matched with the telepathic half-back partnership that he has evolved with out-half Ronan O'Gara since their schooldays at PBC in Cork, and subsequently with Munster and Ireland. And when O'Gara has one of those utopian Lansdowne Road displays – cue v. Australia 2002, v. South Africa 2004 and against Leinster 2006 – the service from his Number 9 is often forgotten. To some, Stringer is the shadow in the wind, but to

O'Gara, Stringer supplies the oxygen that enables him to breath fire into his kicking or passing game. They have been through some battles together, thrust initially into the limelight with Munster in the Heineken Cup in the late 1990s. Two heroic victories over money-rich Saracens in December 1999 and January 2000 cast the now famous double act onto centre stage against Scotland in the 2000 Six Nations.

It was a changing time in Ireland both socially and economically. The turn of the millennium and the Celtic Tiger brought with it an optimism that swept the country. The arrival of Stringer and O'Gara came bang on cue to supplement this flighty excitement that Ireland was capable of achieving beyond the mediocre. In a sense, we were, as a country, dreaming of things that never were – and saying why not? The new caps were young and had no inhibitions, no fears. Three others made their debuts alongside Stringer and O'Gara that day against Scotland in Lansdowne Road – John Hayes, Shane Horgan and Simon Easterby – all brought with them a vibrancy to a team christened Young Ireland.

After the bitter defeat to Argentina in the World Cup the previous November and the humiliation suffered in Twickenham in the first game of the 2000 Six Nations, change was needed and Ireland coach Warren Gatland opted for youth and a daring game-plan in his next match. Gone was the plodding, the turgid rugby, the slow ruck ball and staid three-quarter play. In was adventure, all-singing, all-dancing rugby and the Lansdowne Road audience lapped it up.

'We hadn't beaten Scotland since 1988,' remembers Stringer. 'We were staying in the Glenview at the time. Out of the blue, Warren came up to me before the team was announced publicly and said simply, "We're going to go with you and start you." Obviously, it was shock and I'm there thinking in the foyer of the Glenview, "Am I really good enough for this?" All the doubts come creeping into your head. You're delighted on the one hand, but it's daunting enough to play with the Claw and Gaillimh who have been there for years. In the end, you just go with it. Thankfully, there were four other guys earning their first cap. When you're on your own starting out, there can be nerves. The media stuff was shared then between five of us instead of all the pressure being on one fellow. That made it easier really in the build-up to the game.'

The Twickenham disaster needed to be exorcised from players' minds and to mollify the pain of that 50–18 defeat, Warren Gatland and backs coach Eddie O'Sullivan drew up a revolutionary game-plan. Well, it was revolutionary to Irish eyes which were smiling at full-time that Saturday. To the supporters who saw Ireland beat Scotland that day, it was fast and it was vibrant, and Ireland scored loads of tries in the 44–12 win. The famous 'roar' was back in old stadium. 'If you looked back at the English game, the ball was slow. Everything was pedantic. Warren and Eddie wanted to bring something new to it. Since that week, we've relied on always getting the pace of the game up. We mightn't be the biggest team, but with continuity we could bring it to a pace and a level where the other team can't cope, then you're on a good way to winning the game.

'Our aim was to get the ball away from rucks as quickly as possible and give our backs the space because we had a good backline. Probably for the first time in Irish rugby there was a threat, a real threat out wide. We came off the back of a hiding over in Twickenham. The coaches gave us the licence to have a go. The daunting task of going out for your first cap brings its own pressure but, in a strange sort of way, there wasn't that much pressure on because people didn't really know what to expect from us. "Have a go. What was the worst thing that could happen? Express yourself" were words running through my mind.'

In the dressing room before kick-off, Stringer remembers Gaillimh putting the new lads at ease, Woodie winking and smiling, telling the Young Irelanders to enjoy themselves. And for the national anthems Galwey bear-hugged both Stringer and O'Gara as the Cork duo stood for their first 'Amhrán na bhFiann' and first rendition of 'Ireland's Call'. 'Ah, Gaillimh. Yes. Special moment,' smiles Stringer, 'and do you know I remember we stood in the same positions for the Italy game and the following morning one newspaper had a photo and the caption under it was titled 'Goodfellas'. I think as well just going up for the anthem, it's obviously hard not to be affected by it. It's your first time out on the field with the Irish team. But then the doubts came back to my head again, "Do I remember all the calls? I'm in a position to make decisions. Bloody, hell, I hope all this works out." There is a lot of pressure there. Then the first twenty minutes pass you by. Gone.'

Playing alongside Ronan O'Gara should have lightened the burden, but O'Gara was in Stringer's boat too. Would they be one-cap wonders? Would they sink or swim? 'In the first half, we didn't really click. I threw ROG a few shaky passes and put him under a bit of pressure. He let me know about it ... and still does! To this day, he keeps me on my toes. We got into them in the second half, got a bit more confidence. We were more confident and comfortable and seemed to click a bit better. I always like to think that it's a game of rugby for eighty minutes; that you're doing for eighty minutes this thing since the age of seven. I remember Declan Kidney saying to me when I was a student in Pres to concentrate on what I was doing and not be affected by what was going on around me. Schools Cup matches are big, boisterous occasions. They test your nerves as a young fellow. They were good bloody preparation when I look back now.'

He says he wouldn't normally go back and watch video replays of matches but his earliest memory of beating England gets a few runs now and again. If he likes throwing himself recklessly into tackles, then Stringer serves as Ireland's most famous hand-tripper. His trip on Dan Luger in October 2001 ultimately denied Clive Woodward's side a Grand Slam. It was England's final 2001 Six Nations game, pushed back because of the outbreak of foot-and-mouth in the spring.

Keith Wood described this pivotal moment in the game in the Inpho book *Putting it on the Line*. 'We lead 14–9 [in the second half] and the battle is raging just inside our half when Dan Luger finds a gap and goes haring towards out line. The gap is my fault. I am slow off the ground and in rushing to get into the defensive line more quickly, I leave a gap outside of me and Luger races through. We all chase back but he looks home and dry. If he scores, they will

Tripped up: Peter Stringer involved in one of the great Lansdowne moments when his last-ditch ankle tap prevented Dan Luger (14, England) from scoring a try in the 2001 foot-and-mouth Six Nations.

go on to win the game, of that there is no doubt … but cometh the hour, cometh the midget and Peter Stringer's incredible ankle tap saves the day. We arrive in support and turn the ball over…'

'The midget' remembers the moment vividly. In his home in Cork, his dad, John, has 'the trip' framed. 'Dan Luger had beaten a few guys, but he had beaten me easily when I fronted up to him first. He side-stepped me and rounded me. For whatever reason, I kept going. I normally wouldn't have a hope of catching them wingers. He had to beat Girvan Dempsey after that, and stepped fairly easily as he had done to me. But I think for a split second he had to check and got through without Girvan laying a hand on him. That split second gave me the momentum to catch up with him. Despairingly, I just threw myself out there. I found Humphs [David Humphreys] saying to me afterwards that he had given up the chance of trying to catch him. In the video when I hand trip him, you can see Luger falling and, just before he falls, Humphreys has conceded that he's obviously going to score because Luger's one of the quickest guys in world rugby. And then, as Luger is falling, you can see Humphreys' reaction. I got behind for the ruck and kicked left-footed to touch. It nearly didn't make touch. I was like, "Jesus get into touch, give the lads a bit of a rest." It made it in about the ten-yard line. It was a great feeling. The photograph shows the crowd in the background as Luger is running away from me. Irish fans have their hands on their heads. Yeah, that was a special moment.'

Though England lost a possible Grand Slam, they still were crowned Six Nations champions. No bad feat, but Clive Woodward, Martin Johnson, Lawrence Dallaglio *et al* judged themselves on Grand Slams – though Johnson and Dallaglio were injured for the Ireland game. To witness the celebrations afterwards, you'd think Ireland had won the World Cup, when it was a downcast England team that was collecting the championship trophy in front of the West Stand.

Stringer felt his feet never touched the ground for hours afterwards. He says he floated around Lansdowne for the lap of honour. 'There's a photo of Gaillimh, Woodie and myself. There I am just walking around with two legends. They never looked happier. They had been part of some low days for Ireland. It was my first real experience of really connecting with the crowd, and really seeing how much it meant to them and feeling proud of what we had achieved. England collecting the trophy was weird, yes. When you're disappointed, it must be strange going up to receive a trophy and try to feel happy about it. On the day, we were the team who felt we played better and deserved it and we nearly felt like saying, "Give us the cup!"'

The dressing room was a mix of hugs, champagne spray, tears, weariness and renditions of 'From Clare to Here' led by Killaloe native Wood and 'Stand Up and Fight' – a Munster anthem – by manager Brian O'Brien. The delirium of the young and the brave. Even Taoiseach Bertie Ahern stepped into the inner sanctum to catch a taste of a famous day in Irish sport. 'I remember Ronan going absolutely mad. In fact, everyone was freaking out and seeing the Taoiseach coming in and the lads trying to lift him up on their shoulders (we did it to Marty Morrissey in Limerick for the Munster homecoming) was quite surreal. He remembers England prop Jason Leonard popping in to offer his congratulations. Leonard had earlier sought out his friend and London Harlequins club-mate Keith Wood at the final whistle offering the Ireland hooker a warm embrace. Inside with the Irish lads, his presence and magnanimous actions were a throwback to the great amateur days. 'I remember that. Jase is a great fellow, from the old-school era. "Rala" [Paddy O'Reilly] was there handing him a cup of tea. "There, two sugars, Jase," I think was what Rala said. Jase sat down with his cup of tea, had a chat with a few of us. He's a real gentleman, there was no kind of hesitation about it. He just congratulated us. He's a real genuine fellow.'

After England, the good days continued at Lansdowne. If you call coming very close to beating the All Blacks a good day. As Munster fans discovered in the week of their seismic clash with Leinster in the 2006 Heineken Cup semi-final, the wee man has a knack of picking up big injuries before big clashes – and in Stringer's mind nothing came bigger than the All Blacks in Lansdowne. He didn't want to miss that. He grew up admiring David Kirk, even imitating him in Temple Hill when local hero – and Ireland scrum-half at the time – Michael Bradley was out of sight. 'I injured my ankle the Thursday before the All Blacks game. Just two days before the biggest day of my life. I was a real doubt. I had a fitness test the morning of the game, played the game – how I

137

don't know – and then had a scan on it the morning after. I literally couldn't walk. It turned out I cracked my heel bones. I managed to live the dream against the All Blacks but I was out for eight weeks after that. But I spoke to the Claw while assessing my chances of playing. He never got a chance of playing New Zealand and I felt it might be my only ever chance of playing them.'

Those at Lansdowne remember one of those searing, edge-of-the-seat days at the old ground. After England, we thought we had enough of the drama for one year. Then Ireland got away and led New Zealand 21–7 two minutes after the restart. Fantasy rugby. But eighteen minutes later, the score was 40–24 in New Zealand's favour. Stringer blames himself for one of the tries. 'There I was next to a ruck on my own line, the New Zealand second-row picked and basically dunked the ball over me and over the tryline. I found myself in a position about a foot from the line and it was a case of this six-foot seven-inch guy walking all over me. I was disappointed and blamed myself obviously for that try. We could have taken them that day. But I remember there was some noise there, under lights and it created an even better atmosphere.'

Gatland was close to creating history and many felt his future was secure despite what happened in Murrayfield. The IRFU committee took an alternate view and, on 28 November, the former All Black was summoned to the Berkeley Court in the vicinity of Lansdowne Road and told his services were no longer required. Gatland subsequently went to London Wasps where he coached them to three Premiership titles and a European Cup in 2004 – beating Munster along the way in the semi-final at Lansdowne Road.

138

Stringer, however, will remember Gatts for one token of kindness particularly. 'He wrote me a letter after he finished up just saying he wanted to congratulate me as a player, not after any specific occasion or anything, but to say he had doubts about my size initially and whether I would survive in international rugby. He wrote that, as soon as he plucked up the courage to pick me, every doubt just left him and he saw me as a person and player. The letter is something I hold dearly. It's a great thing to get from a man who wouldn't be renowned for expressing his emotions that often and to get that was certainly very nice. That's something I'll always remember about the man. I didn't know which way to approach him when I came into the set-up first. I found him a difficult guy to relate to – I think a lot of people would say the same. He was very influential at the same time – he would have a quiet word with you rather than make it publicly known.'

A southern hemisphere scalp came sooner rather than later when Ireland defeated Australia in the rain at Lansdowne the following autumn. Stringer was playing opposite one of the world's finest scrum-halves, George Gregan, and remembers someone who spent a lot of time just talking to the referee and complaining. 'It was absolutely miserable. There were puddles of water all over the ground. Sometimes when it's like that, you get into a game more. You're not spreading the ball from touchline to touchline, instead keeping it in close, making more tackles in around the fringes and you can get a real sense of wanting more. We were sliding around and, when you're tackling, it's so much easier than dry ground. There was a real sense that day that we were not going to allow them to beat us in our backyard. The win just brought it to a new level. We felt afterwards that we could compete against these teams.'

Brian O'Drsicoll captained Ireland that afternoon in the absence of an injured Keith Wood and produced one of his finest hours in a green jersey. 'Brian was really special that day. I think intelligence on the field is his greatest virtue – that ability to read a game is impressive. We do a lot of speaking in training with regard to technical play in the backs and Eddie would advise us on what to do and what way he wants us to play. Everybody stands and listens when Drico has something to say.'

Winning a Triple Crown against Scotland in 2004 was a special day for Stringer because he scored a try. He can't remember exactly where he was when Ireland lifted their last Triple Crown in 1985 but he knows this was special to Irish supporters because they don't win that many of them. 'It was quite close at times. Matt Williams had them well fired up because of his association with

139

My Lansdowne Roar: Stringer celebrates his magical try that helped seal Ireland the 2004 Triple Crown against Scotland at Lansdowne Road. 'Normally I wouldn't be the most flamboyant celebrators of tries,' says Stringer.

In the final weekend of March 2004, with Ireland only eighty minutes away from a first Triple Crown in nineteen years, Scotland came to Lansdowne. The first leg of the Triple Crown campaign included a thumping six-try 36–15 win over Wales at Lansdowne; the tries came from Shane Byrne (two) Brian O'Driscoll (two), Ronan O'Gara and Anthony Foley. Ireland were in confident mood going to Twickenham to take on the newly crowned world champions and, in an incredible game, beat England 19–13. Girvan Dempsey scored a memorable try in the corner, and O'Gara kicked fourteen points. O'Sullivan's men kept their championship hopes alive with a 19–0 win over Italy as a gale force wind swept through Lansdowne Road but their eye was firmly on the Triple Crown.

Matt Williams, who at the beginning of the season had left Leinster to coach Scotland, knew many of the players intimately. When Ally Hogg went over to make it 16–16 in the second half, it looked like Scotland would spoil the party. But Ireland upped the ante and pulled away convincing winners on a final score of 37–16. The tries that afternoon were all memorable: born-again Gordon D'Arcy (two), while Geordan Murphy, David Wallace and Peter Stringer added the others. 'The crowd actually stayed in the stadium,' said O'Sullivan of the ensuing match celebrations.

Leinster. He knew a lot of the players and Scotland, we found, were really up for it as well. There were a few nerves at the start of the game but I think when David Wallace scored, it gave us breathing space. I nipped in for a nice one! I felt very proud to score in that Triple Crown win. Normally, I wouldn't be the most flamboyant celebrators of tries, but I was on my knees, and threw the ball into the air. Scoring tries brings out some strange things.'

The big names in world rugby kept dropping at Lansdowne in the autumn internationals. South Africa were next in November 2004 and their coach Jake White, who had already master-minded two test victories in South Africa over Ireland that summer, was indirectly psyching up the Ireland camp, saying only three Irish players would make it into his match-day twenty-two. Some saw his remarks as a slur on Irish rugby. White tried to assuage those remarks later in the week, going on the charm offensive. 'I've huge respect for Irish rugby,' he said. 'The Willie John McBrides, the Syd Millars, the Noel Murphys, Ollie Campbells and Fergus Slatterys are great players, and great people come out of this country. So if it was seen as disrespectful then that is not the way it was intended.'

However, Ireland coach Eddie O'Sullivan – like many who had given their lives to Irish rugby – had an altogether different view. 'Jake's remarks … were pretty much an attack on Irish rugby as a sport,' he said, 'We're as proud a rugby nation as anybody else. We mightn't be as good as South Africa according to the record books but we're proud of our rugby. It had nothing to do with the game, I just felt unhappy about what he said. I felt it was totally unnecessary.'

But the omens looked good for Ireland going into the game. Since their Triple Crown win over Scotland the previous March at Lansdowne, Ireland had won thirteen of their previous fourteen games at the ground. And an altogether new-look South African team weren't used to these parts – especially the capricious nature of the wind inside Lansdowne. The day before the match, the South African kickers came off the field unable to decipher which direction the wind actually blows inside the ground.

Hurt by their failure to build on their Triple Crown defeat by losing two tests in South Africa, Ireland put in one of their most complete performances with debutant open-side flanker, Johnny O'Connor, winning the man of the match award. Sometimes, the coming-of-age comments are thrown about lightly but, that afternoon, Ronan O'Gara put in a quite magnificent performance scoring all of Ireland's points – including a cheeky try – in a 17–12 victory.

'Performance-wise, that was one of our best in a green jersey. In 2000, we were quite close to beating them but we didn't really have that self-belief to really go and win it. But to beat Australia and then South Africa saw a growing maturity in the team. We really clicked as a team and completely outplayed South Africa. ROG sneaked in for a try in the corner! But he had a great day all the same. For Irish rugby and for Lansdowne Road that was another unforgettable afternoon.'

A Triple Crown and a win over one of the Big Three had been achieved in the one calendar year – but, in April 2004, Munster lost to Wasps in the European Cup semi-final. It was one of

142

those hugely colourful days at Lansdowne Road, a packed house brimful with fanatical Munster fans. 'I remember Lawrence Dallaglio recounting the day afterwards that, when he walked out before kick off, he said, "What the f*** is this?" They only had a few hundred over at it. He and his team-mates didn't realise what hit them. But the match itself was a horrible one to lose. Leota got in the corner – myself and John Kelly tried to stop him. I'm still adamant to this day that I held up that ball in the corner where Leota dived. When you lose like we did that day you feel like you let people down. That was the worst part of it. It just felt like the day deserved a victory. But it didn't happen. It was so emotional. We were down, we came back then. There were a lot of tries in it. The lead changed hands so many times and for the supporters it was very emotional. I saw Warren afterwards. Obviously, he shook hands and said hard luck but was delighted for his own team coming back. He was delighted that he had done it against Munster at Lansdowne Road. It was a sweet victory for him.'

For Stringer though, little will surpass Munster's victory over Leinster in the 'Seismic Sunday' clash in the European Cup semi-final at Lansdowne Road in 2006. 'The inter-pro games are always the toughest you're going to come up against. The fact we know each other so well and that it's that bit more difficult to break down their defences because of the way you like to play, it was difficult going out from that point of view. There were no friends that day. Everyone fully realised that there was an opposition there standing in our way of becoming European champions. You hear of boxers who are good friends going into the ring and then belting the living daylights out of each other. It's just when you get into that arena it's not about friends, it's just about being selfish and wanting to win the game.'

It has been a long journey for the Number 9 from Cork. He first travelled to Lansdowne Road with his father for the Ireland–England Five Nations game in February 1987. Perched on the Upper West Stand, he watched Temple Hill and Cork Con locals Michael Bradley, Michael Kieran and Donal Lenihan fashion a 17–0 win. The magic of the place took hold of him that day. 'It was tremendous, the whole thing about going up to Dublin, seeing the match – I wouldn't have experienced anything like it. I'd never seen that number of people before in my life.' Now it's he, a pocket of green (and red!) mischief, who has added to Lansdowne's great days.

Ulster's Triumph

The European Cup, 1999

Simon Mason & Gary Longwell

Seven months after the Good Friday Agreement was endorsed by the majority of the people of Ireland, the feel-good factor emanating from the North transferred itself onto the Ulster team when they lifted the European Cup in Lansdowne Road on 31 January 1999.

It was a day when sport managed to break down the barricades of division, and that was the greatest message of the day.

But rugby in Ireland took off in ways that no one could have foreseen. It was more than simply an Irish province making its claim as the High Kings of Europe, it was more than the sight of David Humphreys and Mark McCall becoming the first Irish players to jointly lift the European trophy. More than anything, Ulster's triumph acted as a catalyst for Irish rugby rejuvenation. It was as if Ulster dropped the stone in the pond and the ripple of hope set Irish rugby free from a decade of darkness.

Twenty-four hours before the final, Ulster coach Harry Williams was predicting as much. 'Of course we want to win for Ulster but we also want to win for the whole of Ireland and make people proud of Irish rugby. I can promise we will do everything in our power to do that.'

Since that winter's afternoon, Irish rugby has experienced a revolution: Munster went on to contest three European Cup finals, before finally winning in 2006, and Ireland have won Triple Crowns in 2004 and 2006 and have never finished below third place in the Six Nations.

Ulster's triumph accelerated the process towards full-time rugby in all four provinces – and accelerated the smooth transition to and assimilation with professional rugby in Ireland. Full-timers could fill up their days thinking about the game instead of being subjected to weights programmes at six-thirty each morning, then hitting the office before embarking on a crucifying training session in the evening.

The European Cup was still only three years old when Ulster started on their 1998–1999 campaign, but it was a baby the Irish provinces took to their hearts and embraced warmly.

The road to the final in Lansdowne wasn't without its problems for Williams, who, at the beginning of the season, was dealing with a squad of full- and part-timers. How could he stitch together a cohesive outfit to take on Toulouse, Stade Français and the English club sides (who had opted out of the European Cup that season)? The incoherence off the park was mirrored in indifferent performances in their first two pool games. A 38–38 draw at home to Edinburgh – albeit an action-packed try-fest with supporters getting a good bang for their buck – Williams only saw problems and called for patience. In their next match, away to Toulouse, the defence leaked five tries, one more than against Edinburgh, in a 38–3 loss and Williams had to draw a line in the sand.

'It was then that some of the players were semi-professional,' said full-back Simon Mason. 'Harry made the decision that we were going to go full-time in the day and to stop messing around with training in the evenings – that made a big difference to the squad.'

Harry's vision seemed the only common-sense idea to bring tangible success to the province, and it reaped dividends. 'We got off to a good start against Toulouse at home in our third pool game,' says Mason. 'The heads were more focused and there was unity, a bit of belief in the side. After beating Ebbw Vale comfortably, we then went to Edinburgh and won 23–12 and effectively secured our place in the quarter-finals with a home draw. I think the aims today haven't changed – you try to get through your group and get a home draw in the quarters and it gives you a hell of chance of progressing.'

Toulouse were in their crosshairs again in the quarter-final but, importantly, Ulster had them at home. The quarter-final was one of those typically fraught Ravenhill nights – the rain teeming down, the crowd in full voice and

Happy Harry: Ulster coach, Harry Williams, who masterminded the first European title win for an Irish province.

146

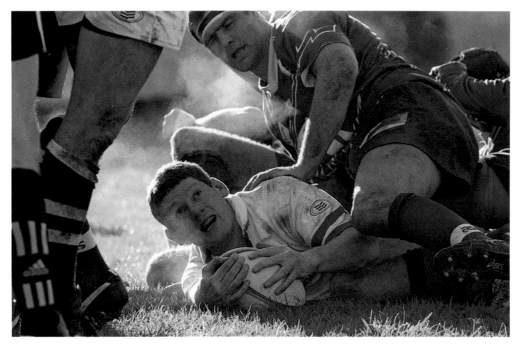

Stephen McKinty scores a try during Ulster's epic 33–27 win over Stade Français in the European Cup semi-final at Ravenhill. Next stop, Lansdowne Road.

an underlying hope amongst home fans that the French might crumble. But Toulouse defied the French convention of flakiness away from their parish and sunnier climes and fought the good fight.

Ulster accepted the challenge and beat the 1996 European champions 16–13 in a cracking cup tie. They had made their biggest European statement to date; now all they needed was a favourable semi-final and the final – and Lansdowne Road – would be their final port of call.

Once again, Ulster found good fortune in the draw, a home semi-final but the opposition was of the Gallic variety again. Parisian club side, Stade Français, arrived in all their pomp and majesty expecting Ulster to roll over, but the Irish province defied its underdog status with the performance of the season in a screamer of game that ended 33–27. Simon Mason kicked twenty points, the tries came from Humphreys and Stephen McKinty.

After the game, Williams walked into the dressing room and confidently told his team that the title was Ulster's. Whether it was a good or a bad thing, he made a statement some thought dangerous, others arrogant. There were those amongst the 20,000-strong support who thought they had witnessed their team peak against Stade Français. 'I remember going into the dressing room in Ravenhill and Harry said, "Our name's on the cup,"' said lock Gary Longwell. 'I think it was then the belief hit us. Harry never said anything cheaply.'

Locked and loaded: Ulster's Gary Longwell on the charge. 'Our game-plan was simple … if we could get the territory, force the mistakes, Simon would punish them every time,' says Longwell.

'It was turning out to be a very special year,' says Mason. 'We started in September by playing in front of relatively small crowds and the team got on a bit of a roller-coaster. The crowds built and built and we got to a memorable semi-final in Ravenhill when 20,000 turned up.'

As the final neared, the sense of expectation grew. Longwell found himself immersed in the menial duties that attend such a mammoth fixture mainly helping out the admin staff at Ulster headquarters in his free-time, 'I remember helping the staff at Ravenhill in the process of sorting out the tickets – we could have comfortably filled Lansdowne three times. I was able to get ninety tickets for friends and family which would be unheard of nowadays but, as players, we got a massive ticket allocation.'

Looking back, it took a team of special men to mobilise 50,000 Ulster people from varying classes and creeds to travel south to bathe Lansdowne Road in a shimmering red and white glow. But the Red Hand support identified with this team in a way no one expected.

Munster have built up a rapport with its people since making the breakthrough in 2000. Their success has been built on the basic ingredients of blood, sweat and sheer honesty along with a

148

team ethic and sense of province-hood that most other European regional sides see as a template for success. But ask an Ulster-man, and he might contend they patented the brotherhood thing first.

The grand relocation of Ravenhill to Dublin 4 began midweek before the match and the Ulster squad and management booked into the Berkeley Court from the Thursday night, a location central enough not to be too far from the madding crowds. There were some supporters milling around the hotel lobby on the Thursday but the trickle became a flood by Saturday afternoon. Some teams might look upon the sight of hundreds of fans in their hotel as a distraction, but this Ulster team didn't mind. It only drove them on. They felt at one with the supporters and, as Mason thought, what would running away to hide solve? 'I think Declan Kidney said something like they floated to Millennium Stadium for the last few miles of their bus journey for their European Cup final in 2006,' recalls Mason. 'We had that feeling too. After getting a tremendous send off from the hotel, we boarded our bus and I don't think the wheels touched the tarmac from there to the ground. All we saw was white and red; it was as if we were being shouldered to the stadium!'

That season, and despite his heroics on Ulster's European odyssey, Mason's international career had hit the rocks. It was close to three years since his last cap and returning to Lansdowne and staying at the Berkeley brought back memories of his first Ireland cap in March 1996 and a 20–17 win over Wales. He knew the routine once, but the memory of it had begun to fade. 'In my own first cap, we beat Wales comfortably at Lansdowne Road. I had dropped out of favour with the Irish selectors yet, a few years on, I felt more rounded as a player. On the Saturday of my first cap, I went down practising the kicking – everything went spot on. We stayed in the Berkeley before my first cap; I roomed with Simon Geoghegan. Simon scored a try, I scored fourteen points. For me, the European Cup final was nearly a second coming.'

Before being hit by the tumult of the European final, Mason longed for some quiet. Late on Friday afternoon, he and his room-mate Stephen Bell (who would be reserve scrum-half against Colomiers in the final) went down to Lansdowne, bounded a few fences and sat in the South Terrace. No talk, just imagining. 'It was absolute dusk at the time, four o'clock on a January after-noon,' says Mason. 'We went down and bumped in over the gate, walked into the South Terrace, overlooking a very surreal situation, "Think about the difference it would be in twelve hours time jammed packed with 50,000 people," I thought to myself. I remember sitting there thinking back to earlier eras of Ciaran Fitzgerald, Trevor Ringland and Triple Crowns and the first inter-national I ever went to. I was with Brian McDermott when Ireland played Scotland in 1988 to watch the likes of Trevor [Ringland] and Philip Danaher at full-back. All these memories came flooding back.'

They knew the whole of Ulster was behind them, but the messages of goodwill that poured in from every walk of life both moved and stirred them: the British Prime Minister, the Irish President, GAA teams, the other three Irish provinces, Ireland internationals, Limerick rugby folk, Dublin 4 clubs – everyone passed on their best wishes.

149

It stunned Harry Williams, says Mason, and the Ulster coach decided to turn all these gestures into something even more positive. A master of psychology, Williams posted all the messages in the team meeting room in the hotel. On match day, he asked that a selection of them be posted on the dressing room in Lansdowne. 'Harry hung up all letters of goodwill, faxes and cards. Our team room was awash with good luck from Tony Blair to Mary McAleese,' remembers Longwell. 'Everyone from both sides of the community in the North sent their wishes. All the Gaelic teams sent faxes to us. I think every player spent hours walking the room reading them all. It was those things that got us going. The weight of the support that was behind us was incredible and moving.'

The positive atmosphere Williams had created rubbed off on the team 'On paper, we were not a great team,' says Longwell, 'there were certainly teams that seemed a lot stronger than us. I think from the amount of belief we had in ourselves, we all got on so well as a group as well, it was going to take a special team to beat us.'

Williams had wonderful people skills, according to Mason, who says there was a sense you could arrive in the morning despondent or unhappy with your game or down in the dumps in general and, after a meeting with the coach, your confidence levels would be back up again. 'He was more of a manager; he just had that ability to exude calmness upon people. It was around that time when I was overlooked a few times by [Warren] Gatland and Harry was the first to be talking to me saying, "You are the first on my team-sheet. You're really important to me." He really had a good way with people. When you get to that level, you need someone to be cool, calm and collected. The demeanour he showed in the stands was very similar to the demeanour of the Harry Williams we met every day. To be fair as well though, if someone needed a telling off, he would say it.'

The pre-match warm-up saw Ulster strike the first psychological blow to their opponents. Or, more precisely, the supporters did. They transformed Lansdowne into a rawer and wilder version of Fortress Ravenhill. Colomiers realised they had entered the bear pit of Irish rugby and, on days like that, it is intimidating for any visiting team. 'I know in the final Colomiers were beaten during the warm-up,' recalls Longwell. 'They left the pitch early. We looked at their demeanour and they didn't look ready for battle. We knew something was wrong with them.'

Mason added, 'It disrupted Colomiers players. They obviously hadn't got there on a fluke – they'd been away to Perpignan and won and got to Lansdowne on merit. But I think the day was just too big for them. I feel the crowd and the whole occasion drove us on, and that was one of the reasons why we got such a comfortable winning margin really in the end.'

After Colomiers had left the field, the Ulster team contrived to pump up the volume even more inside the ground by exercising a pre-rehearsed warm-up routine. Colomiers were lucky not to have seen this as they might have just thrown their eyes to heaven, packed their bags and gone back to France. 'A couple of guys who had played in England saw that Gloucester always do a lap of the pitch before the match to get the crowd going,' Longwell explains. 'We did that, and the noise was unbelievable. All our friends and family were sitting in the East Stand, so the whole

Kicking King: Ulster's Simon Mason proved a prolific kicker for Ulster throughout their 1999 European Cup triumph. Here the Scouser is about to kick one of six penalties in Ulster's momentous 21–6 triumph in the final at Lansdowne Road.

team lined up facing the stand and did a big salute before the game. The noise hit us as hard as a French tackler but we felt good after it.'

It was then Mason felt that no team was going to beat them, that Williams' words after the semi-final came back to him – their name *was* on the cup. 'I just felt it was going to be a day of destiny for us. We were all very nervous because it was just such a big occasion but there was definitely a feeling that no one was going to beat us and certainly not Colomiers, without underestimating them.'

The team ethic had worked for Ulster ever since that away win in Toulouse in the pool stages. Each man trusted the other inside or outside him.

Mason saw the Band of Brothers philosophy grow within the team during their road to glory. 'I think the whole Ulster thing that year was a bit like how Munster has done it over the past few years. Certainly, this year it's great to see them winning but their wins have very much been based on team work. You obviously have your O'Garas and Stringers and O'Connells who stand out, but it's always been very much a team effort. I think Irish rugby is very much based on that anyway. We were always a good team as individuals – there were no outstanding players except maybe for Humphreys who did the kicking, obviously a class player, and Andy Ward, but there were no real individuals who stood out. Coming up to the final, for me personally, I just felt confident in the team especially defensively in the likes of Jonathan Bell in the centre. I could concentrate on my job and, when the opportunities arose, I was able to slot them over.'

Colomiers seemed to lack spirit. Stories even seeped from their camp that players who had got the team to the final were now cast aside in favour of a few returning stars. Their coach Philippe Ducousso came in for the strongest criticism. Still, how many coaches could have afforded to leave out players of the calibre of Jean-Luc Sadourny and Fabien Galthié? But their names alone could not beat Ulster. Sadourny's and Galthié's fitness was called into question before the game. Sadourny came back for the semi-final after a seven-month injury and Galthié had been out for four months before their win over Perpignan. Galthié was the biggest doubt and the scrum-half was undergoing fitness tests the night before the match. On the day, their impact was minimal.

Humphreys launched a litany of garryowens early on in the game into Sadourny's territory, and the French international full-back contrived to make a host of handling errors to a background of whistles and catcalls.

It was Ulster's pack that surprised most people and, in the loose, Longwell, Mark Blair and Stephen McKinty applied enormous pressure on their counterparts that, ultimately, created the penalty opportunities for Mason.

Colomiers' opening ten-minute spell was their best, with Laurent Labit giving the French an early score. But Ulster's pack was thriving and, though the French took exception to some of Welsh referee Clayton Thomas's decisions, the Irish side deserved to go in leading 12–3 at the break thanks to Mason's four penalties in the first half. 'Lansdowne Road – she's always a tough customer,' says Mason. 'With the breeze blowing around you had to take an element of risk. In terms of my confidence, I had always been a confident kicker. Once I got off to a good start, I never thought anything was going to faze me.'

'I think, from about thirty minutes into the game, I honestly believed in my heart we were

152

going to win – I couldn't see us losing,' Williams said after the game. 'The French seemed like rabbits trapped in a car's headlights.'

'A lot of credit was down to Harry,' says Longwell. 'We had a game-plan and we really stuck to it. I think we went behind very early on and got a bit carried away but we had a chat before the game kicked off again. "Back to the game-plan, stick to the game-plan," Harry kept telling us. Looking around the dressing room, you should have seen the fire in people's eyes. Some sat and listened. Others you had to take down off the ceiling they were so pumped up and anxious to get back out on the field. I knew it was going to work for us. There was just a supreme confidence about us that day and, in front of 50,000 Ulster fans, there was no way we were going to lose the match.'

Longwell will never forget the impact the injured Mark McCall had on the side in the days leading up to the match and isn't surprised that he is now a top professional coach. 'He didn't let on, but he must have been absolutely devastated not to be on the pitch. He went round having chats with players, and he just made you feel ten feet tall. He was just such a motivating character, just one of those guys who said the right things at the right time.'

Two minutes after the break, David Humphreys, masterminding the game from out-half, dropped a goal and, from there to the finish, Ulster squeezed the life out of their opponents, with Mason adding two more penalties. 'I got a lot of good press for kicking the goals – effectively like soccer when you score the goals. But I was only doing my job. The pack including Allen Clarke, Justin Fitzpatrick through to the likes of Andy Ward, and all those lads stood up and were counted on the day and put the pressure on the French to create those opportunities. That was the story of our season – every player just gave 100 per cent in every game.'

Longwell admits the game-plan was the simple rugby equation – territory and pressure equals penalties. 'Our game-plan was simple really when you look back, but damn hard work. If we could get the territory, force the mistakes, Simon would punish them every time.'

And so they did, Mason applying the finishing touches after his forwards scavenged and hunted in the bear pit. 'The conditions weren't too bad for kickers,' recalls Mason. 'It was a dry ball. It wasn't raining. It wasn't a bad day. It was a little bit blustery, there's always a bit of wind moving around the old stadium. It's a big open stadium, these days you see the international kickers when they're playing at Twickenham or Stade de France, they've got an enclosed stadium, the grass is perfect, there's very little wind but, ironically enough, Lansdowne Road was always a great test of any goal kicker. Rather than make me nervous, the day lifted me, I had no negative thoughts that day which is not normally like me because, as a goal-kicker, you're thinking of the worst. Maybe it was the fact there were so many Ulster supporters around, the cacophony of noise. It's just an incredible atmosphere.'

It wasn't the most entertaining of spectacles, but the occasion was magnificent enough to merit a place amongst the great European finals. As Mason says, 'The final itself wasn't a great rugby match but I thought we did enough on the day to outplay them and take our chances. For me, personally, I felt a lot more mature, getting to that European final. The first few international caps go by you in a bit of a daze, but it was great for me to come back more mature after those few years, out of the Ireland scene.'

Mason was born just outside Liverpool and followed the Reds on many a Saturday from the Kop End at Anfield, standing amongst probably the most loyal set of the supporters in English football. There was no doubt in his mind that the Ulster supporters acted as a sixteenth man at Lansdowne that day. 'I'd played on the Irish side and I'd played at Lansdowne Road, at Twickenham, but I'd never experienced anything as intense as that. Having stood on the Kop for many years, this was as close as you could get to this football atmosphere where it was really intense. Munster have proved the same with the support they have at Thomond Park.'

The final whistle was greeted with an almighty roar, one which had been absent from Lansdowne Road ever since Gordon Hamilton's try nearly knocked Australia out of the World Cup quarter-finals in 1991. In more ways than one, the win signalled a sort of liberation day for Irish rugby. Ulster achieving the unexpected meant that Irish rugby would no longer be the bridesmaids of world rugby.

This was Ulster's day, the pitch invasion that followed more akin to September days in Croke Park. 'It would have been nice to parade around the stadium with the trophy and to have spotted your family,' remembers Mason. 'I was reminded of it the time I saw Tyrone lift the All-Ireland trophy for the first time in 2003 – that sea of red and white brought back memories of our European triumph. It also reminded me so much of the red of Liverpool on big Anfield nights … it's just one of those things you never forget in life really. And what an experience.'

It was a bright day for Ulster and the people of Northern Ireland and, for once, they could celebrate in unison. Rugby had succeeded where so much else had failed. 'I wasn't born in Northern Ireland but I was aware of the history of the place. Living there was just a fabulous experience. The people up there are so warm and I get back as regularly as possible because I have so many friends there. Sport can sometimes transcend a society. As a sportsman, you try not to get too involved in politics but, when you're living in Northern Ireland, it's always there, it's part of the culture of the place you're living in. The win happened in a period when there were a lot of positives coming out of the province anyway. We always look on the negatives in life. That day there were so many positives and just reflected Northern Irish society at the time. You just have to look at Belfast over the last number of years – the heart of the city is great. Around that time there was a real feel-good factor. We united a few people even if it was just for an afternoon.'

Longwell couldn't help but be moved by the whole day. 'It was one of those sort of things that united the province. It happened before with people like Barry McGuigan – everybody in the province got behind him. We felt like that – people wishing us well from all walks of life. We had a function in the Stormont Buildings, after. All the politicians were there: Seamus Mallon from

European Cup final, 30 January 1999: Ulster players Gary Longwell, David Humphreys and Andy Ward celebrate with fans. 'We felt like we were playing for the whole province,' says Longwell.

155

the SDLP and David Trimble and they knew each of us by name. I know Seamus was at the semi-final as well because we met him afterwards. I think everybody had a bit of common sense around the thing. Problems were forgotten, and everyone was behind the team. We felt we were playing for the whole province.'

Williams, perhaps sums up best what this red-letter day in Lansdowne really meant. 'It was a very, very special day. For Ulster, that day was more than just winning the Heineken Cup – it was a coming together of communities. It didn't matter what church you went to, what game you played or anything, it was just a wonderful, wonderful day where everybody came together.'

Wanderers FC

Founded 1870

Tucked snugly between the West Stand and South Terrace is Wanderers FC Pavilion and, on match day, this building is a hive of activity acting both as a bar to the general public and as a dining room for corporate lunches. The upstairs is leased to the IRFU while downstairs the walls are bedecked with photographs and memorabilia of the club's long and proud history, though the formation of Wanderers remains a controversial subject. Lansdowne FC's founder, H.W.D. Dunlop, claims that Wanderers came into existence in 1870, after a group of Trinity students needed opposition for the university team because, at the time, there was no other club in Dublin. Jacques McCarthy, a well-known rugby writer of the time, dates the foundation of the club to 1871–72 and records Richard Milliken Peter as its founder, a man who is also considered the father of Irish football. Born off the Adelaide Road, Peter became Honorary Secretary of Wanderers and became Honorary Treasurer of the Irish Football Union when it was founded in November 1874. He played a huge part in unifying Ulster with Leinster and Munster after a war of words had broken out between representatives from the North of Ireland FC and Leinster representatives after an inter-provincial match in Belfast. Ulster claimed that there were no representatives from North of Ireland, the one active club outside Dublin, on the IFU and, after showing they had the better players after winning the international, wondered what right Dublin had to form a union without first consulting Belfast. They formed an opposition union – North of Ireland Union – but, eventually, and thanks to Peter, a compromise was reached that each should nominate ten of the twenty players who were to play England in London on 15 February 1875.

Paul McWeeney writes in his centenary history of Wanderers FC that 'the first Wanderers team to be recorded for posterity was that of 1877–1878, and a glance through the names indicates the degree of dual allegiance with Trinity'.

One of the more interesting characters to emerge from Wanderers was Frederick Moore.

He joined the club at the age of twenty-one and was a member of the club for seventy-one years until his death in 1949. He became curator of the Trinity College Botanic Gardens in Lansdowne Road and is credited with transforming the gardens into a world-renowned amenity, he was awarded a knighthood in 1911. Moore was extremely dedicated to his club, stating, 'Once a Wanderer, always a Wanderer.' Capped four times for Ireland, Moore became president of the IRFU in 1889–1890, and his passion for the game was reflected in the fact that he didn't hang up his boots for Wanderers until the age of forty-four.

During the 1879–1880 season, Wanderers were obliged to move from their original Clyde Road headquarters because the land was required for tillage purposes and moved to Lansdowne Road where Henry Dunlop leased them a field. Today, they also have a clubhouse and playing fields on Merrion Road to cater for the club's various teams.

The club is proud of its contribution to rugby football, having provided eighty-seven Irish international players, five captains, and one captain each of England and Australia, in addition to one captain of the Lions. Many Wanderers have represented Ireland since the formation of the national team. In its earliest years, Coo Lynch, Tom Crean, Robert Johnstone and A.W.D. Meares were notable internationals. James and Joseph Wallace were two famous brothers to have lined out for Ireland in the early part of the twentieth century while it's recorded that the first Wanderer to tour New Zealand with the Lions was Paul Murray. One of their more famous sons is Ronnie Dawson, who captained the 1959 Lions tour to Australia and New Zealand. Andy Mulligan, who was flown out late in the programme as an injury replacement, figured in the victorious fourth test. Ireland legend Mike Gibson spent one season in the Wanderers colours, while other Ireland internationals from the club include Ronnie Kavanagh, Kevin Flynn, Jack Notley, 'Boldy' O'Neill, Gerry Culliton, Paddy Kavanagh, Jim Flynn, Robbie McGrath, Alfred McLennan, Willie Sexton, Tony Ensor, Mick Fitzpatrick and Philip Matthews. England internationals include J. Gregory, J.A. Middleton, C.J. Newbold and P.D. Young, while four Wanderers – A. Slack, D. Frawley, L. Walker and P. Howard – have represented Australia.

Their roll of honour includes one All-Ireland League Division Three title (2003), as well as fourteen Leinster Senior cups, Five Leinster Senior League titles and five Metropolitan cups. They also hold the distinction of having three VCs: Major T.J. Crean, Major Robert Johnstone and Lieutenant F.M. Harvey.

Tony Ward

Out-Half

1978–1987

It is sometimes said that Tony Ward arrived on planet rugby in the wrong era. You always get the impression that the former Ireland out-half would have thrived in these professional times. 'Wardy' was a superstar, a great Number 10 who was never far from the public eye and filled as much newspaper space as George Best.

It seems now that Irish rugby followers never saw enough of Ward's talents to fully appreciate his skills. When he looks at Ronan O'Gara, Ward identifies with a player who shares many of the same qualities he had as an out-half. And, to many, Ward was a star player but one, alas, who never got to win a Triple Crown.

Though that was a big disappointment, his career is peppered with many happy moments from Lansdowne Road. While a student at St Mary's College in Dublin, he first got hooked on the colour and uniqueness of the Leinster Schools Senior Cup and a dream of one day of running out at the national stadium.

In 1966, he saw the late Shay Deering lift the cup for Mary's at Lansdowne Road. Ward looks back with fondness on those days as a starry-eyed teenager following his idol's movements. While a first year at Mary's, Ward also wanted to lead his school onto Lansdowne Road for Leinster Schools Senior Cup final day. 'We were a tiny school in the suburbs, we didn't win too many cups,' says Ward. 'I was at the 1966 final when Shay Deering's team beat Newbridge – that's where the hero-worship for Deero began. This guy in my eyes was amazing. In 1966, Mary's were actually expected to win it. Tom Grace was on that Newbridge team at the time but Shay Deering's side beat them. But in 1969 when we won the cup again, I thought we had had no right to win. We beat Terenure in the final 10–9. Conor Sparks was captain of Terenure – he was a big star in those days. I remember Johnny Caffrey blocking down an attempted drop goal that would have won the game for Terenure. Mary's held on. Derek Jennings was the Mary's captain and seeing that win was a huge influence on my wanting to play rugby for the school.'

Attending St Mary's offered Ward the opportunity of watching Ireland play at Lansdowne Road on international weekends. Securing a ticket through his school, Ward, like hundreds of schoolboys from around Ireland, watched from the South Terrace, giddy with excitement and quietly dreaming of one day playing there for Ireland.

'We used get the schools tickets for the Lansdowne Road end. When I was in first year Shay's twin brothers – Kevin and David – came in and they made the schools team and Leinster schools as well. They were in my class so we used attend the Five Nations or any of the internationals in Lansdowne. After the match, the Deering family used to always gather underneath the posts at the Wanderers end of the ground. We'd all go onto the pitch and gather there. Everyone did in those days. No steward would stop you at that time from getting onto the pitch, everyone just went onto the field and gathered in different areas and chatted for half an hour afterwards. It's just the way it was.

'As a youngster, my fondest memory was of me and Terry Kennedy (who would go on to play on the wing for Ireland), who was in my class at school, trying to meet the President of Ireland at Lansdowne. Eamon de Valera used to attend the rugby matches in a big black old Rolls Royce or Bentley – it was the famous Dev car anyway. After the game, the car used to be driven in near the Wanderers Pavilion. Dev would presumably be having a cup of tea and cakes afterwards and then himself and Bean de Valera would come out of the VIP area and get into the back of the car. It almost became a ritual for Terry and me. We had the timing perfected. Half an hour after the game, we would always be outside the Wanderers Pavilion waiting for the black car to come in. We used to run up, as old schoolboys used to do, and we'd always be the first two at the doors of the car. There'd be a queue of people, but we'd be the two right at the door when the president and his wife got in. We convinced ourselves that he knew us so well. That was a big thrill.'

As a youngster, Tony admits going to more soccer than rugby games at Lansdowne Road, but he witnessed many great rugby moments at the ground. 'One of the famous games I will always remember is the Ken Goodall try in 1970. Ireland won 14–0. It was a big upset at the time against a great Welsh side and Alan Duggan got a try in the corner. But in 1973, there was a famous reaction to John Pullin's England team as they ran out in Lansdowne Road. It was a very special moment. The applause was spontaneous. Today it might be done by some DJ on a pitch orchestrating the whole thing but it was a genuinely felt feeling for what they had done [in travelling despite receiving death threats from the IRA].'

Ward says he owes a lot to his coaches at St Mary's, Fr D'Arcy and Fr 'Wally' Kennedy, who groomed him as an aspiring out-half and when he was made senior captain in his final year, there were high hopes of attaining another cup. Ward led Mary's onto Lansdowne Road for the semi-final of the Senior Cup against High School. 'It was my first time running out at Lansdowne as a player. I was captain of the senior team in 1973 but we were beaten 10–9 by High School – they went on to win the final, the only year they ever won it. John Robbie and Ian Byrnes were the half-backs for them. Rodney O'Donnell was on our team. We were unbeaten all season and had hammered everyone else in 'friendlies', including High School. To this day the biggest disappointment in my rugby career without a doubt – including being dropped in Australia [in 1979] or not being on a Triple Crown team – was losing that day.'

To compound his disappointment in a season that promised so much, Ward was overlooked for the Leinster schoolboys team that year. Ollie Campbell – a player he later had to battle with for the Ireland Number 10 shirt – and Ian Burns were the out-halves chosen that season.

Ward was also a talented soccer player and it seemed he would play League of Ireland football with Shamrock Rovers after his Leaving Cert. 'For me the earliest memories were all in the 1960s and I was hugely into soccer as well. I remember seeing Waterford play Man Utd at Lansdowne after they won the European Cup. It was a year after they won and the team contained all the stars including Georgie Best. Then, in 1973, Louis Kilcoyne organised a team – North and South combined – under the name Shamrock Rovers to play against Brazil in rugby headquarters. It was one of those great occasions where even the crowd appreciated the enormity of it because of the historical political implications.'

Tony Ward made his debut in the Ireland senior side against Scotland in January 1978, and his inimitable style and ability to boss the pattern of play brought with it expectations of the dawn of a new era for Irish rugby. Ireland had failed to win a game for two seasons so naturally there was a massive weight of expectation resting on Ward's shoulders.

He was not alone that day. Three others made their debuts with him – centre Paul McNaughton, flanker John O'Driscoll and second-row Donal Spring. It was also the day Johnny Moloney captained his country for the first time. The pair chatted for hours before the game and Ward remembers receiving plenty of messages of goodwill particularly a pleasant note from former Ireland out-half Barry McGann, who assured the debutant that everything would be fine playing in front of a home crowd.

One thing Ward will never forget was the crescendo of noise he felt the moment he ran onto

Tony Ward (centre of shot) makes no secret of his delight after Stewart McKinney crossed the line for the only try of the game. It came during Ward's first cap against Scotland in 1978 Five Nations at Lansdowne Road.

the field. He does not know where the streak of confidence that attended his game that day came from, but the famous Lansdowne Roar played its part in raising his standards. In essence, Ward was dancing inside. 'Once I got in a nice garryowen early in the game, I felt fine,' he says, remembering one of his first few moments in an Ireland senior shirt. Ireland won the game 12–9. Ward kicked two penalties and converted Stewart McKinney's first-half try.

Grand Slam winning Jackie Kyle watched from the stands that winter afternoon and said afterwards that Ward made a fine debut at out-half, adding, 'I would not be despondent about Irish rugby after that performance.'

'Certainly, my first cap, because you're so nervous for your first game,' said Ward, 'will stay with me forever. One of my abiding memories is arriving in the car park. This was before the Wanderers dressing room was built underneath the stand. It was the last season we togged out in the old Lansdowne Pavilion which was down in the corner near the Havelock Square terrace. There was an uncovered stand in that corner and the changing room was underneath that. I remember when we got off the bus before the game, I was so scared, so nervous. The pipe band or army band was warming up but the sound the bagpipes made was so eerie. I will never forget the feeling – it went right through your system. I remember thinking you just want to be at home with your mummy! Ridiculous thoughts come through your mind because you're so uptight and so nervous. That was my abiding memory of arriving in Lansdowne. We won 12–9 and in the last few minutes Scotland got a penalty. Dougie Morgan was the captain, a scrum-half, but he declined to go for goal to make it 12–12. It was very kickable. Instead, they went for the win because their logic was they wanted to stay in the hunt for the Triple Crown. That's how big the Triple Crown was at the time. We defended and held out to win 12–9.'

The wind that blows through Lansdowne Road today has remained as difficult as ever and throws up the ultimate challenge to the most metronomic of kickers. Ward converted a poetic effort against Scotland on his debut. It was hit so sweetly even the touch judges went running back to their positions on the touchline before the ball had completely gone over the bar. He still sees goal-kickers today grimace as they attempt to convert into the most precarious and most difficult wind conditions in a world rugby stadium. 'When I do RTÉ commentaries, I talk about conditions before the game, and I make the same point over and over again – and anyone who has played there will tell you the same thing – you cannot judge the wind at Lansdowne Road. If you look at the flags on the Lansdowne Road/South Terrace end and you'll see them blowing one way and then you look across the far side and blowing differently but not quite as heavily. It's just the design of the ground. The fact that it's not fully encircled means it blows in all around the place. It's a very, very hard ground to play in or to kick tactically, particularly for those who are not used to it.'

If Ward had to make do without a kicking coach in his playing career, then life on an international weekend was made more difficult by not having the opportunity to practise at Lansdowne on the days leading in to an important match. 'When you look now at the professional players, they have everything laid on for them. I remember in our day you weren't allowed near the pitch beforehand. I remember being down there once and seeing Ronnie Dawson running a team off the pitch when he happened to be going by on the Saturday morning and they were out doing some lineout practice. You had to get very, very special permission to go on the pitch to do any kicking. Occasionally, you did, it was never a given – you had to look for the permission to do it. Today, on a Thursday or Friday they go off and do their kicking. That's standard now. Another factor in probably not allowing us on then is that we didn't have tees. You had to make your own divot on the ground.'

Ward had grown up in a golden time for Welsh rugby and while he religiously watched *Match of the Day* on BBC 1 on a Saturday night, *Rugby Special* on Sunday afternoon was also compulsory viewing.

Ward was to be a central character in the Ireland–Wales 1978 Five Nations game. 'That was the great era of Welsh rugby. That was when it was at its zenith. You had all the greats – J.P.R.

Williams, Phil Bennett, Gareth Edwards – it was just a never-ending list of greats. You got to see Welsh rugby pretty regularly on the BBC and they were megastars at the time. When I arrived on the team in 1978, we all stayed in the one hotel. And you literally spent the two days beforehand trying to avoid each other. It was a ridiculous carry-on. One day, I had to get into the lift with the Welsh guys. There was about seven or eight of them – it was packed. Genuinely, I thought they didn't know who I was. I kept my head down and there was total silence until I pushed the button to get off. We were on the third floor and they were on the fourth and when I got out, Gareth said, "See you tomorrow, Tone." I remember being on a high that Gareth Edwards knew my name.'

Ward might have been on a high after Edwards' recognition but he was saddened by the quality of rugby on view in the test match. 'Against the Welsh in 1978 it was a very dirty game. They were seeking a third consecutive Triple Crown and they won 20–16. Sadly, it was a really tempestous game. Gareth and J.P.R. retired after that game – they said that finished it for them. They just found that the game had become too physical, too dirty and they decided enough was enough that the pressure was too much.

'There was an incident during the game where Gibson was playing centre and he chipped a ball over J.P.R. down at the Lansdowne Road end of the pitch. As Gibson was running around him, J.P.R. took him out of it. It caused a furore at the time. It was a professional foul. They got a late try from J.J. Williams but we might have won that game had we got the six points for J.P.R.'s foul.'

In 1979, Ireland drew 9–9 with France. 'I have two main memories of that game. In those days, you were allowed tap the ball to yourself for a free-kick and then have a drop goal. Towards the end of the game, it was 9–9, we got an indirect penalty or free kick on the 22 in front of the posts, I tapped it to myself, and it was blocked down by one of the French back-row forwards. I also remember getting a knock on the head in the first half of that game from Jean-Pierre Rives. Early on, I tried to do a side-step but caught his stiff arm on the side of my head. I was concussed. At half-time, I had to go into the dressing room for some attention. I literally couldn't see. It was a migraine. What I saw was a desert and just heat shimmering. I just had to go in and get some tablets. In those days, the teams stayed on the field at half-time. On my way back onto the field, I ran to the French huddle without realising it. I literally just came out and veered towards them. It was very embarrassing. But I don't know how I got through that game. Those were the days when you had to stay on field.'

During his playing days, Ward came under the influence of Ciaran Fitzgerald whom he describes as the greatest ever Ireland captain. To say that Ward was moved by one of Fitzy's team talks would be a complete understatement. Fitzgerald was, according to Ward, every inch the army captain in the dressing room and he remembers days when he could have run through the old dressing room walls at Lansdowne such was the almost manic delivery of the Fitzy speech.

'The coach wasn't allowed onto the pitch at half-time then. He had to send out a message with the man who brought us the oranges. It was the captain who did everything. When you consider captaincy now – Ciaran Fitzgerald was the best Irish captain bar none. Don't let anyone tell you otherwise. He was so far ahead of everybody in terms of preparation and work for the match. Whether it was talking to individuals and putting it all together or pressing the right buttons individually and collectively, Fitzy was in a league of his own. He's just one of those guys, a motivator supreme. He was one of these guys when he asked you do something, he looked you in the eye. You know what he's asking you to do, he's going to do himself whereas others will bulls**t their way through it and you get to learn very quickly the captains who are all "we're going to go out there and get stuck into them all … etc." But with Fitzy, it was never like that. He was just unbelievable. And, thankfully, he has two Triple Crowns to show for it because the guy was torn apart inside after the 1983 Lions tour. Then the captain just had to do so much, whereas now, with respect to Brian [O'Driscoll] and everybody else involved, everything is done for them. Now, even at half-time, the coach, the defensive coach, the kicking coach all have their few words in the dressing room – there's little time for the captain to speak.'

But it was the way Fitzy handled the captaincy that impressed Ward. 'You handle different people in different ways. Captaincy in our times was so important and, I believe, it's how you handle personalities. Ciaran would tell one guy, "You're the greatest in the world and I want you to go out and prove it today," and he would do it. That delivery was for the likes of me for example. He would tell another guy, "If you don't do it today, you're f****king gone." There were guys who would need a kick up the arse and he would respond enormously. Different people respond in different ways. There's no overall way in doing it but the great captains were the ones who knew what worked.'

After all these years, Ward holds fond memories of the old stadium. Nothing gave him a greater feeling than running out onto the national stadium in any game. 'Because I'm Irish, running out on the national stadium always meant so much more than watching on television or simply going there to watch a game. And, I must admit, even in latter days as you go out and play Leinster Cup games or inter-pros when there were two men and a dog at it, it still gave you the thrill – you were still playing in Lansdowne Road, it's still special. I don't care what anyone says. The national ground is special and I think it will be again when it's rebuilt for the generations to come.'

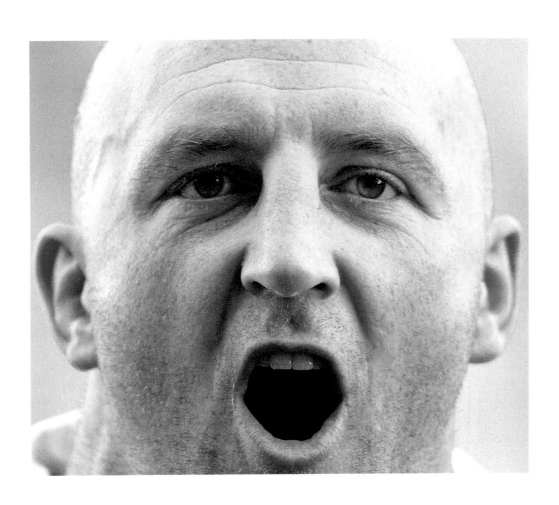

Keith Wood

Hooker

1992–2003

Keith Wood sat on the bench against Australia at Lansdowne Road in 1992, watched one of the unluckiest hookers of Irish rugby John 'Spud' Murphy earn his first and only cap and then disappeared. Wood had intended to hang around a bit longer, be in selectors' faces a bit more. Little did people realise then the enormous legacy he would leave Irish rugby after eleven years wearing the green.

'I came out of nowhere,' he says in relation to his call-up to the Irish bench against Australia that afternoon. But if he feels he sprung from the abyss, Ireland could not even have dreamed up a more dedicated, warrior-spirit. Lansdowne Road seemed to roar a little louder when 'Woodie' was on the ball.

The doyen of rugby writers, Frank Keating, described the fifty-one-times-capped hooker as 'a potato on speed', in reference to the most famous bald pate in rugby whenever Woodie embarked on one of his trademark breaks up field. This image is everlasting – the face would contort, ice in the eyes as he'd face down his opponent with a sometimes mad-cap stare, the shoulders would be hunched and he'd make more yardage than most back-rowers on any given day. On a rugby field, he was as close as a forward can get to being a free spirit. Wood performed his functions as a hooker, but he was a non-conformist of sorts on the field – he refused to play to type.

He was very much the focus and talisman of every Irish team up to his retirement after the 2003 World Cup quarter-final loss to France in Australia. He could have hung around for another year and picked up a deserved Triple Crown in 2004 at Lansdowne Road, but his body had been put through the ringer once too often and he decided enough was enough. In a sense, he was the iconic figure behind Ireland's renaissance, a believer in our worth as a rugby country, a symbol of what could be achieved. Above all, he was a winner and a champion.

He suffered so many disappointments and setbacks and black days – and he was a survivor of fifteen operations – for Irish rugby, that we forget sometimes what drove this most driven of sportsmen to the top of his game. There was the highpoint of beating England in 2001, with a breath-taking try in a win that went a long way to erasing the endless stream of bad memories.

Keith Wood's late father, Gordon, won twenty-nine caps for Ireland as a prop forward between 1954 and 1961 and, in the late 1950s and 1960s, was part of famous triumvirate in the front-row which included Syd Millar and Ronnie Dawson. His son would do him proud.

It was in a test match against the Aussies, in 1994 in Ballymore, Brisbane, when Wallabies coach Bob Dwyer singled out the Killaloe native as a potential great.

Woodie played his first full international against the USA that November in Lansdowne Road. The Eagles were plucky and organised, he remembers, but the confidence gained after an encouraging tour to Australia gave the Irish a feeling that they would overcome their opponents. They didn't feel invincible but were confident enough to put teams like the Eagles to the sword. This Ireland managed on a 26–13 win. 'We were fairly comfortable with the idea that we'd go in and beat the States but it was bloody tough. They were very capable at that time.'

Wood's first Five Nations game came against England in 1995 in Lansdowne Road and, despite the loss, he has an everlasting memory of the day and the atmosphere. 'As a superstitious youth I always came out last and, on the first Five Nations game I played, I was blown away by the noise as I slowly climbed the twelve steps up to ground level and then floated the remaining steps to the pitch. It was the worst weather I had played in. We were well beaten by Will Carling's side and I, personally, got the crap kicked out of me. But that was it; I was hooked. I had played in autumn matches but this was altogether different. I was addicted to the buzz, to the wearing of the green and to Lansdowne.' The 1995 Five Nations was an unhappy one for Wood and Ireland. Throughout his career, Wood would – sometimes even recklessly – challenge for ball, putting his body on the line. And, after losses to England and Scotland (he was injured in Murrayfield), he missed the remainder of the Five Nations championship.

There was something to put a smile back on his face (and that of Irish rugby) when Nick Popplewell, Peter Clohessy and himself packed down together in the front-row in a Barbarians

169

Keith Wood playing with the Barbarians and wearing his club socks (Garryowen), as is tradition, has the fabric of his shirt tested by Ruben Kruger of South Africa. 'We didn't play in a particularly Baa-baas style,' says Wood of their 23–15 win. 'But it was a great game, and a really great occasion for Lansdowne.'

side that defeated South Africa 23–15 at Lansdowne in April 1995. It will always remain a high-light in his career. With Simon Geoghegan also on the side and recording a splendid try, it lifted Irish rugby and the mood of the country – if only for an afternoon and if only for a Barbarians side. 'I loved it. It was my one and only time playing for the Barbarians. I remember the English were not allowed to play – the only guys from England who were allowed to play were those not in the English squad. We didn't play in a particularly Baa-baas style. Instead, it was real, hard nitty-gritty stuff, but it was a great game, and a really great occasion for Lansdowne.'

The shoulder injury which had eaten away at Wood's season returned to haunt him during the World Cup campaign in South Africa in 1995. After only nine minutes against Japan, he had to retire with a dislocated shoulder. But when he returned for the autumn internationals in November 1996 and a test against Australia, his leadership qualities on the field and his motivational abilities in the dressing room were rewarded with the Irish captaincy. Here was someone who could optimise mental focus in a team. 'I was only approached that week to take on the captaincy. I was slightly taken aback. It was very much a case of me being the only one who could be captain at that stage. We had a distinct dearth of leaders in the team. An awful lot of the guys had retired at that stage like [Philip] Danaher and Brendan Mullin, so I might have been the only obvious choice. I remember Gerry Murphy saying a couple of years before when he was making me pack leader, "He doesn't shut up anyway so we might as well give him an official job."'

The platitudes – 'glorious defeats' and 'valiant losers' – were the words ringing in the ears of the Irish team after they came close to doing the impossible against Australia in 1996. But Wood saw this test match as a classic example of an opportunity lost. 'It finished 22–12 with a try in the last minute. They were leading 15–12 and we were pushing the game, trying to get there and we could and should have overturned them. We lost in the last couple of minutes which was bloody annoying because we had played very well in a difficult enough kind of scenario. Leading out Ireland at Lansdowne was pretty special, though I just wish I had been leading them to win.'

This was another one of those 'difficult periods' for Irish rugby. The 1996 autumn internationals series begun with a whimper – a loss to Western Samoa, the most damning indictment of their performance being the ability to fashion only a single try while the Pacific Island side crossed the Irish line five times. The inevitable cull followed the week of the Samoa match and, when glory was snatched from them against the Wallabies, there was talk of turning a corner. More or less the same team lined out against Italy in early January 1997. But there was no corner turned, Ireland lost 29–37 at Lansdowne and it marked another downer, a players' and coach's nadir.

170

Players may have found the weight of expectation unbearable, but Ireland's first full-time coach during this period, New Zealander Murray Kidd, was under severe pressure to deliver. While the Australia match represented progress and a step forward, the loss to the Italians at home in front of Irish fans in dire need of some New Year cheer, watched the team regress even further. It was another nightmarish day at Lansdowne and, while some players' reputations suffered, the end was in sight for Kidd. A few days after the Azzurri rocked Irish rugby, Kidd met with IRFU officials and a severance package was agreed.

Some said Kidd could not connect with that Irish side; others that he was ahead of his time but, ultimately, it was an uncomfortable time to be an Irish player according to Wood. 'It's very hard to talk solely on those sort of terms,' admits Wood. 'A lot of those things can be taken quite comfortably out of context. We would have had five coaches in four years, and none of them were in for such a long period of time as to make a telling contribution. It was a time when we changed coaches at every available opportunity and that was at very little value to us. We needed to have a coach come in, have a level of control and balance within it, which, ultimately, didn't arrive until [Warren] Gatland came in. What we needed so badly was continuity for coaches and continuity in selection.'

Brian Ashton took over as new coach, but the injury woes continued for Wood. A shoulder injury in another loss against France fourteen days after the Italy game meant an early championship departure. All these injury setbacks were becoming the norm in his career and, from the Lansdowne stands, the latest appeared extremely painful on impact. 'I was carrying the ball and I had a feeling I tripped over Thomas Castaignède. I landed on my elbow and I popped my collar bone. It was pretty painful, not as painful as you think, once you do all the ligaments, once they all go, there's no real pain.'

On the field, the signposts towards improvement were encouraging, but it was dangerous to talk of an Irish revival. It had to be whispered. And ever so quietly. Ashton, with the reputation as a bit of an eccentric but whose expertise lay in cultivating dashing backline moves now hoped for progression. The IRFU seemed chuffed with their man. A win over Wales at Cardiff Arms Park seemed to confirm their selection of Ashton as being the man to lead Irish rugby through a turbulent time and the early years of professionalism. Wood thought Ireland were on the up too. If they weren't winning, at least they tried to find solace in a good performance. 'I thought we had turned a corner in a lot of cases; where once we had a situation where nothing had been going our way at all, now we started by stringing a couple of good performances together.'

But heavy defeats at home to England and away to Scotland eroded their confidence. The margin of the defeats and taste of unpalatable displays in these two games was hardest to digest. Ashton had been offered a six-year contract before the trip to Murrayfield.

Wood returned for the autumn international against the All Blacks in November 1997, scoring two tries in typically Woodie fashion. He always cut a dashing figure for a forward, he loved to bound around the park, glide into backlines, felt oh so comfortable ball in hand and, with his penchant for putting boot to ball, he was never shy to attempt a drop goal if the opportunity arose. Most of all, he gave every last ounce of energy for the cause. He was combative, wholehearted, rugged, battle-hardened – many wondered if he could ever play a bad game for club, province or country.

Wood remembers some kind of protest taking place at Lansdowne but it wasn't one calling for Ashton's head on a platter or attempts to slag off the Irish team. Indeed, it was rare to see the like at Lansdowne Road but, on the day Ireland played the All Blacks in 1997, the travelling support displayed black-and-white posters of protest: 'No Hart – Bring back Josh.' The Wednesday before the match, Josh Kronfeld, a legend of All Black rugby, lost his Number 7 jersey to Andrew Blowers.

The tremors of Kronfeld's demotion were felt back in New Zealand, particularly in South Island where Kronfeld was revered – news of his demotion made front-page headlines there. Apparently, coach John Hart replaced Kronfeld in order to shake things up a little and tried to justify his decision by arguing it was for the benefit of the squad. But his decision was odd, especially in an era when the All Blacks rarely rotated and always strived to put their best team on the field.

The posters calling for the reintroduction of Kronfeld flashed around Lansdowne Road, but darting around the park indefatigably was the figure of Keith Wood whose two first-half tries had put Ireland into an unexpected 16–15 lead. Wood's heroics – not for the first time – brought

Lansdowne Road to its feet. His second try saw him out-sprint winger Jeff Wilson after Eric Miller hacked on. Sometimes, you looked at Wood and saw him as the original comic-book hero; Ireland's first Superman before the cape was passed on to Paul O'Connell.

Kronfeld's replacement also put an end to Wood's time on the field, with a tackle that aggravated an already dodgy ankle. Looking back, Wood says he doesn't buy in to hackneyed comments of 'being on top of the world' after scoring a few tries against the All Blacks. 'I don't go in for trite comments. Yes, it is fantastic, yes it is unbelievable when you get the buzz. The buzz when you're going over the line in Lansdowne is incredible and I often describe the noise in Lansdowne as being like the beat. It was like a heart beating between a high and a low sound. You couldn't hear and distinguish individual noises and voices and suddenly there was a beat to the place and that was fantastic. I scored a couple of tries. I never went on that mad "look at me, I scored a try" thing. I could honestly tell you that, if you looked at the tries I scored, it's rare that I jump up and down after scoring them. You're there to score them, you're there to try and get a score on the board.'

Part of Wood's legacy to Irish rugby was his fresh soundbites at press conferences, his ability to accentuate the positive and to truly believe in those players around him. Deep down, he himself had tremendous self-belief and it always came through in his pre-match comments. 'I remember saying beforehand we had a 25 to 1 shot of beating them and I was getting roundly criticised in the press afterwards. I would say, "You asked me a question and I gave you an honest answer and if it's too honest for you, I'm not going to be offended by the fact that I'm being honest."'

Brian Ashton was often termed a maverick genius by English journalists and, as if to prove that he was capable of the unexpected, he announced a team packed with fresh faces for that All Blacks test. He brought in five new players, it was a bold move by the coach, but he felt the new caps deserved their chances and added that they would spice things up after the bitterly disappointing conclusion to the previous season's championship campaign. But facing a seasoned All Blacks side was no place for young men. Kevin Nowlan, John McWeeney, Conor McGuinness, Malcolm O'Kelly and Kieran Dawson were thrown into the lion's den and they, and the Irish team, were tossed and turned and torn to pieces by the All Blacks.

Four players at least saw another day out in green; for St Mary's winger McWeeney it was the beginning and the end of his Irish career. Wood felt for those new boys, particularly for those that never came back. 'We'd a distinctly unsettled team. We had five new caps, some who were never really seen again. From a coach who was living in England, who had a lot of talents but selection wasn't one of them. Because he didn't know half the players, he may have seen them once and picked them. To do that for the test against New Zealand was wrong.'

And this All Blacks team, still hurting from their World Cup final defeat to South Africa in 1995, were a formidable bunch and seemed to hit the field in every test match to prove a point that they were still the greatest. Ireland lost 63–15 and the level of the All Blacks dominance could be measured in one fifteen-minute spell in the second half when Ireland could only get a hand on the ball twice, such was the All Black's control at ruck time, their recycling abilities and their sheer physical strength in all areas of the field.

It was a defeat Irish rugby didn't need.

The All Blacks side consisted of Taine Randell, Frank Bunce, Buck Shelford – great names who underachieved at World Cup level. To have them perform at Lansdowne Road was then a rare occurrence; many saw the All Black jersey as having a mystical quality and the sight of it can instil a sense of dread into the opposition. Wood doesn't agree. Even during their Haka, he admits he used to find it difficult to keep a straight face. 'Mystique no, never did. Never saw that card, to be honest. I respected the players, yes. You respect the players you play against and you give them the respect they deserve. I always looked at the Haka as being a pretty good promotional tool for the All Blacks but the history of it was something that was never major for me and, for anybody who thinks that's a chip-on-the-shoulder comment, all you have to do is look back to the infamous match in 1973 between the Baa-baas and the All Blacks and you see the poor old New Zealanders doing the Haka – it looks like a group of Morris dancers. It's only developed into something of note after the fact, in a very publicity orientated world and they used it to fantastic effect. I always had huge admiration for the distinct lack of respect [David] Campese's showed by kicking a ball around on the 22 while this was going on. I myself used laugh at it and giggled, winked and smiled, just to see whether it would provoke any sort of reaction.'

He suffered an ankle ligament injury in that game and had to retire in the second half. Ireland wondered if he would have scored more, but for the creaking ankle. 'Hardly likely, they were kicking me up and down the field at that stage.'

After a loss away to Italy five days before Christmas Day 1997, a doomsday scenario had been painted for the upcoming 1998 championship, while Ashton's uneasy relationship with manager Pat Whelan was brought into the media mix. Failing to beat Scotland in the Five Nations match at Lansdowne Road signalled the end for Ashton. He wrote a letter of resignation to the IRFU explaining he got an attack of shingles but his disillusionment ran deeper. He later hinted that he should not have taken the Ireland job, he didn't understand the Irish psyche and that he probably should have attended more All-Ireland League games.

Wood admitted later that the 16–17 defeat to Scotland was one of the lowest points in his rugby career.

Gatland was parachuted in from the west of Ireland where he was coaching Connacht and on his arrival, Irish fortunes changed for the better. 'The change really for me was in Paris in 1998. We were expected to be hockeyed by France but we didn't make too many mistakes. If we'd defend pretty well and we'd work hard and all that, then we're going to be in with a good shout even though we weren't doing anything particularly entertaining. We were back playing with old, Irish, honest endeavour.'

A positive Five Nations followed, Ireland just lost out to Wales and there was no capitulation

173

to England. 'I never went in for all those major turning points or not. It's hard to make that straight call. A turning point is when you win. OK, that can sound kind of cold as well. When you look at it, we were not a great team for a long chunk of time and we tried bloody hard and we played as hard as we possibly could. But we weren't quite structured enough whatever the reasons were. Ultimately, there were things that started to resolve themselves as soon as we got a lot of the structure right, we got consistency in the team right, we got good performances out of it, we got monkeys off our back by beating teams, by beating France in Paris (2000) and beating them at home the following season, by beating England (2001), beating Australia (2002), South Africa (2004) – all these things are cumulative. And, because all of them were working and sorting out for us, we were then able to say yes, this is a turning point. You can't call them turning points at the time, but you can see them for what they were after the fact, and that doesn't necessarily mean you don't regress during that. You do know it's the start of something bigger and better.'

He savoured the victory in October 2001 at Lansdowne Road that deprived England of another Grand Slam. His try was a moment where Lansdowne saluted forward innovation in a move rehearsed on the training ground and brought exclusively to Broadway Lansdowne. Or, pertinently, it was borrowed from the Lucien Mias book of lineout peeling. Mias, a French lock of the

174

No way through: Scotland halt Wood from scoring the game's first try in the 2000 Six Nations. The floodgates eventually opened in the second half as Ireland ran out 44–22 winners. Wood's late try brought the biggest cheer of the afternoon.

1950s, discovered a ploy that was really difficult to stop. His idea saw forwards launching off the lineout and peeling round the back. It was a devastating strategy and defences, particularly forwards, had little time to react.

The sight of Wood barrelling over the line – and over Neil Back – is one of the great Lansdowne moments. 'It was one we had used a couple of years beforehand and, for some reason, we tried it once or twice that week. Well, once in training during the week, once that morning, once in the pre-match warm-up and we tried it in the game. It was good because it was simple: a simple throw to Mick Galwey, a simple pass on to Anthony Foley, a bit of unadulterated brilliance by Foley, you can't see it on the tape but I can tell you that it was. He passed a dead ball, which meant there was no weight on the ball, it was there in the air, so it wasn't going in any particular direction. It was such a perfect ball, I could have run any angle, I think there could have been a little subtle interference by Eric Miller at the back to stop them getting at me and then it was a little canter to run over the line. I had to score from there. I was going at full tilt and because of Foley's pass being perfect.'

He tried a drop goal before half-time – 'it was a bad decision, pure stupidity but luckily I got away with it' – and Ireland went into the break leading 11–6. An upset was on the cards. 'There was a turning point in that game. In the second half, I made a mistake, left a defensive hole and Luger ran through. We tried to chase back but he looked home and dry but [Peter] Stringer came across and ankle-tackled Dan Luger. It was incredible stuff.'

This was Ireland's third game in four weeks and, with twenty minutes left on the clock, England were raising their game as the Irish tired. 'Everyone ran themselves to a stand still. I remember badgering the ref to blow the damn whistle and, when he did, there was joy, but relief too.'

He'll never forget Jason Leonard's gesture at the end of the game. Team-mates and best buddies at Harlequins they had to scrum down opposite each other for eighty minutes. 'Immediately after the game, all the England players walked off the pitch except for Jason. He walked out onto the pitch to find out where I was to congratulate me and I remember saying in my speech that night that that was a mark of a sportsman. He must have been shattered at losing a Grand Slam but went out of his way to show that he was happy for me.'

Keith's late mother, Pauline, stalled his dash for the dressing room and beside his mother was his sister, both overwhelmed with emotion. Inside the dressing room, he led a rendition of 'From Clare to Here'. 'We were helped by what you might call an arrogant selection by England. They were picked on past form, not on present form and we felt we could intimidate a lot of their players. Halfway through the match, I recognised some of their lineout calls, and Malcolm O'Kelly told me they were the Lions calls that had been used on the Lions tour [to Australia] that summer. We actually used their [English] lineout calls … they said afterwards that they weren't the Lions calls, but they were. That English team was eminently beatable and yet they nearly beat us. That was a huge thing to get over, that was one of those bogeys we had to get over and, subsequently,

'For me, and every Irishman, Lansdowne
Road is where my Six Nations memories
lay and I can probably sum up what the
whole thing means by recalling what has
to be the best day of my Six Nations
career in October 2001 when Ireland
beat England.' Keith Wood's expression
is of a man who has experienced so many
false dawns, but who has finally got to
beat one of the big boys on his home patch.
This game was originally due to be played
in March but, because of the outbreak of
foot and mouth across Britain, the game
was put back to October. England were
going for the Grand Slam, but had to
prepare for this game without totemic
figures, such as Martin Johnson and
Lawrence Dallaglio. Lansdowne has
never had a day quite like it. It was
never noisier, according to Wood. 'The
tears came straight away when the
national anthem struck up,' he said later.
Wood scored a memorable try in the first
half on a day when Ireland pulled off the
shock of the championship. 'In truth the
actual rugby was just the half of it,' said
Woods. 'Personally, it was a golden day
when everything came together. In
retrospect, it was one of my very last
appearances at Lansdowne Road and
it is special for that reason alone.'

Wood tries to break through the New Zealand defence during the 2001 autumn international. 'That was a game we should have won,' says Wood. 'It was the angriest I'd ever been after a game.'

178

when you look at the English team, without the likes of Johnson and Leonard and others, you say to yourself, yes, we can beat them – with Johnson at the helm, England was a much harder team to beat.'

He reacquainted himself with the All Blacks in November 2001. A Hickie try pushed Ireland 21–7 ahead and, for long time, they kept New Zealand on the back foot. Eighteen minutes later, Reuben Thorne, Doug Howlett, Aaron Mauger and Jonah Lomu crossed for tries to make it 40–24. It was typical All Blacks, ruthless to the last. 'That was a game we should have won and that was a game we lost for a variety of reasons. It was the angriest I'd ever been after a game. We were in a position to do it and we didn't and if you're looking for a turning point that could be one of the biggest.'

When Wood retired, a great leader was gone, but he contributed profoundly to Irish rugby's revolution years. 'With me going, with Claw going, Gaillimh going, we were guys who went through an awful lot of the bad times – we had some good times too and it was a phenomenal part of my life. We now have a group of guys in there that almost expect to win. They don't have that sort of negativity in their background. I'd like to think we didn't have a huge amount of it either, but we're still tainted by the fact that we lost an awful lot of games when this present crew has won an awful lot of games. I take great pleasure in the fact that they win and I would like to think that I had a lot to do with it in that a lot of things had to change. But I've always said and I believe totally the winning of those matches are of the fifteen guys that start. Everything that they've learned over the past ten years is an experience for them to get to that day.'

Since Wood's retirement Lansdowne seems a less boisterous venue. He was capable of energising a whole stadium and electrifying 49,000 spectators with one barn-storming run into space or into a thicket of opposition shirts. Woodie was one of a kind. He has returned to Lansdowne since retirement as an expert BBC analyst and can be seen on a Six Nations day on the sideline below the West Stand curling the collar of his coat around his neck from the cold and the breeze. 'Without the crowd, the ground is a cold windswept great edifice long past its prime,' says Wood. 'It seems to live for the big occasion; it comes to life, struggling one last time to hold its place. It has an atmosphere and a noise level all of its own.'

Gareth Edwards

Scrum-Half, Wales
1967–1978

Gareth Edwards arrived at Lansdowne Road for his first senior Wales game in the old ground in March 1968. He was just twenty, but had heard much about the friendly Irish, the unique Lansdowne atmosphere and had watched news of games at Dublin on cinema screens in Wales. 'This will be grand,' he thought.

That spring afternoon, he walked into the Lansdowne Pavilion, nestled cosily between the West Stand and Havelock End Terrace. 'Like a little house in the corner,' mused Edwards. He recalls that the dressing room looked like someone's front room – quaint in an Irish sort of way. 'It was a surreal setting, so welcoming and cosy, but it seemed there wasn't enough room to swing a cat in there. It was a contrast to the reception you got from the Irish team when you hit the ground!'

After nearly ninety minutes of rugby, he was seen galloping back to the sanctuary of the dressing room as quickly as possible, because the atmosphere had become fairly heated outside. Though Ireland won 9–6, his debut at Lansdowne would be remembered for all the wrong reasons. Then again, he wasn't entirely culpable.

The debris accumulated around the perimeter of the field was a result of an Edwards 'drop goal' and the contentious refereeing decision that gave the score. The build-up to the drop goal wasn't a play Edwards or his team had premeditated. He had intended passing along the line in his own unique style but changed his mind in the last moment. He does remember connecting sweetly with the ball but may be sorry he ever did. 'I hit it very well, it travelled straight and true, but the ref was watching the Irish back-row line for possible offside, and he looked up just too late to watch the ball swing. I thought for a moment that it might very well have gone over because the ball just swirled in the wind and turned around the post. I think the ref thought it was going to go one direction and he was cricking his neck to sort of see it go over and the next thing I knew he had given it. I think there were 40,000 in Lansdowne that day that didn't agree with him!'

The result of Edwards' drop goal was the sight of a mini-riot breaking out on the terraces. He was told on the bus to the match that the Lansdowne crowd was very knowledgeable but after his kick, he hadn't too much time to ponder the merits of the Lansdowne crowd. The ball was retained by the Irish supporters, and then bottles, tin cans, even fruit were hurled onto the field – though nothing was thrown at any player. Then sections of the crowd began to spill onto the field as well. 'There was a lot of controversy surrounding that drop goal. I remember there were loads of coins, loads of Guinness landing all around us. There were enough coins to have taken care of us for a night out in Dublin! It was mayhem really. The game looked like it would end up a draw. I don't think any of us were hit but some of us were laughing at the sight of all these objects being hurled down from the terrace.'

184

Approaching full-time, the Welsh players harboured a suspicion that the referee might add as many minutes of injury-time as was possible in an effort to assuage 'the angry mob'. And, ten minutes later, Mick Doyle touched down on a patch of grass in the corner near the then Lansdowne Pavilion – a patch that, years later, would become known as 'Currow Corner' – and the game ended almost immediately. 'I remember a lot of injury-time so Ireland had an opportunity to score a winning try right down near the dressing room, which I think was a bit more than a coincidence than just the fact they had scored in the corner. As soon as the try was scored, it was a case of us saying, "Lads, let's go away from the referee now into the safety of the dressing room." The try just won the game for them in the last minute but it seemed like an age from our point of view. And from Ireland's point of view, justice was served when Doyler scored in the corner.'

'I don't want to remember it thank you very much,' says Edwards of Wales' 14–0 loss to Ireland at Lansdowne Road in 1970. While the Edwards drop goal from Wales' previous sojourn in Dublin was still vivid in the Irish memory, the Ireland players had also been particularly hurt by the beating they received at Cardiff Arms Park the previous season when the principality went on to win the Triple Crown – and some were fired up by the punch Noel Murphy received when Welsh forward Brian Price ghosted from a ruck and hit the Ireland flanker. It was Murphy's last international match for Ireland.

The retribution was cold and calculated. Wales were squeezed and suffocated. The result didn't exactly precipitate rioting in the streets in Wales, but there were plenty of inquests afterwards in the Valleys. The star-studded Welsh side, men of genius in red jerseys, never got close to Ireland in 1970. In the aftermath, they started looking within themselves in an effort to solve that great post-match post-mortem of 'where did it all go wrong?' Edwards says it didn't take much to solve the puzzle of that day, the visitors learned something very important – you never underestimate the Irish, especially on their home patch.

'They were all over us. We all played badly. Barry [John] and myself at half-back had a very torrid time. Ken Goodall was quite sensational – well, all the Irish forwards were really. There was no response from us at all. Barry McGann slammed over a beautiful drop goal and I remember Alan Duggan and Ken Goodall scoring fantastic tries. It was a comprehensive defeat – 14–0 doesn't sound much by today's standard, but we were very well beaten on the day. We lost a match that we thought we might conceivably win. As a commentator of the time said, "We were lucky to get nil!" When we went to Ireland we always knew it was going to be tough, we had experienced players with us at that time, but we were a well-deserved second, so well beaten, we were never able to play at all. We never really got off the ground and the Irish took a grip of proceedings from the very beginning. We all had a bit of a nightmare really.'

And though the greatest Welsh scrum-half of all time was rubbing away the tears of a comprehensive defeat, he was later saddened by the news that Ken Goodall would be moving to rugby league the following season. 'Ken was the star of that game in 1970. He was a great loss to British

185

The Dixie Dive: Flying Lansdowne winger, Alan 'Dixie' Duggan scores a spectacular try against Wales in the 1970 Five Nations at Lansdowne Road. Ireland won 14–0 with the late Ken Goodall also scoring a try.

Make way for the legend: Spoken of in the same elevated tones as Jack Kyle, Mike Gibson was one of the finest out-halves/centres of world rugby between 1964 and 1979. Here 'Gibbo' is challenged by Gareth Edwards (tackling), Mervyn Davies (with headband) and J.P.R. Williams (right) in the 1973 Five Nations.

and Irish rugby. I played all too briefly with him in the 1968 Lions tour but I have so much respect for him. As a Number 8, he was such a talented player and though we had Mervyn Davies, Ken was right up there with the very best and, of course, if he hadn't gone to rugby league, who knows what the future would have held for him.'

The fall from grace of the Triple Crown champions at Lansdowne Road brought with it feverish inquests and consequently gossip throughout Wales. Some of the stories got quite personal and showed how far people and newspapers would go to finding the solution for a sudden collapse of form. 'There were definite inquests in Wales. I can laugh about it now but the rumours were that the Welsh team were fighting behind the scenes and, on the Friday night before the game, they were out having drinks and fighting on the lawn outside the hotel. Then they were saying that myself and J.P.R. Williams were fighting after the game because my girlfriend had gone to J.P.R.! Such was the sting of the defeat that the Welsh fans felt there had to be more than just the fact that Ireland were so much better than us.'

Wales and Scotland did not travel to Lansdowne Road in 1972 because of the political situation in Northern Ireland, and so Ireland lost out on an opportunity to play the 1971 Grand Slam champions. Wales were a team of all talents, playing a brand of rugby that today would mark them out as innovators and entertainers.

Whether the Lansdowne Road faithful had their appetite sated by the excellence of some of their own like Mike Gibson, Barry McGann, Tom Kiernan, Tom Grace and Fergus Slattery, the Welsh team brought with them a mystique almost as impenetrable as the All Blacks. Superlatives were spun out lavishly by the media in an attempt to paint as effusively as possible the talents of Edwards, John, Gerald Davies, Williams and Phil Bennett or their much-vaunted Pontypool front-row of Price, Faulkner and Windsor.

Amidst the hype and hoopla of Welsh rugby, the potential and capabilities of the Irish seemed to have been undermined. Indeed, the Irish team was not far off winning a Grand Slam.

'In 1972, we didn't go over and that was a huge disappointment for us but the political scene wasn't conducive to travelling. I know England did go the following year. The players were quite prepared to play but the WRU made the decision and said no. It's easy on reflection to look back but people in the union were very concerned and the threat was very real as we all know. The union said, "This will not be the players' decision, this will be our decision," and they pulled the plug on it.'

When Wales travelled to Lansdowne in 1974, Edwards recalls it was probably a better result than the team could have envisaged. Still, it was a stadium where this Welsh team had yet to break loose, cause mayhem and win respect from the Irish public. But the vagaries of the wind coupled with a litany of incomprehensible decisions by the referee left Wales playing a more conservative brand of rugby, alien to their innate attacking instincts. Free expression had to wait for another day. The game was less about inventiveness and playing with abandon and more about a sleeves-rolled-up attitude – a very un-Welsh thing especially for this group of superstars.

'By that time, the Welsh team was maturing. We were playing some great rugby coming into that match. Then we came to Dublin. There was a very strong wind, as there tends to be in Lansdowne. We played very well into the wind in the first half and I just thought, 'If we turn around – and I think it might have been 6–6 at half time – there's a chance of winning this. All we have to do is win a few balls and keep Ireland down there.' We got penalised out of the game in the second half whether it was justified or not, but, naturally, I'd have a blinkered view about it. We were hard done by. The referee was penalising Wales in the lineout for pushing and, having played with Willie John McBride over a number of years, I knew exactly who was doing most of the shoving! But that's only a whinge,' he says with a smile. 'It was an awful game spoilt predominantly by the wind. But we had the advantage in the second half. We had the wind and I thought surely it would be a matter of time if we could at least get a couple of penalties, Phil Bennett would put them over, we weren't too concerned about how the game would be won, but we never got into the position to get it. We only got a few penalties in the second half and the match finished at 9–9, which was a huge disappointment to me. I think both sides nullified one another. We had to wait a few years before we had a decent game of rugby against one another at Lansdowne Road.'

187

When the curtain was pulled back for their meeting in Dublin two years later, it was time for the Welsh to put on their most extravagant show. Edwards, so often 'the man' in Welsh victories, capped off one of his most inspiring displays with a try in a 34–9 victory. Still, Edwards would let you believe that scoreline was deceptive, that somehow Wales sneaked a win. 'That was a very, very tough game. It was only in the last fifteen minutes that we pulled away. It had been very tough, very close and it all just came together. The 1971 side were all that much younger. We were young but there was a lovely way about the game we played which was more mobile. We had control of the pack and we could also play an expansive game. In that period of time – 1976, 1977, 1978 – we won three Triple Crowns in consecutive years and two Grand Slams. We only lost out narrowly in Paris for the third Grand Slam. Unlike 1970 and 1974, we were able to hold on and match Ireland's aggression – and we were then able to ride the storm so to speak.'

Sadly, we were to see the last of Edwards at Lansdowne Road in 1978. He went on record afterwards as saying that the game had got too physical, that the fun had gone out of it for him. Most of the Welsh players felt Lansdowne resembled Carisbrook for a day and certainly Edwards felt he was in the House of Pain. 'I put it on record as saying that the game was so physically hard that I thought, "What am I doing here? I'm not really enjoying this." It's a peculiar thing to say, you know. The responsibility and the intensity of the occasion was just wearing me down.'

He remembers a couple of stand-out moments despite the nasty undercurrent. 'We had a wonderful start and I thought this is too easy. I remember turning to Gerald Davies and saying, "Gerald, I don't like this because it's too easy!"' But, as soon as he thought that way, the opposite always seemed to happen. Nothing goes to form or how you would expect it at Lansdowne. And if it's believed that Lansdowne Road does strange things to players, it certainly had done strange things to great Welsh sides in the 1970s. 'When we thought we were going to do well, we came away with our tail between our legs.'

But nothing is easy at Lansdowne Road and Ireland dominated the next hour of the game until the Welsh side showed its experience and resolve. The forwards knew it; they knew they had to get their hands on the ball because they hadn't seen it for about an hour.

'Our pack eventually got a hold of the ball, drove down the middle of the field and worked it into a position. The improvisation of the Welsh back division meant we were able to conjure up a try in the dying minutes which I suppose epitomised the way we had played and that we had been together for the last few years. It showed our spirit and character. And if we were to put our names on the record books, then Ireland had contributed significantly by pushing us to the very, very limits. That try in the last minute won the match for us. We trundled off into the dressing room and there was hardly any noise because the boys were shattered, nobody was shouting or jumping up and down. We were just far too physically tired to do anything else. I remember the delight on the faces of the selectors who came in, but the boys just sat there, too tired to even take their shirts off. "You don't realise what you have achieved," I think is what they said to the

188

team. Nobody responded. Don't get me wrong – there was obviously great delight and elation but people were just completely shattered. I remember well that I had to go down the corridor from the dressing room to do some television work after getting dressed and changed. About an hour afterwards, lots of the forwards were just sat there, the Pontypool front-row were sitting there in their shirts – they were absolutely drained.'

After the match, Edwards met up with his tormentor-in-chief that afternoon, Fergus Slattery. He remembers Slatts was 'all over the place in a flanker sort of way' that afternoon, trying to dictate which way the game should be played. 'We've discussed that game with a laugh many times since. I remember saying to him afterwards, "Christ, you were clattering everyone, Slatts." He said, "No I didn't." Then one of the Irish lads, S.A. McKinney turned around and said, "Yes you did, you clattered me as well!" We all had a laugh about that and had a good drink as well.'

Edwards worked for the BBC after his playing days ended in 1978. The charm of Lansdowne, the laid-back attitude of the people and the miracle of the BBC technicians around the commentary positions still amaze him to this day. 'The ageing stadium was always causing panic for the BBC technicians. I'd be sat in the commentary position with Bill McLaren just before kick-off, panicking about the transmission and whether or not we could get through to London. Then minutes before kick off, Bill and myself find somebody hanging by the windowsill tapping a few wires and meddling around with switches and some one would say, "That'll be all right now." Or I could be standing on the field ready to do a live piece to camera on *Grandstand* which was starting at one o'clock I'd be thinking, "My word, we haven't got London. What's going to happen, what's going to happen?" And with a minute to go somebody taps a thing or pulls something and suddenly I'm saying, "All right, we're through." So it always worked by and large. But, many's the time, we were left biting our knuckles wondering whether or not it was going to work.'

From a playing point of view, Edwards has mixed memories, but has always found Lansdowne an enchanting arena. 'There's a terrific atmosphere there. It seems everybody is just poured into the stadium. It defies logic really the number of people you get into it. It's an electric atmosphere, a wonderful arena in which to play rugby. We came off the wrong side of results on too many occasions, though the crowd certainly get behind their team and make it a very intimidating place for anyone to play.

'The new Lansdowne Road is long overdue … but we in Wales have great memories of the old one – where else would you have a major sporting function with a main line station underneath? It will be sad when Lansdowne Road changes in one way because I have very, very fond – and not so fond – memories but the ground will live long in the memory. Whenever you play at Lansdowne Road, the game always seemed to play at a huge pace, hundred miles an hour, there was no time to take a deep breath, have any kind of control of the whole thing.'

At least Lansdowne can be thankful to have housed a great Welsh team and a scrum-half gem like Edwards.

189

Gavin Hastings

Full-Back, Scotland
1986–1995

Before Gavin Hastings, Lansdowne Road had seen some exciting Scottish full-backs. Hastings, however, was of a different mould, a giant of a full-back at six-foot two, his attacks from deep were characterised by a potent cocktail of power and aggression.

But his greatest virtue was his reliability under a garryowen, a much-loved tactic used by Irish kickers to unsettle a visiting full-back, particularly in the early stages of a test match. Hastings rarely fumbled one and, while it is easy to label him Mr Dependable, he was far from a one-dimensional figure. The greats rarely are.

The taunts from the crowd as Hastings rose to gather a garryowen might unsettle some full-backs but Hastings had bottle and nerve, positional sense and bravery to deal with the most unattractive of Lansdowne's 'executive high balls' which were invariably mixed into the unpalatable swirling wind that so often ghosted around the old stadium. When thrown a challenge like that, he never shirked his responsibility and, many was the time he won over a Lansdowne crowd that way.

But it was Hastings' metronomic place-kicking that seduced people most and won the respect of opposition fans. He kicked so consistently from place, drop and hand, often from the most acute of angles, that people figured that even if you blindfolded him, he'd still strike as dead-eyed as an arrow hitting its target.

Hastings never looked nonplussed when dealing with a garryowen and dealt ultra-coolly with those deposited high into his area. 'As soon as a garryowen was put up, I would know instinctively whether I was going to be inside my 22 or outside my 22 – in other words, would I be able to mark the ball? But if I was inside my 22, I instinctively knew whether or not the chasing attacking players would be able to get to me roughly the same time as the ball. So, I worked out whether I

192

Under pressure: Hastings holds on to possession despite pressure from Keith Wood. Michael Bradley and Paddy Johns (far right) close in on the Scottish full-back during the 1995 Five Nations.

had to jump up for the ball to catch it in order to secure the possession or had time to make the mark. Now all this happened in a split second just because I instinctively or intuitively knew that that was the case. I just can't understand people today in the full-back position not knowing whether or not that is the case. Apparently, they don't have awareness of who is around them or what players might be following up from the opposition. Some people nowadays mark the ball and there is no one within fifteen yards of them. Quite why they mark the ball I have absolutely no idea. The only time I would ever mark was when an attacking player was coming on to me and was going to absolutely cream me. That all happened within a split second of the ball being kicked.

'With a swirling wind at Lansdowne Road, you had to just be so focused on trying to be aware of your surroundings – where you were, where the touchline was, where the posts were, where the 22 was and how much time you had. I was always pleased when I did get the response of the crowd having dealt with a kick positively and properly and with a good kick to touch. The job of the goal-kicker obviously is to try and get the ball between the posts and you have to concentrate on that fact and whether there is a host of catcalls and whistles or silence, you have to block all that out and concentrate on putting the ball between the sticks.'

Hastings settled in to becoming the darling of Scottish rugby quite comfortably. In some aspects of his play, he mirrored Andy Irvine but, essentially, he was cut from a different cloth than the 1970s icon of Scottish rugby.

An instant hero in Scotland on his debut after landing six penalties in an 18–19 win over France in Paris in the first round of the 1986 championship, Hastings was the one player on everyone's lips when he made his Lansdowne debut that March. Hastings and his team-mates arrived high on confidence; Ireland were stuttering into the last round of the championship with that most awful of millstones hanging around their necks – the prospect of picking up the mythical Wooden Spoon. The thought of suffering a whitewash was as uncomfortable a burden as any player could carry.

The first sighting of Hastings at Lansdowne brought as much giddy expectation as the return of the much-adored Tony Ward to the Irish Number 10 position after an absence of two years. Footballing skill is always welcome at Lansdowne and both Hastings and Ward had the capacity to surprise and entertain. They didn't disappoint.

It appeared Ireland was set to avoid a whitewash having lead 9–0 at half-time. But despite their best display of the season – and plenty of memorable Wardie cameos at out-half – Ireland couldn't close the deal. Scotland and Hastings could – though the latter felt a draw would have better reflected the evenness of the exchanges. 'We scored a try and I remember missing a fairly easy conversion. By rights, we should have gone 12–9 up then. Then, right at the death, Michael Kiernan had a penalty from a not dissimilar position from mine – obviously at the other end – and he missed this penalty inexplicably, and we won the match 10–9. I always felt I should have

Phil Orr: Playing his fiftieth game for Ireland, Orr holds his hands to his head in disbelief as Michael Kiernan misses a penalty in front of the posts in the last moments of the Scottish game in the 1986 Five Nations.

194

kicked mine to make it 12–9 and Michael should have kicked a goal and a draw would have been the correct result of all. I felt very relieved too, that my miss, which wasn't a difficult conversion, hadn't cost Scotland the match. And if I did score, I would have bet on Michael Kiernan to put his over right at the death to level the match.'

The decibel levels when Ireland scored inside Lansdowne Road rose to a different level during those times than in the last days of Lansdowne, and Hastings believes the roar had a more 'throaty' texture than any of the stadia in which he had played around the world, particularly in his second visit to Lansdowne in 1988. 'When you ask my memories of playing at Lansdowne Road, it would be the noise and the passion of the crowd. When Ireland scored, for me it was the noisiest place ever that you could play rugby in those days. The noise of the crowd when Ireland were running in some tries particularly that day was, for me, a sad noise to hear because it represented the strength of the Irish team but equally was something that was very, very strong and has remained with me to this day. Whilst we might have played a get-out-of-jail card in 1986, there was certainly no way we could play that in 1988. From my perspective, we did get well beaten on that occasion and deservingly so.'

Ireland put the Scots on the rocks with a 22–18 win, a day Ireland's pack subdued its counterparts in most areas of forward play, particularly in the back-row where Philip Matthews, Willie Sexton and Mike Gibson enjoyed their best afternoon as a unit opposite the Scottish trio of Iain Paxton, John Jeffrey and Finlay Calder. Ireland denied Scotland at source and, starved of primary possession, the Scottish backs, including Hastings, sparked only fleetingly. The full-back, as commentator Bill McLaren said afterwards, 'was made to move from one side of the field to the other. They [Ireland] blocked every porthole that was there.'

Ireland enacted their tactics to a tee. Indeed, afterwards captain Donal Lenihan praised coach Jim Davidson for his thoroughness in the preparation and that the game-plan he devised subsequently sacked the Scots.

But it was the two Irish tries that caught Hastings' eye, both a product of forward industry and back-line magic. 'We started well and created some opportunities but the Irish defence put down markers early that day and I remember we were down inside ten minutes. The Number 8 [Mike] Gibson made the initial incision. Then that brilliant competitor Michael Bradley fed my good mate Brendan Mullin and it passed through [Paul] Dean's and [Michael] Kiernan's hands before Brendan took the last pass to dive over in the corner. I won't say where I was for that try! Paul Dean was really good that day, too, and set up the second brilliantly for Hugo MacNeill. I was very conscious of the fact that Ireland had very dangerous backs. People like Paul Dean, Brendan Mullin, Trevor Ringland and Keith Crossan and Hugo MacNeill at full-back were class players – a sort of golden generation and I always felt these guys were tremendously talented. I did become extremely friendly with Brendan Mullin and Phil Matthews, who was a great blindside flank for Ireland over many years. I always used look forward to the nights out in Dublin with these guys.'

Even though Hastings enjoyed the post-match Dublin social life and a (self-professed) love of Guinness, the idea of coming to Lansdowne Road made rugby worth playing. As amateurs, these opposing players only had a single chance to play against each other each year and, in a strange sort of way, the bonds became tighter.

195

Professionalism, and the familiarity built up between opposing players through Celtic League and European Cup ties, has severely weakened the bonds that once tied. 'We didn't have the European Cup matches – most guys would play rugby in their respective countries. There were a few guys who were playing for London Irish and I might have come against them during my time with London Scottish. However, it was only a result of visiting these places – and coming to Lansdowne Road once every two years – in my mind that's what made them so unique, so different and so special to play at. It was so different and that was why I think you could create a fortress at your home ground because the players from other countries didn't play you there apart from when they played for their country. In a way one of the aspects of modern-day professional rugby is that everything is very much too familiar than it was in those days, and when you have familiarity you're not so frightened as you would be with going to some absolutely brand-new ground for the first time.'

In Hastings' early years of playing test rugby, the cult of the out-half gained a lot more news space, particularly in Ireland where the Campbell–Ward contest for the Number 10 shirt was discussed *ad nauseum* from the start of the 1980s. But Ireland were never short of a progressive pivot, who could cajole and orchestrate the game at stand-off and Paul Dean is one Hastings rates very highly in the pantheon of great Ireland Number 10s. 'I found Paul [Dean] to be a cross between Tony Ward and Ollie Campbell – not quite the flair of Tony Ward, but he was certainly very, very dependable and he was capable of making a break in a way Ollie wasn't. But Ollie remains a legend of Irish rugby. I remember Paul deservedly winning a place in the 1989 Lions tour, alongside Craig Chalmers of Scotland. I always felt Paul was an astute tactical kicker – he was always capable of making a very good break, had some excellent players outside him and I always felt the Irish three-quarter line in those days was very, very dangerous.'

He also admired the qualities of then Ireland scrum-half Michael Bradley. 'Bradley was a tremendously competitive player, in the mould of Gary Armstrong [of Scotland]. For me, they were both very combative players, had great energy and enthusiasm and their performances were tireless on the field. They engaged each other to raise their games to the levels they had set. That's what you need from team-mates – you need team-mates to stick their head above the parapet. As well as Gary Armstrong and Roy Laidlaw, they were typical characters who could do that.'

As testament to the demands placed on rugby players six years before the onset of professionalism the plight of Armstrong is worth telling. Armstrong went into retirement prematurely in 1989 and returned to the game again in 1994. 'Coming from a Border town, he just really couldn't afford to take time off work,' says Hastings. 'In those days, I think latterly certainly, you are likely to get compensated by your employers or the SRU would compensate for any loss of earnings and, equally, you had to be let off work. I think in those very early days Gary Armstrong was struggling getting away from his business and just taking the time off that was necessary. It's extraordinary

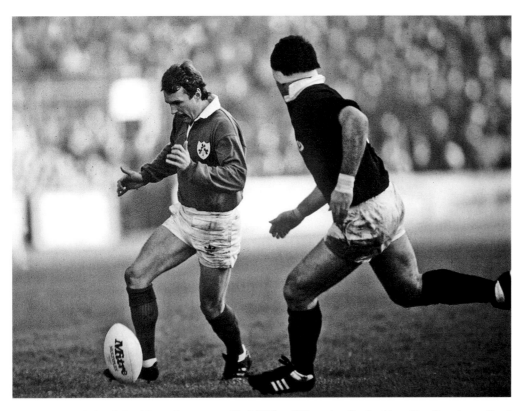

Dean of rugby: Ireland's Paul Dean demonstrates his dribbling skills against Scotland in 1988 at Lansdowne Road.
'I found Paul to be a cross between Tony Ward and Ollie Campbell,' says Hastings.

197

to think now that one of the greatest players of his generation was struggling to get time off work to play international rugby. It's unthinkable in terms of what happens nowadays.'

Hastings returned from the 1989 Lions tour to Australia a hero, but was strangely relieved of his kicking duties for what turned out to be Scotland's Grand Slam season. When they came to Lansdowne in 1990, Scotland discovered a formidable Ireland team up front but bereft in the backline – described by one writer as Ireland's 'Achilles heel'. With no spark in the Irish backs, Scotland capitalised and won 13–10 thanks to two tries from Derek White. Hastings wasn't entirely cast as understudy to Chalmers and was given the opportunity to kick a couple but the strong wind undid any momentum he had built up.

'I didn't kick in 1990 for whatever reason and I don't know quite why. I went on tour with the Lions in 1989 – first choice goal-kicker then – and 1990 was the only season where I wasn't first choice kicker. I think I only took a couple of kicks that whole season. I was living in London at the time and playing for London Scottish and Craig was playing in Scotland for Melrose – perhaps he was more in the public eye and it was decided that Craig should take the kicks. Anyway, I was struggling a wee bit with my kicks. I don't recall exactly the reasons behind it but I didn't really kick at all during that whole Five Nations Grand Slam winning year. Maybe that's one of reasons we won the Grand Slam!

'That was our first game. We came over to Ireland first up. We had a bye in the first round of the championship but we played then on four consecutive fortnights. We had a very strong back row with Finlay Calder, John Jeffrey and Derek White. For me, they were the epitome of Scottish breakaway forward play – they were always scampering around the field, really just generating mayhem and causing havoc in opposition defences. I think for one of White's tries – it might have started with a break from Sean Lineen in the centre – he passed inside to White, who was always there in support and he went over close to the posts. Amazingly, we always seemed to leave Lansdowne Road with a sneaky little victory – in 1986 it was 10–9 and, in 1990, we squeezed a very close victory. So that was that. We were content as always in those days just to get off the mark, and playing away from home was never easy – it's not easy today and wasn't easy then. To get your campaign off and running was a good start for us.'

Hastings being grounded by Irish Number 8 Brian Robinson watched by David McIvor, Gus Aherne and Philip Matthews during the 1992 Five Nations at Lansdowne. Scotland won 18–10, Hastings giving an exhibition of place-kicking.

The saddest days for Irish rugby – but happy enough for Scotland – were in Hastings' next two visits to Lansdowne Road in 1992 and 1994. In their 1992 match, it was a grim afternoon to be Irish and most unpleasant for the Ireland players who had to withstand a barrage of abuse near the end from the crowd. Jeering and slow handclapping were other tools used by the crowd to communicate their frustration at Ireland's inept display. But this was a strong Scotland side that put Ireland to the sword with a 18–10 victory. Hastings gave an exhibition of place kicking, arching over two touchline conversions after tries from Tony Stanger and Andy Nicol. 'Again, as ever, it seemed to be always damn windy,' says Hastings.

The 1994 game between the sides at Lansdowne ended 6–6, a poor return from Ireland after the euphoria created after their 13–12 win in Twickenham a fortnight earlier. Though described universally as a bore, those at the game attested to the strength of the prevailing wind that spoiled proceedings. Indeed, the ferocity of the wind led some commentators to write that age-old regulars at Lansdowne could not recall the last time a game had to be played under the same conditions. The game was a non-event – except for an injury to Hastings. 'My abiding memory of that whole day is I got some staples put in my forehead and I think I went off before half-time and came back on with the head all bandaged up. I went out to have a couple of pints of Guinness after the game. It was probably ten o'clock when I was delivering my post-match speech at the dinner, and I could feel the staples pushing back out of my head and physically coming out of my head because it was so damn hot in the room. There was blood and a bit of sweat rolled into one dripping down onto my nose. I finished my speech anyway, and I went over to see the team doctor explaining that these staples were coming half way out my head. So we both had to return to the team hotel and he had to stitch me up. I'm grateful to him because I don't have a big scar. That was my abiding memory of that 6–6 draw!'

Hastings was always very grateful to get a victory at Lansdowne Road. 'The Irish might say that if we're going to lose to anyone, they'd probably feel happier losing to the Scots. It became a bit of happy hunting ground for us.'

Yet, like so many visiting players, Hastings became subsumed with emotion and nostalgia at the news that the old Lansdowne is near its end. Hastings offers a most fitting tribute to a great stadium, one where he and Scotland enjoyed their best days. 'It's a shame in a way a ground as graceful an old lady as Lansdowne Road will be coming to an end. In every sport, as in life, a mixture of the old and new is what is best and I think that is what makes Ireland and Lansdowne Road so unique. Logistically and health and safety wise, the thought of "let's just build a railway line under it" and every time the train comes along the whole stand shakes, all this stuff, you could argue it's a disaster waiting to happen, but equally that's the Irish for you – it could only ever happen in Ireland. I say that as a compliment, not as a criticism and that's what makes Lansdowne so unique and wonderful in the eyes of so many people – myself included.'

199

Martin Johnson

Lock, England

1995–2005

England's Martin Johnson played four times for his country and twice for Leicester at Lansdowne Road between 1995 and 2005. He never lost there. Famously, in 2001, he couldn't play; instead the giant lock was confined to a seat in the West Stand sporting a grey fleece and nursing a broken wrist from a club game seven days earlier. The image of Johnson that afternoon is of a restless giant, frowning with head in hands as England allowed another Grand Slam to slip from their grasp – their third in three seasons.

He felt the stadium shudder that afternoon when Keith Wood, his former Lions team-mate, crashed through Neil Back for a decisive first-half try and, when the final whistle went, Johnson just wanted to get the hell out of Dublin as quickly as possible, not be beckoned towards a presentation rostrum to accept the championship trophy, which England had won by topping the Six Nations table.

Johnson has said that England always perform best with a healthy dose of fear and there certainly must have been a healthy measure of anxiety and anticipation before his first England game at Lansdowne Road in January 1995 and, if he felt he was entering the eye of the storm, he didn't think he'd be entering it literally. During the national anthems, the hulking six-foot six-inch lock from the midlands experienced a bit of trouble keeping his balance while belting out 'God Save the Queen'. 'It was one of the windiest days I can ever remember,' he says. 'We were getting blown sideways in the anthems.'

If the wind was an unwelcome visitor during pre-match protocol, England's game-plan ran ever so smoothly, almost as in defiance to the prevailing weather conditions. Opting to play against the wind, the visitors eschewed their kicking game; instead quick-tap penalties were the order of the day as the English forwards rucked and mauled and ploughed their way through a physically inferior Ireland. This England team was built in the image of their coach Jack Rowell – big, grizzled warriors, who guaranteed their wide men quick and clean possession. In that first half, England buckled down and adopted the correct tactics against the breeze and went in leading 12–3 at the break.

Essentially, it was game over at that stage and, for Johnson, the butterflies had disappeared from the pit of his stomach and the fear had dissipated. 'We were playing into the wind in the first half. Kyran Bracken was scrum-half and he said, "We can't kick a penalty into touch, we should just tap and go and keep hold of the ball, and really keep the ball away from Ireland because as soon as we lost the ball they could kick it virtually seventy or eighty yards down the field if they wanted." We got right into the game and took Ireland on up front. We had a good pack and we had Dean Richards.' In that team, Richards was a colossus and his performance in the back-row alongside Tim Rodber and Ben Clarke was immense. This trio especially never allowed Ireland to break the gain-line or sneak a few yards around the fringes. Ireland were obliter- ated in the first-half.

Even Ireland manager Noel Murphy, himself a back-row expert, took time out afterwards to lavish praise on Richards' prowess. 'Dean Richards was great for England, he is the kind of man you need on a day like this.'

'We just drove it and mauled it and, because we had the urgency of having to play into the wind, it really actually worked in our favour,' continues Johnson. 'It was one of the best first halves I had with England really.'

Wave after wave of concerted English pressure yielded two tries in that first half. Lansdowne could scarcely believe the might and force of England as the players moved relentlessly down the field with Will Carling and Ben Clarke each running in a try. 'Early on, we just tapped and went. It gave us the sort of initiative to try and get into the game. When I think back, if our game-plan back-fired, we could have been twenty points down in those sort of conditions.'

The lineouts would prove crucial in the first half. Ireland were willing to kick to touch with a boot-the-ball policy, the most sensible option with a gale to their backs. But whatever lineout play existed in the first forty minutes, England dominated. The two Martins – Bayfield and

Anthony Foley, on his Ireland debut, halts Martin Johnson watched by English duo Dean Richards and Martin Bayfield during the 1995 Five Nations. England won 21–8. 'We had to be mentally tough because Lansdowne can be a real cauldron, but it's a great place in which to play,' says Johnson.

Johnson – were imperious. And a problem area for the Irish was compounded with the forced retirement on half-time of Neil Francis who sustained a rib cartilage injury. It's something Johnson remembers. 'Neil Francis' injury was a big blow for Ireland; I thought he was a very good player, a very athletic guy.'

At the break, England knew they had Ireland by the throat but the expected squeeze and follow-on humiliation of the Irish never materialised. Still, Ireland continued to suffer in the lineouts with Bayfield and Johnson stealing and making themselves a right nuisance on Ireland's throw. In the loose, Anthony Foley and Keith Wood did their best to stem the ferocity of England's power-play – emanating particularly from the sustained driving from the back-row triumvirate of Rodber, Clarke and Richards.

Ireland braved it out in the second half; and Anthony Foley notched a late try on his first Ireland outing to keep the final score somewhat respectable at 21–8.

In an era when Irish teams fell away dramatically in the last twenty minutes, it was during this period that the home team's truer side came to light and, if Ireland had performed like that for the previous hour, they might have been close at full-time. The 'ifs' and 'buts' of the performance came up in the post-mortem; as always it is the preferred lexicon of the vanquished to heal sore wounds and deflated egos.

That afternoon, Johnson's colossal shadow was cast across Lansdowne for the first time in a masterful second-row display. Lansdowne might not have known it then, but his giant silhouette was to haunt many Irish performances over the next ten years. 'With the wind, we didn't play any bit near as well; in fact we then changed the way we played and weren't anywhere near as successful, and the only points we scored came from one more try. But we really killed the game off. If Ireland came at us, we were able to turn it over and go fifty or sixty yards down the field with the breeze. That was crucial.'

England took the Grand Slam that year – big players and big characters helping them along their road to glory. 'That was our first game of the tournament and, the thing was, we hadn't played anyone majorly big the previous autumn. Yes, we put big points up against Canada and Romania – but they weren't top-flight opposition. In fact, we hadn't had a tough game since the tour to South Africa the year before. It was a new side too and the win gave us huge confidence as well. That first forty minutes, I'll remember forever. We know too that Ireland were going for hat-trick of wins over England. We had to be mentally tough because Lansdowne can be a real cauldron but it's a great place in which to play.'

Keith Wood's words in the aftermath of their 1997 Five Nations match at Lansdowne Road succinctly sum up the reasons behind Ireland's 46–6 pummelling at the hands of England. Wood was injured for the game but writing in *The Examiner* he pointed to the power of the English forwards, with Johnson in the engine room, as the catalyst to Ireland's dramatic collapse: 'They overpowered us; they pummelled us. They were much heavier and never relented. Normally, a team picks certain scrums to give a special effort and attack. Not so England, not for a second. I remember a scrum with about ten minutes to go, it seemed to be of little consequence but they gave it everything.'

Wood added that the superior weight of the English took its toll and Ireland ended up doing an awful lot of defending which, consequently, sapped the energy from his team-mates. 'It wasn't a lack of fitness; it's just that the huge men in the back five of the English scrum took the heart and soul out of our men. They concentrated on taking every ounce of resistance out of the Irish. It's not nice to look at, it's not pretty but it's bloody effective and enabled them to finally turn on the style in the last few minutes. It's easy to become downhearted in those circumstances. You have to be fair and say England played great rugby in the closing stages.' England's backs paraded their wares to stunning effect running in five of their six tries over the eighty minutes – but five of those tries arrived in the last seventeen minutes.

It could have been so different had Ireland taken their chances, according to Johnson. 'I mean, after seventeen minutes Ireland were leading 6–3 and then Denis Hickie beat a couple of our boys, space opened up and he could have reached our line. But, somehow, he slipped or tripped over and we escaped. Eric Miller got badly concussed early on, too, which worked for us because he was in his best form of his life at that point. I remember it being fairly even in the first half, then Johnny Sleightholme scored to give us a bit of an advantage going into the second half.'

Johnson admits that a new-look England could not get into any discernable rhythm in the first half, as they knocked the ball on, made fundamental errors and conceded a succession of penalties. Ireland were 6–11 behind at half-time but the loss of Miller and Eric Elwood (who had departed two minutes after Miller's twelfth-minute exit) proved hugely detrimental to the Irish game-plan, and the chain of creativity was broken. As Wood says, 'It is unsettling to lose two key decision-makers. We were relying on Miller's speed and Elwood's experience and to miss both was a major handicap.'

Once Andy Gomarsall sauntered over in the sixty-fourth minute, England turned up the heat and Ireland melted into oblivion. England played champagne rugby, fizzing in attack as Ireland were flattened by the chariot. 'The last fifteen minutes was when the damage was done,' says Johnson. 'Ireland tried to run it, but we just picked up the pieces. At the end, they were playing catch-up rugby and that's no easy thing when you're under the cosh.'

It was a demolition, a humiliation and a huge regression for Irish rugby still grappling tenuously with professionalism. England appeared to be light years ahead, and Ireland were incinerated. Who was there to shout stop? Ireland looked to coach Brian Ashton. Ashton had to take the flak for the shambles all around him. Afterwards, in an effort to conceal the cracks behind another public humiliation, he stated, 'There is no quick fix for the ills of Irish rugby. It would take two or three years, not two or three weeks to put things right.'

It wasn't such a bad diagnosis. In 2000, though under a different coach (Warren Gatland), Ireland won three consecutive Six Nations games, including a win against France in Paris, all of which marked a turn in Irish rugby's fortunes.

'I didn't know Brian at all at that point [in 1997]. All I knew is that he was associated with backs. He was on the television the week before talking about being involved with England at various other levels. He said that he wanted Ireland to win; obviously he was coaching against his home country and he felt quite mischievous about it. Brian just wanted to coach – being a head coach is just an entirely different thing. He maybe got that feeling with Ireland when things started to go a little bit wrong for him, they didn't really have that belief in themselves. The score turned into a rout, but we weren't forty points better than Ireland. There was real silence in the crowd especially near the end. They started to leave early as well. As the away team, to come and play the way we did, was a great feeling. We even had Jeremy Guscott on the bench and Austin Healy came on as a replacement to win his first cap. I thought we had a pretty strong squad: it was Hilly's [Richard Hill] debut season in the Six Nations, Lawrence's [Dallaglio] second season, Shawsey's [Simon Shaw] first season. It was a fairly exciting time for us. There was almost a changing of the guard from two years ago. No [Brian] Moore, Richards, Bayfield, no

Rob Andrew. We should have won the Grand Slam – we lost a hell of a lead against France in Twickenham afterwards.'

The British and Irish media reasoned before England's visit to Lansdowne Road in 1999 that Ireland had the best tight five in the northern hemisphere and their deduction seemed rational enough given Ireland's exciting win over Wales in Wembley and England's struggle to overcome Scotland. The big question was could Ireland actually do it? In the Lansdowne press box, there was a pool organised in which predictions are made on the final outcome. Most journalists – both British and Irish – went for a home win.

The pre-match predictions and theories around England's frailties in the tight five only served to galvanise their pack, and they ran roughshod over Ireland in ruthless defiance to the soothsayers. Richard Cockerill, Tim Rodber, Martin Johnson, and the back-row of Richard Hill, Neil Back and man of the match Lawrence Dallaglio annihilated the Irish pack while there appeared such easy and smooth cohesion between England's backs and forwards. 'We got a rugby lesson today,' said Ireland coach, Warren Gatland afterwards.

England elected to play against the wind in the first half and, Johnson says, 'We laid the foundations for our victory down in the first twenty minutes.' Memories of 1995 seemed to be relived as England retained possession superbly and for seemingly enormously long periods against the elements. 'I think we got the tactics right again. Even against the wind, we were dominating possession which frustrated the Irish. They were still very good defensively and, perhaps, we should have got a few more points inside their half.'

Indeed they should. During this opening period, Ireland had a mere 20 per cent of possession and their lineout imploded – England took possession from four of Ireland's throws in the first half. Tim Rodber and Johnson were claiming ball at will, and gave them another platform to drive at an Irish pack already under pressure. 'Lansdowne was very quiet during the opening twenty minutes. I suppose there was a lot of pre-match hype around Dublin after Ireland's impressive victory over Wales but the noise quickly subsided when we took charge up front. I think the Matt Perry try showed us at our best – forwards driving up the middle and the backs forming good lines behind which enabled Perry to finish off in style for the first try. Still, there was only two points between the sides at the break.'

Johnson points to the influence his one-time Leicester team-mate Eric Miller had on proceedings after his introduction in the second half. 'When Eric came on there was more purpose to the Irish play and I think his sense of urgency was one of the factors Ireland brought the score back to 15–12 with about ten minutes left on the clock. Ireland displayed typical fervour and passion but our defence did really well.'

Teenage sensation Jonny Wilkinson lined at centre for England and, at just nineteen, showed maturity beyond his years landing his fourth penalty in the sixty-third minute to push England 20–12 in front and, though David Humphreys replied with a penalty, England's forwards – Johnson,

Dallaglio and Back, in particular – helped settle the game when Tim Rodber scored a try in injury-time. The overwhelming feeling around Dublin that evening was that Ireland were lucky to keep the final score so respectable given England's powerful demonstration in the rudiments of rugby forward play.

The game, however, wasn't without its controversial moments. There was a suggestion after-wards that Cockerill had taunted spectators at Lansdowne at the final whistle. He ran down the touchline giving what he recalled later as a 'routine victory gesture'. Cockerill pleaded innocence afterwards, 'I don't want my action to be misinterpreted. England have been criticised all week and, when we scored, it was clear we had won the match. I gave the spectators a routine victory gesture – with two fingers held up showing that we had won.'

The sense of relief for England at this victory was echoed by their coach Clive Woodward, 'That was the biggest game since I became coach – bigger than New Zealand, Australia or South Africa – it put them all in the shade because we simply had to win.'

'It was a pretty tough game. It wasn't over till it was over,' says Johnson. 'It was a hard slog. This was Lansdowne Road and any win there has to be savoured. It was a transitional England team and a good team. Again, a team that should have won the Grand Slam but lost to Wales.'

In the spring of 2001, England were playing an all-singing, all-dancing brand of rugby, and looked shoo-ins for a Grand Slam. Their plans were disrupted after an outbreak of foot-and-mouth disease across Britain, and their Lansdowne date was pushed back to late October. In a rugby players' mind that constitutes a new season and, after a disappointing Lions series in Australia, many England players had lost form – and, in Dallaglio's case, picked up an injury. Momentum can be difficult to carry over from one season to the next and, if you factored in their catalogue of injuries to key players, England's chances of a Grand Slam win in Dublin diminished by the day.

All week at the England camp, the key mnemonic had been T-CUP 'think clearly under pressure', but their minds weren't right as they went into their first international of the new season without many key players. 'In spring 2001, we'd beaten everyone out of sight. I think we broke a record for most number of tries or points scored, we had a really quick and fit team. Iain Balshaw played at full-back and we were bringing Jason Robinson off the bench for those spring games. We just ran teams off their feet really.'

Fate seemed to be conspiring against Woodward and his team, and Lawrence Dallaglio, Johnson and Phil Vickery missed their biggest game of 2001 – the Grand Slam tie in Dublin. The sight of Johnson confined to a seat in the West Stand as his team crumbled under the feverish intent of Ireland is a lasting image. All he could do was close his eyes and wish matters on the field would resolve but that didn't happen. The biggest and most impressive figure in English rugby was powerless. 'I broke my hand the week before playing for Leicester after about twenty minutes. I played up to half-time. It's not a ridiculously painful injury, and I remember the physio

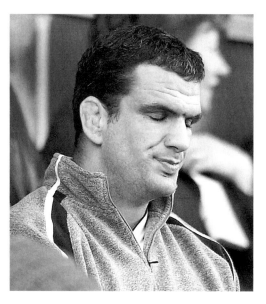

Not again: A dejected Martin Johnson as Ireland score a try during the 2001 Six Nations match between Ireland and England at Lansdowne. England allowed a Grand Slam to slip through their hands for the third year in a row.

208

saying, "You'll be all right" but you could feel the bone rattling in my hand. Lawrence got hurt, I broke my hand, Phil Vickery was out, Balsh had lost a bit of form during the Lions tour, so it was difficult before we even hit the field. We probably made more breaks in that game than we did in the previous two. I had been very frustrated watching it. We tried to play some beautifully attractive rugby in our own half of the field and we kept turning the ball over. When you go away and you concede the first try – which we did – it makes it an awful lot harder and Ireland scored a really well-worked try. Then we had five opportunities in that game late in the second half but the referee penalised us a few times. Even at the end, I remember saying to Clive, "If we keep hold of the ball here, we'll score a try" and I was sure of it. Ireland defended well, but we tried to play too much rugby in our half, which was crazy.'

Ireland's win precipitated the greatest outbreak of emotion – on the field by the players and in the stand by the supporters – since the Triple Crown win in 1985. The irony of it all was amazing. A dejected England team had just won the Six Nations Championship but they only spoke in terms of Grand Slams. Reluctantly Johnson, along with captain for the day Matt Dawson, accepted the trophy and trooped off disconsolately. Ireland, on the other hand, did a lap of honour. 'For Ireland it was real big, emotional win. I said if we won I'd go on the field. If we lost I was saying to Clive I'd rather not go down and collect the trophy. When we lost, I'd rather not have won anything. I don't think the preparation was right either. The guys were in Ireland all week which I thought was a mistake. I think the best way to prepare for those games is to come in on the Thursday afternoon when you've two days to get ready for it. I think we made the mistake off the field. But it's all about who wins the game – and we didn't win the game, Ireland won the game. We would have much rather given them a clap and walked off because it was as flat as it could have been in our camp. We'd lost another Grand Slam – it was getting beyond a joke at that point really.'

At a press conference the week of the Grand Slam showdown in Lansdowne Road in 2003, you could sense England were ready for battle. In the interviews, there was a cold steeliness in their carefully chosen words. The pressure was on them to deliver but they were used to that and, once and for all, they wanted to break down the barriers of underachievement, which, in their vocabulary, amounted simply to their inability to win Grand Slams. Even Neil Back was not going to allow heckling from the Munster contingent in the Irish crowd (the 'back-hander' controversy from the 2002 European Cup final from Cardiff was still fresh in their minds) distract him from the task in hand. The rugged flanker delivered his words with a determined delivery, no cadence, each word emphasised flatly for optimum effect. 'No amount of intimidation from any fan in any stadium in the world has affected my performance in a negative way.'

The message was clear, England were on a mission.

In the match, England dominated in every sector, their forwards crucified their counterparts in open play and the Lansdowne crowd was silenced. England won 42–6 and Johnson, at last, could lift the Six Nations trophy as Grand Slam champions.

Johnson believes that the scoreline didn't reflect a fine Irish performance ('better than 2001') but Ireland caught England in a mean mood, after years of hurt had built up inside them in their crusade to lift a Grand Slam. 'Ireland probably played better than they had two years before in

many ways. It was just opportunity taken. We played into the breeze and, early on, we were under a lot of pressure. I remember Geordan [Murphy] playing very well – I thought he was Ireland's best player that day. For the first try, we got them under pressure in a scrum, won the turnover and Lawrence scored a try. Jonny dropped two goals to make it 13–6 at half-time. In a way, the game was a reverse of 2001 because Ireland were having opportunities and were counter- and counter-attacking and played a very wide game as we had done two years earlier. We defended very well and got a couple of chances when Ireland could have scored. Jonny's tackle on Maggs was a big one in the first half and there were a couple of other occasions as well where we could have been 13–3 down at half-time.'

With the pack in control, Jonny Wilkinson came into his own at out-half and, before half-time, dropped two goals with his so-called weaker right foot. 'I mean Jonny dropped one

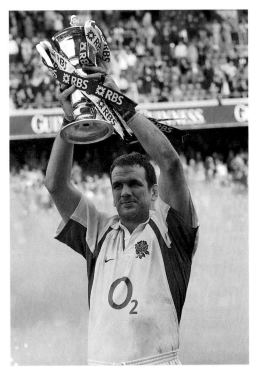

Cup of cheer: Johnson lifts the championship trophy in March 2003, this time as Grand Slam champions.

Reluctant champions, 20 October 2001. Even though they had topped the 2001 Six Nations table, England players are devastated at losing out on a third consecutive Grand Slam (and their third in three seasons losing out to a Celtic nation) when Ireland overturned them 20–14 at Lansdowne Road. Jason Leonard does his best to console Mike Catt (left) and a crestfallen Jonny Wilkinson, whose stunned expression is one of the most remarkable post-match shots in sports photography. The outbreak of foot-and-mouth disease across Great Britain forced the Ireland–England tie to be rescheduled for October. England had waltzed through their first four fixtures in the spring, but the élan and panache and free-scoring style which had marked out their performances in those games were decidedly absent when they came to Lansdowne. An injured Martin Johnson was forced to watch it from the lower West Stand. 'I was saying, if we win, I will go on the field,' remembers Johnson. 'If we lose I was saying to Clive [Woodward] I'd rather not go down and collect the trophy. When we lost, I'd rather not have won anything ... We'd lost another Grand Slam – it was getting beyond a joke at that point really.'

just before the half, to bring it from 10–6 to 13–6 which is quite a big stretch. We just took points at key opportunities.'

At the start of the second half, England were making mistakes and could not build on their score – a trait of the Woodward teams was to build on leads. 'We made a few mistakes, the referee penalised us and we were getting a bit frustrated with things. There was no score for the first twenty minutes in the second half and then [Mike] Tindall broke through two tackles to score. Before Mikey's try, Ireland were pushing to get back in the game and, if they had even got three points at that time, the game would have had a very different feel about it. But with Mikey's try, you suddenly had a fourteen-point gap and it's a long way back in the modern game. Will [Greenwood] then intercepted Geordan who was trying to force the game and Will was helped over the line by most of the England pack. Really, we got on the back of Ireland chasing the game. It was one of those games where the score didn't reflect the pattern of the game; but, then again, we didn't think the score reflected the game in 2001. The most important thing was our attitude. We would have taken a one-point win and everyone would have been happy in the England camp, and outside the England camp. There were no illusions of playing attractive rugby and sometimes it gets into people's heads about how they play. I say – just win at all costs, however you have to. We played a lot less rugby than we did in 2001 – we just happened to score tries and get points.'

The day, however, will be remembered for Johnson's refusal to move to a particular side of the red carpet for the arrival of President Mary McAleese. England positioned themselves on the left-hand side of the pitch (looking from the West Stand) where Ireland usually line up for internationals. When Johnson was asked to move his players twenty metres to the other side, he refused point-blank. 'We were getting a lot of grief from the Irish fans – because obviously, they were up for the Slam as well. But we had our heads on – we weren't taking any rubbish. I walked out to the side where we were going to play from and I didn't know anything about it being Ireland's lucky side. I just walked out to the side I was going to play, lined up and I remember seeing the Irish boys walk down behind me and the team. I wondered what they were doing. I thought they were going down to the North Terrace end of stadium to gee the crowd up. Then the guy came out and said to me, "You gotta move." I said, "I'm not moving anywhere mate. Just get on with the game." And then the crowd went crazy because I obviously gesticulated at the guy. The crowd was getting noisier and noisier and it became a stand-off. Then, I thought we couldn't, and shouldn't, move. It would have looked like we were backing down. If they'd been clever, they would have got the referee to ask us to move – I would never have refused to do it for the referee because that's before the game kicks off. Then they sent someone else out and he said you got to move and I said, "I'm not moving anywhere, just get on with the game."'

It appears England were not informed about correct Lansdowne protocol, 'We don't even think about it – in most stadia the changing rooms are on either side of the tunnel and you naturally go to your side. In Twickenham, if you're on the left-hand side, you walk onto the pitch on the left-hand side. In Lansdowne, it's not like that because the changing rooms are next to each other down the same corridor so there's no natural way for the teams to walk out. I've seen it on video afterwards and the whole red carpet controversy looks like a pause where nothing happens. The president then came out and we got on with the game. Irish people said to me, "You made the president walk on the grass" but we had the carpet in front of us.'

Johnson returned for his final game in Lansdowne Road in 2005 when Leicester Tigers defeated Leinster in the European Cup quarter-final. It was a game Leinster were expected to win but,

Get on with the game: Johnson point blank refuses requests to move to the other side of the red carpet before England's 2003 Grand Slam win. 'We had our heads on – we weren't taking any rubbish,' says Johnson.

with Johnson at the helm, the Tigers smothered the Irish province's free-wheeling style and one of the most iconic figures of world rugby maintained his winning record as a player at the ground. 'I was thrilled with the response from the players. It was a great occasion too – to fill a stadium like Lansdowne for a European Cup game was brilliant. It went right for us that day but all wrong for us in the semi-final afterwards. I remember I came over as well in 1997 for a European Cup game against Leinster and really snuffed a win against a really good Leinster team in our very first midweek European Cup game at Lansdowne. It was a good win against a Leinster team that included Paul Wallace, Malcolm O'Kelly and Neil Francis.'

Michael Lynagh

Out-Half, Australia
1984–1995

In 1984, Michael Lynagh arrived in Ireland, twenty-one years old and poised to make his mark in this part of the world. Already earning rave reviews and gaining kudos in Queensland, where since the age of eighteen he had occupied the Number 10 jersey, here was an aspiring star on a tour of Ireland and the UK and part of what is regarded as the greatest Wallaby side of all time. They were the Eighth Wallabies and became the first, and only, Australian side to win all four tests on a Grand Slam tour.

'Noddy' Lynagh went on to become one of the world's greatest out-halves, a self-appointed kicking machine (at one time he held the record as top points scorer in major internationals with 911 before that record was overhauled by Neil Jenkins on 1,049 points). On his first tour on these islands, Lynagh amassed ninety-eight points in eleven games.

He was proud to have played, however fleetingly, alongside the great Mark Ella, who, at the end of that 1984 season, stepped down from international rugby. The king had retired prematurely but the rising prince was readying himself to take the throne of his idol.

Australian management approached the 1984 test against Ireland annoyed and frustrated at developments off the field. Twenty-four hours before the third leg of their Grand Slam tour, a three-man disciplinary committee handed hooker Mark McBain a two-week suspension after an incident that arose in the England game. Coach Alan Jones discovered McBain in tears when news reached the team hotel. The three-man committee found McBain and Peter Wheeler of Midlands guilty of fighting and it evoked a strong reaction from Jones. 'Both players deny the charges and say they did not hit each other. Mark is in tears tonight and I must say I weep for him.' The incident overshadowed the build-up to the game; this bombshell dropped so close to an international test only further ignited the Aussies' desire to put Ireland to the sword.

Ireland, meanwhile, had come out of a Five Nations whitewash with bruised reputations and were badly in need of a lift of some kind. Enter the Messiah, aka Mick Doyle. The arrival of Doyler and his promise of an exciting and brash attacking rugby philosophy reinvigorated Irish hopes. The Currow coach's mantra was simple: run the ball at every opportunity. But he also had a set of forwards capable of combating Australia up front.

And this is what Lynagh discovered in his first match at Lansdowne Road – an ultra-committed Irish side with Doyle's 'give it a lash' philosophy written all over their game. Lynagh saw a commitment in the tackle area, and remembers Donal Lenihan and Willie Anderson giving the three Steves of Australia – Williams, Cutler and Tuynman – a horrible time in the lineout.

Only in the scrummaging did Australia prove more powerful while, behind their front eight, they possessed a backline of all talents, which mesmerised the four home unions throughout the tour. And it proved the difference in their 9–16 win over the Irish.

Lynagh lined out at first centre; and inside him stood the mercurial Mark Ella, who directed play as any good out-half should, scoring a try and two sweet drop goals over the eighty minutes. It was an even first half and only a Lynagh drop goal separated the sides at the interval. Lynagh vividly remembers the only try of the game. 'Mark [Ella] had levelled matters with a marvellous drop goal and I think we upped our game after that and played with more confidence. I was able to break through the Irish cover, which had been fairly difficult to break down all afternoon. I laid off to Matt Burke, but Michael Kiernan came across to tackle him. Earlier Kiernan did brilliantly to deny Campese a certain try but Burkey, despite being dragged to the ground, did well to lay off to Mark Ella who ran in for the try. We won 9–16 but, as we expected, we got a bit of a battle from the Irish. From memory, I didn't kick particularly well that day but we scored a nice try. Ireland were always really tough at Lansdowne Road. Still, I was disappointed with the kicking side of my game, which might have made the victory a little more comfortable than it was.' Australia did create multiple try-scoring opportunities, but Ireland's fervour and brashness kept the final scoreline decent and their reputations intact. It also proved a baptism of fire for twenty-year-old Trinity student, Brendan Mullin, who lined up opposite Lynagh in his first full Ireland international.

Michael Lynagh in action on his Lansdowne debut in 1984. Mark Ella was the out-half on this Grand Slam tour, 'Noddy' Lynagh lined up at first-centre. The Wallabies triumphed 9–16 against the ultra-committed Irish.

Australia's next visit to Lansdowne Road was for a World Cup quarter-final on 20 October 1991 with Nick Farr-Jones' assertion that it would be 'a tragedy if Australia were to lose against Ireland' ringing in their ears. Coach Bob Dwyer added further pressure to the mix saying Australia hadn't reached their potential as a team even after a successful summer victories over England, Wales and New Zealand.

If there was a growing sense of trepidation in the Aussie ranks, Ireland talked up their chances with captain Philip Matthews viewing the match as the perfect opportunity to do for Irish rugby what Jack Charlton's soccer team had done for soccer in Italia '90. He even went as far as to say Ireland would beat the Wallabies.

The heady old Irish ingredients of passion and pride were on full view that afternoon, the forwards giving it welly up front, while Ralph Keyes enjoyed arguably his best day in the Irish out-half shirt. But Australia's backline oozed class and the team included top performers in David Campese, Lynagh, Nick Farr-Jones and Tim Horan.

It might seem a little thing to spectators, but the playing of your country's national anthem is a great time to get the adrenalin moving. That day, the band forgot to play 'Advance Australia

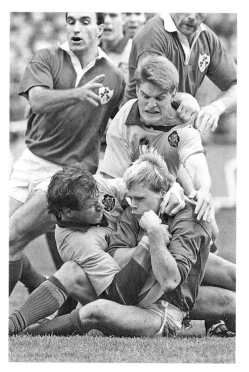

Ground force: Irish wing Simon Geoghegan (right) on the ground tries to keep the ball against Australian flanker Simon Poidevin (left) and centre Tim Horan during the quarter-final of the 1991 World Cup. Australia won 19–18.

218

Fair' and the sight of the Wallabies looking around wondering what they had done to deserve such treatment must have left them thinking the gods had conspired against them. To them, it was the ultimate slight whether it was because of the early kick-off (one o'clock) or the seriousness of the occasion, the players tore into each other – literally – from the kick-off. Philip Matthews landed an uppercut on Willie Ofahengaue, then Neil Francis joined in before Ofahengaue smacked Nick Popplewell in the head. Lynagh maintains the non-playing of their anthem and the sight of the Irish picking a fight strengthened their resolve. 'Phil Matthews set out to hit Ofahengaue from the kick off – that seemed to stir our boys up. As the game wore on, I don't think we were surprised by the Irish resistance at all. We knew a lot of their players and we knew the game would be fairly tough.'

The Wallabies had started in a fashion Ireland supporters had feared – a relentless phase of attacks and an early try courtesy of the dashing David Campese who scorched forty yards under the posts. You could sense then by the silence of the crowd that thoughts to the effect, 'Oh no, not another trouncing' were running through their minds. It seemed Ireland would capitulate but that wasn't the case in a bizarre but uplifting afternoon in Dublin 4. Ralph Keyes kept Ireland in touch but Campese struck another hammer blow when he notched his second try in the second half. Ireland refused to buckle and courageously and unbelievably were within sight of a World Cup semi-final when Staples and Jack Clarke combined to put Gordon Hamilton through for a try in the corner. Lansdowne erupted. Keyes followed up with an immaculately struck touchline conversion. It was dream stuff.

Ireland 18 Australia 15: it would have made some final scoreline and, with four minutes left on the clock, all that was left for Ireland to do was hold onto the ball. Even Nick Farr-Jones' pre-match fears of an impending 'tragedy' were beginning to unfold. 'We got fairly comfortable with the way we were going in the game – made a lot of breaks, missed a few opportunities, scored some tries. I think it was Ralph Keyes who kept the Irish ticking over,' says Lynagh.

Australia were three points down with four minutes left but, in typical southern hemisphere style, refused to panic. How often has Lansdowne Road seen the calm but deadly response of southern hemisphere opposition in moments we might consider a crisis? The Wallabies worked their way down field and, in a sophisticated and clinical fashion, created the try that crushed Irish hopes of a massive scalp. Rugby would have to wait another day to steal children's imagination, fused at that time to Jack Charlton's soccer team. 'You look up at the scoreboard and there was only a few points between the sides at any stage,' says Lynagh. 'It's a strange sort of thing to be saying, but we always felt that we were in control of the match. However, with four minutes to go, we weren't. Of course, we were particularly concerned at that stage. But if you start worrying about the game being over, you can't focus on what you need to be focusing on, and that's actually scoring points to win. We didn't really think of the negatives as such, but more how do we get out of this and win the game and that's what we ended up doing.'

Lynagh, the acting captain after Farr-Jones departed through injury, calmly assembled the players and said, 'Guys, we will kick long, we will go for the field possession and we will win possession. If you get caught with possession, just keep on driving towards the Irish line, hang on to it, we'll get a scrum and we can win.'

Lynagh was at the beginning and the end of what proved to be the match-winning try. Having initiated the move from a scrum outside the 22, the ball was briskly moved to Campese, who scampered for the corner. Brendan Mullin brilliantly tackled him, but the mercurial winger managed to find Lynagh who had looped around the three-quarters and dived for the corner. 'It was a particular play that we practised a lot at training and we had done in few games previously. We devised it around the star of the Irish defence, Mullin. We had practised it a lot so under a stressful situation, we decided to use it again and in the end it paid off. It's a good example of showing when you come up with a plan, you practise it and under pressure it seems to work.'

Lynagh had the option of a drop goal but trusted his instincts and went for the try. 'I was unaware that had we kicked a drop goal it meant that we would win the game through try count or whatever it was. I thought let's go and win the game and so I spurned the opportunity to kick for a drop goal and got the try. Who is to say I would have got the drop goal anyway? Those last four minutes were my best moments because I was captain and to be able to turn potential disaster into a win felt good in that role. And also, I think from that moment, we felt within the team that we were a unit that could do things, which we saw the following week against the All Blacks. I do feel that those four minutes against Ireland after Hamilton scored were a real crucial turning point for us in that particular tournament. That gave us a lot of confidence. Before that, we played OK in bits and pieces, but we hadn't really worked together – we were threatening to do it and, when we needed to, we went up that extra gear. I think that really defined that 1991 team as a successful unit. That was the moment that really defined us.'

Australia coach Bob Dwyer paid tribute to his backline afterwards, admitting it was their best

219

performance all year but, sitting in the West Stand that afternoon, he said that he found it difficult to conceal his nerves as his legs turned to jelly, 'We talked all week about how tough it would be, but it was even worse. My knees have still not stopped shaking and I suspect only a shot of Irish whiskey will have the desired effect.'

The Aussies hired a PR company to handle their dealings with the media during the 1991 World Cup, a move that proved a wonderful success with plenty of access to their camp. The management and players' openness and refreshing insights filled up many a journalist's jotter and, certainly, four days before their World Cup semi-final against the All Blacks, the Wallabies won over the assembled press corps with their amicable manner and memorable *bon mots*. It contrasted with the All Blacks' guarded responses in the lead up to one of the biggest matches ever played at Lansdowne Road.

If Dwyer's comment about needing Irish whiskey to steady the nerves was refreshing, consider the words of his flanker Simon Poidevin who, to that point in his career, had played Ireland on four occasions. He created a ripple of laughter when he described the Irish team as 'a collection of lunatics – very skilled lunatics – running around at speed' but, on a more serious note, placed Keyes' performance on a par with Ollie Campbell as a kicker.

It's not every day Lansdowne Road gets to host two of the southern hemisphere's heavyweights in a knockout competition, but seven days after Ireland caused more than a tremor in world rugby, the tournament's joint-favourites, New Zealand and Australia, descended on IRFU headquarters for the World Cup semi-final.

It turned out to be a great tie, as the Aussie backline duo, Lynagh and Campese sparkled. The All Blacks, despite losing, still brought their own sense of mystique, vigour and style to the occasion and, as their captain Gary Whetton said afterwards, 'at least we bow out in style'. 'I think it was definitely our best game of the World Cup, particularly in the first half in terms of attacking opportunities,' says Lynagh of their 16–6 win, 'and in terms of creating opportunities it was outstanding.'

New Zealand's preparations were thrown into disarray when Michael 'Iceman' Jones refused to play on a Sunday on religious grounds – the greatest flank-forward in the world missed the biggest game of his career. In his place, came Auckland flanker Mark Carter, though Jones' action didn't provoke any hostility from fans because of his huge popularity. Hopes of a second successive final appearance ebbed further away, in the build-up when news that full-back Terry Wright was out through injury.

During the game, Australia produced the tournament's most breathtaking display of attacking rugby in the opening half. It was simply brilliant stuff. Campese didn't take long to set Lansdowne alight once again – his hitch-kick had become part of an amazing repertoire of moves for beating defences. The hitch-kick saw him first jog and tease and then suddenly there was a one-and-a-half, then a two-and-a-half-step with one leg rising high in front of him and he was gone.

The great Campese: After breaking Irish hearts in the World Cup quarter-final, David Campese returned to Lansdowne to inspire the Wallabies to victory over the All Blacks in the semi-final. 'One of the great joys of Campese's play is that he never knows what he's going to do next, so neither does the opposition!' says Lynagh.

His local Queanbeyan newspaper in New South Wales called it 'Campese's struggletown shuffle'. As he himself famously said, 'My mind doesn't know where my legs are taking me.' But Campese had more than one string to his mellifluous bow – a great runner and a devastating finisher as well, he gave Lansdowne more than his share of great moments. Michael Lynagh says, 'One of the great joys of Campese's play is that he never knows what he's going to do next, so neither does the opposition!' Campese broke Irish, and subsequently All Black, hearts and went as far as saying during the tournament that he likes to play in the northern hemisphere away from the pressure and the criticism he came in for Down Under.

'I thought our first half was one of the best forty minutes that I have been involved in,' continues Lynagh. 'The second half showed that as a team we had a number of ways of winning games. We could score tries, we could kick, had a good forward pack and then we could also defend if we had to without the ball because New Zealand had most of the ball in the second half. Particularly in the first forty, every time we got ourselves into a position, we really did make it count. Look at the plays we scored from – Timmy Horan's try and David's try. They weren't planned moves. We were playing off the cuff, just reacting to one another and the opposition in front and, I think, that's what showed in what was a pretty special outfit.'

Campese's first try will never be forgotten. After Lynagh set up a ruck in midfield, Campese came off his right-wing position and took off on a diagonal line across field with a host of New Zealanders following him before squeezing in at the Lansdowne Road corner. Certainly, a try you couldn't teach. 'If anybody thought it was a pre-planned move for me to go up to the opposition and take on the All Black back-row, I wouldn't have agreed to do it to start with. That's where the ball came out, I saw a bit of space and off I went. Campo came back from the right wing and took the pass.'

Lynagh kicked a penalty after thirteen minutes and, six minutes before half-time, was central to Australia's second try. He chipped through for Campese who neatly gathered and then picked out Tim Horan with a deft pass.

New Zealand tried valiantly for a try of their own but it never materialised. However, they did deliver on their reputation as a skilful, ball-carrying team capable of fifteen-man rugby. But the Australian defence survived a series of assaults on their lines. It was heroic stuff from the Wallabies proving they could mix the champagne rugby with a blue-collar attitude. The world champions never opened them and the All Blacks' only reward was two Grant Fox penalties.

222

I'm not a bad scrum-half either! Lynagh (centre left) of Australia passes the ball out from a maul during the World Cup semi-final against New Zealand at Lansdowne Road. Australia won the match 16–6.

'In the second half, we had to defend and we did. We probably knew – and no disrespect to the English – that this was the final. Both the Australians and the New Zealanders knew that, whoever won that game would go into the final as strong favourites, given that New Zealand had already beaten England in the first game of the tournament. I felt there was a lot of leadership out on the pitch that day – it wasn't just Nick and myself. There were a lot of guys out there that Bob actually picked to do a job and they delivered. I really think that was key; there was a bit of maturity within the team and some useful enthusiasm as well. It was a very happy World Cup odyssey. I thought it was a particularly good time in Australian rugby. The team, the guys I played in that period were outstanding but I played in a period over fifteen years with a lot of guys and a lot of different oppositions.

'We knew how good the All Blacks were and how good they were back then. And a win against the All Blacks is a momentous occasion and we hadn't had a lot of wins over them in the previous few years. We did beat them in 1990 for the first time and then during the summer and that gave us confidence going into the World Cup semi-final. It definitely was a cause for celebration because they were such a good team. To beat them at Lansdowne and play so well was just terrific.'

Interestingly, New Zealand assistant coach John Hart went on record hoping Australia would go on and win the World Cup because of the style of play they employed. England were criticised in many quarters for employing conservative tactics and for never using the ball outside their Number 10 – and Australia did go on to beat England in the final at Twickenham.

When Australia returned to Lansdowne Road just over twelve months later, the hopes of Ireland replicating their World Cup heroics never manifested themselves. The Wallabies were simply irresistible though Lynagh, who captained the tourists on the 1992 tour, departed the game with an injury with twenty minutes left on the clock. He was on long enough, however, to mastermind the try of the match in the first half: another chip through and beautiful hands from Campese, Ofahengaue and Kearns put Jason Little through.

The Wallabies proved they were real world champions coasting to 17–42 victory; Campese scoring again at his favourite ground to bring his tally to fifty-one international tries. 'I went off with a dislocated shoulder,' recalls Lynagh. 'I had tackled somebody on the ground, he passed the ball and whoever it was tried to jump over me, I put my arm up and grabbed his leg and he took my arm with him and took the shoulder out of its joint. So that was the end of my tour. It was the first time I went off in a test.'

Every time he returns to Lansdowne as either spectator or, most recently, as a Sky Sports pundit, he is consistently reminded of the day he broke Irish hearts with his match-winning try in 1991. 'Sometimes, if you are in a hurry, it's a bit difficult. After the European Cup semi-final [Munster v. Leinster] in 2006, I was in a hurry to catch a plane. Unfortunately, I wasn't staying the evening but it was a bit hard to get out of the place. The Irish kept reminding me of 1991 and saying, "I'll never forgive you for that."'

Colin Meads

Lock-Forward, New Zealand

1957–1971

One team and one player dominated world rugby throughout the 1960s and Lansdowne Road shared their company on a mild December's afternoon in 1963. New Zealand came to town, but the thousands who came to the match came to see Colin Meads, a champion of the game's old values. He was part of an All Blacks team peopled with special players, but no one carried an aura or a reputation as great as Meads. Already a legend, his fame grew even more in retirement and, such is his standing amongst the New Zealand populace that the *New Zealand Rugby* monthly magazine voted Meads New Zealand Player of the Century and the NZRFU chose the farmer from King Country as the greatest All Black of all time. In a country laden with so many greats, there was no dispute and no tribunal – Meads was simply the greatest, an icon. In the New Year Honours list of 2001, he was made a New Zealand Companion of Merit, the equivalent of the by-then scrapped knighthoods.

To his team-mates, Meads was known as 'Pinetree', but to commentators he was euphemistically known as 'the enforcer' because of his involvement in a host of controversies. Opposition players regarded the lock-forward, who won fifty-five caps and dominated the game from 1957 until 1971, as a teak-tough player, an uncompromising performer feared by many but respected by all. Bill McLaren tells a good story of Edinburgh University's Earle Mitchell who, on his debut, was down to mark Meads in the 1967 test against Scotland (a game in which Meads became only the second All Black ordered off in a test when Irish referee Kevin Kelleher dispatched him for dangerous play). After the game, friends of Earle enquired how Meads had fared and Earle replied, 'I just looked him straight in the eye and told him I would not tolerate any nonsense from him during the game. But,' he added, 'I whispered it.'

Meads, along with a star-studded All Black XV, came to Dublin on a wave of hysteria and brimming with confidence, having clocked up seventy-five points in their previous two games, albeit against provincial competition – Midland Counties and South Western Counties.

Lansdowne Road is an enchanted place at the best of times, but there is an extra thrill when the All Blacks are in town. But, after eighty stirring minutes against a Tom Kiernan-inspired Ireland, Meads and his colleagues ended up extolling the virtues of Ireland's play – the best team performance they came across on their tour. In Alex Veysey's biography *Colin Meads: All Black*, Meads refers to the 1963–1964 tour of Britain, Ireland and France and criticises the northern hemisphere teams' defensive outlook and inability to score tries in open play, but it's hard to think he had Ireland in mind. 'From the first match against Oxford University, when we might have expected some sign of intent from the British teams to meet us halfway, the Oxford backs stood as flat as last year's beer not only on our ball but on their own.' Meads emphasises the benefits of second-phase rugby which, inevitably, leads to more attack-minded rugby and, as a consequence, more tries. On the 1963–1964 tour, he discovered that the teams he came up against were boring conservatives, who preferred to play simply off set-pieces. 'Ours was winning rugby but, more than that, it was try-scoring rugby. We scored sixty-four tries through our centres and wings. The British public are strongly inclined to demand attacking rugby miracles from touring teams while setting out themselves to negate any such possibility.'

His lash out at the British attitude to rugby is plain but Ireland served up the rugby of their lives to nearly pull off the shock of the century against the – almost – all-conquering All Blacks. 'It was a great tour,' remembers Meads. 'We got beaten early in the third game against Newport and I think that was, in many ways, a blessing because we didn't have to carry that mantle of being unbeaten. The Irish game was a real cracker. I enjoyed it, naturally, but the greatest disappointment of my rugby career was when we didn't get back to Ireland in 1967 because of the foot-and-mouth outbreak.'

He liked the Irish climate and the hospitality, and likened Lansdowne to Athletic Park, Wellington, but, most of all, he loved Ireland's rugby. He played opposite Willie John McBride and, today, the two still share stories about the game. 'A lot of stories revolve around what went on between Willie John and I. Willie tells it differently, but I got flattened in one lineout and it was Willie John because Wilson Whineray saw it. Willie tells it that he went back amongst their forwards to sort someone out and Bill Mulcahy says, "What the hell did you do that for?" And Willie said, "Well I had to do something, he [Colin] was all over me pushing and shoving." Then Bill Mulcahy said, "That's all right for you, now we're all in for it!" I think in the next lineout, Willie got a little tickle up front from some of our players and he thought it was me for a long time afterwards. I had to tell him it wasn't – our skipper did it to him.'

Visiting teams are never sure what kind of Ireland they'll meet in Lansdowne Road but you could hardly say the All Blacks were insecure in their own ability. The odds were certainly stacked against the Irish, especially up front where they conceded nearly a stone a man against the New Zealand front eight. But Ireland came desperately close to causing the greatest upset of the time. New Zealand were on guard, according to Meads, and they could sense from the off that the Irish were up for the game. 'We were always aware of it at the time. Rugby in those countries in those days was a lot stronger in comparison to today, but I always remember that Ireland game as one of the great games. We didn't know what Ireland had; we hadn't played against any of them before, it was a new experience for both sides. Apart from Bill Mulcahy, Ronnie Dawson and one or two others, who had been with the 1959 Lions, we didn't know many of them at all.'

The great irony of the day was that the men in green conjured up all the magic, not the fabled All Blacks. The wizardry came from the Irish backs, scoring a try fashioned from a blend of good hands, speed of thought and great finishing. Johnny Fortune's try and Tom Kiernan's nonchalant conversion had Ireland in the lead until the sixty-second minute and, even then, Lansdowne dared to dream of celebrating its finest hour.

The story of the game is stirring and the try is worth retelling again and again. Meads was in the scrum near his own line and saw that Ronnie Dawson got a quick heel. 'Initially, Tom Kiernan had sent a sixty-yard kick down field to find position well inside our 25 – Tommy was doing that all day. He had an amazing ability to find touch from long range from slender angles.' Indeed, throughout the game, Kiernan outshone his opposite number, the revered Don Clarke, and got three fifty-yard touches from slender angles. Clarke was a legend in New Zealand but, that day, it was Kiernan who had his reputation enhanced by a thoroughly rousing display. Debutant Alan Duggan had come off his wing to bolster numbers in the open and take a pass from Jimmy Kelly, 'Dixie' Duggan cut through a chink of space between two All Black shirts. Duggan was snared and swallowed up but still managed to get the ball away to the outstretched arms of centre Jerry Walsh. Displaying adroitness and speed of thought, the second centre lobbed the ball over Pat Casey's head into the waiting arms of the unmarked Fortune and the winger scored. Some All Blacks complained that the pass was forward, but Lansdowne rejoiced at another golden moment.

The All Blacks were stung but, through their awesome set of forwards, struck back with a Kel Tremain try in the thirty-fourth minute. It is worth naming the All Blacks pack because New

228

Colin Meads was voted the greatest All Black of all time by the NZRFU. Here 'Pinetree' Meads leaves a plethora of Ireland players sprawling on the ground during the 1963 test at Lansdowne Road.

Zealand will never see their likes again: Wilson Whineray, Denis Young, Ken Gray, Allan Stewart, Colin Meads, Kelvin Tremain, John Graham, Stan Meads (Colin's brother). Still, one New Zealand writer wrote after that game that the Irish pack was 'the toughest and best pack seen in the tour so far'. Meads says that, 'They took the game to us and we had a hell of a hard tussle. As regards Kel's try, we were pretty close to the line; there was this scrum formed and Kel was a great flanker and would be at the end of anything close to the line; a very strong and big loose forward. Wilson Whineray was our captain and he was a very mobile prop, great ball skills, great handling of the ball and loved running with it. By world standards, he wouldn't have been one of the strongest props, but he always held his end up and was a great support player in the lineouts and around the field.'

Ireland might well have felt unfortunate that they got on the wrong side of a referee's decision thirteen minutes from time. Scrum-half, captain and man of the match Jimmy Kelly initiated the move sending a beautiful pass to centre Pat Casey. Casey running from well inside his own half was faced by two All Black defenders but chipped the most delicious of cross kicks under the New Zealand posts. In one split second, a dozen things happened. An All Black defender was hit hard by an avalanche of green shirts, the ball spilled over the line and in came flanker Eamon Maguire to touch the ball down. The referee was slow to arrive at the action and adjudged that Maguire had knocked it over the line and awarded New Zealand a scrum. Ireland protested that they got a hand to the ball. 'That's always the case until after the game!' jokes Meads. 'There was probably some reason we protested, we should have got more penalties, I don't know, but that's the way it went. I always remembered the great time we had in Dublin, we had a great social, a good after-match function, a great dinner. The Irish were good sportsmen, good to play against. It was one of the hardest games of our tour; it was a real cliffhanger and one of those games that could have gone either way.'

As for his impressions of Lansdowne, Meads was charmed by the venue. 'It was one of the good stadiums in those days, a good rugby stadium, the crowd were right beside you, right on top of you and that sort of thing. It's a good atmosphere and obviously very good for the home team, they really got into it. It was little bit like Carisbrook in Dunedin but I tell you it was more like the old Athletic Park in Wellington [which was pulled down and a rest home was built there] but it had a huge open stand on one side.'

In the end, Meads left an incredible mark on his first and only game at Lansdowne. And was just glad to get the win.

The View from the Stands

Ray D'Arcy

Radio & Television Presenter

When he started playing with – as he likes to term them himself – 'the grown ups' at Cill Dara RFC, a minibus of J2 daytrippers would be organised for a Five Nations Saturday to Lansdowne Road. Those were happy pilgrimages, says D'Arcy – a couple of stops for a few sociables were par for the course before they'd pile into the South Terrace like a movable scrum for another Ireland international. Bill McLaren used say Lansdowne Road had a 'certain hilarity', and D'Arcy was witness to plenty in his time as a supporter.

'There was one particular guy, who played hooker with Cill Dara. We all thought he was a complete lunatic – he used hook the ball with his head before the rules changed! We were in that South Terrace for one particular game. Hugo MacNeill was playing full-back and I can't remember which team we were playing but they got a scrum right between the posts on the 22, or the 25 as it was known then. Hugo, being the full-back, was the last line of defence. So the opposition split their backs, and Hugo had to decide which way they were going to go. Then our hooker shouts out, "Go left, Hugo," and Hugo went left. The other team went right and they scored. So we blamed our man for that particular try!

'I was there in 1985 when we won the Triple Crown with that famous Michael Kiernan drop goal. I was in the South Terrace at the far end of the field. Kiernan had his back to me when he lofted over that score. I just wish I was in the other end but the place went bonkers. Still, it was great to go along and see your country win.'

D'Arcy took up rugby at eleven. A keen sportsman, he also dabbled in hurling, Gaelic football, soccer and badminton, but settled for the oval ball in adult life. He lined out at first centre for Cill Dara's Junior 2 side, which were a fledgling club at the time, not a rugby stronghold, but the spirit was good and the pride-in-the-parish mentality was prevalent many a Sunday when the jersey was pulled on. At the time, the club had to borrow a field from the Irish National Stud and used to shower in a stable. 'It was real lower end stuff!' says D'Arcy. He played to the age of thirty, adding 'I copped that you can make up for lack of talent with loads of determination.'

D'Arcy came from a working-class background, but rugby in Kildare is classless and the environment suited the passion he brought to the game. It's why he shares – despite his Leinster roots – an affinity with Limerick and Munster rugby. 'The rugby in Kildare is quite egalitarian – it's like Limerick as opposed to Dublin. You'd have privates in the army playing alongside officers, guys working in the ESB and teachers and farmers. Definitely, I would feel more passionate when I was playing than when I was following Leinster or Irish rugby.'

At Trinity College, he remembers seeing Brendan Mullin on campus; the centre setting out on what became a distinguished career with Ireland. But commuting from Kildare made D'Arcy's commitment to rugby in the university impossible.

In recent years, D'Arcy has found himself lifted and moved by Munster's European odyssey, and there was no way he was going to miss the 2006 European Cup semi-final between Munster and Leinster at Lansdowne. The week of the match, his morning show on Today FM consisted of dedicated slots to what many considered the biggest game in Ireland's rugby history. To the presenter, it was a local battle, pitching the country lads against the city slickers, and Ray came up with an idea to solve his own sense of identity crisis: wear a jersey that was half-red and half-blue. The idea was good but the jersey never made it to Lansdowne and, instead, he stood in neutral colours in the Havelock Square Terrace amongst the Leinster fans. He says he was 'stunned' by the Munster performance.

'Most of my best memories are of Munster and I'm a Leinster man myself. Leinster never arrived that day. It was a disaster. There's just an honesty about Munster's play. That's not to say that other teams are different or dishonest, but there's a sort of passion – a raw passion. It is that egalitarian thing in Limerick when it comes to rugby – there is no elitism about it. And when I used hear Limerick people go on about the Claw and Gaillimh and legends of the past, to stand in Thomond Park you say "this is real stuff". Leinster never caught my imagination in that way. For the European Cup semi-final, I was very quiet but I was with a mate of mine. He's not a huge

The smile says it all: Munster out-half Ronan O'Gara runs in the match-clinching try in the eightieth minute against Leinster on Seismic Sunday. On his shoulder is his Cork Con team-mate Donncha O'Callaghan celebrating the moment. In the background, Girvan Dempsey (left) and Brian O'Driscoll look on in disbelief. The red side of Lansdowne erupts. 'A stunning try and a stunning performance,' says Ray D'Arcy.

rugby fan, but prefers the day out. It was embarrassing really after a while – Leinster just folded completely. Even from the kick-off, Leinster knocked on and it was a sign of things to come. There was a sort of a despondency amongst Leinster supporters. The Munster support was over-whelming. You would think that it being virtually a home game for Leinster, that they would out-number Munster. But there was no comparison. It's difficult to describe. Even a purist would give out about the bodhráns, but bodhráns bring the extra few decibels to the whole thing and red is a stronger colour than blue.'

He sees the new generation of rugby players, their absolute fear of no one – the Brian O'Driscolls, Denis Hickies and Ronan O'Garas – as symbols of Ireland's new-found confidence.

Woodie scores: Keith Wood scores one of the most famous tries ever in Lansdowne Road against England in 2001. From a lineout peel, the Ireland captain barged headlong over the English line. David Wallace is in support. 'To see Keith's joy as he walked around the field after the final whistle was a special Lansdowne moment,' says D'Arcy.

'It's like our whole approach to everything changed. It hasn't swept through the whole country and there are still areas of Irish life that are the way they are. I did my Leaving Cert in 1981 and studied economics. We had to read about the economy and I remember being embarrassed by our economy which isn't something a sixteen year old should be thinking about. It was just so unbelievably bad. That seeps into your personality, your self-esteem and self-confidence, and then you fast forward to the late 1990s, twenty-first century, the country is booming and that has permeated most people's lives.

'This generation of Irish people could challenge the best in the world and that came out in sport, that came out in rugby, in business. So you had people like O'Gara and Stringer who demonstrate a professionalism and attitude that wasn't there before. Keith Wood is a prime example as well. You see him on the BBC now and he's a very assured and insightful contributor and was a player who really believed in himself and his country. I thought his finest hour came against England in 2001 in Lansdowne Road. His try was something special off a lineout and to see the joy on his face as he walked around the field after the final whistle was a special Lansdowne moment.'

Professionalism has been good for rugby in Ireland, the provinces and national side are prospering but D'Arcy can't help thinking back to how life used to be on the rugby pitch. 'When I started playing with the adults at seventeen, the lads were still having a cigarette at half-time. The whole ethos and approach has changed and the whole professional era has brought that on as well. I don't think you'd see even a J2 team smoking now at half-time. I don't know what would have happened if rugby hadn't gone professional.'

Martin Murphy

Operations Manager

Martin Murphy has been Operations Manager at Lansdowne Road since the game turned professional in 1995, and has overseen the move from rugby as simply just a game to an occasion and a huge corporate event, all of which requires meticulous planning and co-ordination. Still his most basic function remains constant – to ensure the safety and welfare of the players and the 50,000 spectators and that the whole event passes off smoothly. A former lock-forward with Wanderers, part of Murphy's remit is to co-ordinate all the arrangements for internationals as well as playing a central role in the big European Cup ties that have graced the stadium; his own standout days being Ulster's 1999 triumph as well as the Munster–Leinster semi-final in April 2006.

Murphy's role is multi-layered and more than just simply arriving with a key to open up the main gate for referee and players, supply a ball and allow the game begin. 'There's a core team of staff (seventy-five people are employed by the IRFU in total in four different locations around the stadium) that are involved in event management – they've other roles as well and other duties, but we're all pulling together as part of a team. The planning process starts the closer we get to the events. We'd send out notice to the authorities of the matches well in advance. We also have a liaison committee which includes ourselves in the IRFU, the guards, the fire and ambulance people and the local authority. We meet and there's a detailed planning meeting that deals with all aspects of the event and afterwards there is always a debriefing. We have meetings with our head stewards and briefings for stewards and ongoing training for them. For one of the big internationals – like the English or French match – we'd have 1,400 working behind the scenes and that would break down into 700 stewards, catering staff, programme sales people, bar staff, plumbers, electricians and maintenance people that are on site the day of a match.

'There is a quite a level of activity for own staff and for contractors working on site leading up to matches. These are big events – 50,000 people, corporate hospitality. It's very satisfying to see a game run off smoothly. We do the pre- and post-match event as well. There's a team dinner and pre-match lunch and it's great when it all works and it generally does. You can have minor hiccups along the way and it's not an easy stadium to manage; it's quite difficult because it's old and not round. More than 50 per cent of the capacity is on the terraces – that's great from the point of view of atmosphere, but the terraces are not symmetrical. It's a big operation to manage packing the terraces. Because, unless you control and manage the terraces, you'll have the late comers and they'll all be at the edges and there'll be loads of room in the middle, so you have to get people and pack them in and get them to various segments of it. The guys we have doing it have been doing it for years, we have systems in place and they can communicate with each other and the guards are there as well and they're an integral part of the whole operation. There'd be fifty gardaí on duty on a match day.

'I'll be sad to see it go, but I'm looking forward to a fantastic new facility. I played for Wanderers in Lansdowne and it was fantastic to play out there. But it's time to move on because people expect greater comfort at many different levels. The modern spectator deserves a different element of comfort. Croke Park has set a great benchmark and a fantastic standard of facility, something that you won't find in many locations across Europe and we have to be up there at the same level to provide the same sort of facility for people. It's not just the match now – it's the occasion, the event, it's the experience of the day. We're lucky here, there's a pattern for people coming to Dublin for those matches – you're straight out of Lansdowne Road and into the local hostelries. That will continue in the new stadium which is a great advantage.'

239

Eddie O'Sullivan

Coach

He arrived like a whirlwind on 19 February 2000. Eddie O'Sullivan's backs brewed up a storm against Scotland, a team Ireland had not beaten since 1988 and people at Lansdowne started to talk about a revolution in Irish rugby. The confidence, the strut and winning attitude of this new Ireland team were the emblems of the Celtic Tiger.

Eddie O'Sullivan arrived as assistant coach to Warren Gatland for the beginning of the 2000 Six Nations to liberate a backline badly in need of oxygen and width. Post-Lens (the site of the 1999 World Cup quarter-final loss to Argentina), Irish rugby craved a new beginning and it didn't take long for Gatland and O'Sullivan to dream up a blueprint to get Irish rugby back on track. Everyone was getting fed up with the regular derailments.

But Irish supporters learned to suffer one more time after Lens. The team and management took another kick in the guts when England quite simply ran amok at Twickenham in the first game of the 2000 Six Nations.

In the parallel rugby world of the European Cup, Munster were capturing the imagination of the country. Heroic wins over Saracens, home and away, the honesty of their rugby, and the way they tapped into the national psyche confirmed that the province should have more representation on the national team.

Gatland and O'Sullivan plumped for youth and natural-born leaders like Mick Galwey for the visit of Scotland. There were five new caps, all of whom later played a massive part in Ireland's Triple Crown wins in 2004 and 2006.

The men of the south, who won their first Irish caps against Scotland in 2000, included half-backs Peter Stringer and Ronan O'Gara – the 9 and 10 who had partnered each other from underage at Cork Con to Munster schools rugby at Pres and who were cutting an elegant swathe through the 1999–2000 European Cup. Then there was John Hayes, and the return of old warriors like Mick Galwey and Peter Clohessy. It is no coincidence that Munster's success story and odyssey in the 2000 European Cup coincided with the Irish rugby team's emergence as a genuine tier-one nation. Also debuting that spring afternoon were Simon Easterby and Shane Horgan.

As conquerors of England in the final game of the 1999 Five Nations, Scotland were in confident mood, clutching to a proud twelve-year unbeaten record against an Ireland regarded as perennial wooden-spoonists. However, Ireland played like men possessed – none more so than Galwey and Keith Wood, the latter's bullishness and give-it-all attitude on the field apt expression for the frustrations suffered over the previous six years. 'I was only assistant coach at the time and it was my second game involved with the senior team,' says O'Sullivan. 'My first game was at Twickenham and we got a ferocious hiding. Everyone knew at that stage that it was time to change, and to put in a lot of new faces. A lot of the guys I had been involved with at Under-21 level [where O'Sullivan won a Triple Crown in 1998] changed the dynamics of the team. We brought in a younger back-row and more backs, and we changed our game-plan to running with the ball from set-pieces rather than using the forwards alone to take it on. It caught a lot of people off guard, I think. The game-plan revolved around set-piece attacks from the backs rather than using the forwards and driving lineouts.'

The new caps emerging on the national scene seemed to inject a vibrancy that set Ireland rolling during the campaign. 'It's a massive leap up from European Cup level. No matter what anyone says, nothing prepares you for test rugby. It was a fiery baptism for the five new boys in Lansdowne Road but it's great place to start your career, in front of a home crowd. For Shane Horgan, it was his first time playing on the wing. He was a centre all his career, and got a try in that first test. Then we had a new back-row – Simon Easterby, Foley switched to 8 while Dawson stayed at 7. John Hayes started in the front-row, while Peter and Ronan were both thrown into the deep end. They were all very important decisions. It just happened to click at the right time and kick-started everything for everybody.'

Keith Wood's superb leadership and drive around the park, Malcolm O'Kelly's peerless display

Eddie's Boys: Cian O'Mahony (12) celebrates Ireland's Under-21 Triple Crown win in April 1998 with team-mates David Wallace (left) and Ronan O'Gara (right).

in the lineout and notable performances from all five debutants, were the foundation for a wholly unexpected 44–22 win.

After going 10–0 down inside twenty minutes with Kenny Logan scoring a penalty, a try and a conversion, it took twenty-two-year-old fly-half *wunderkind* Ronan O'Gara to direct a move which also involved Denis Hickie and Kieran Dawson and ended with Malcolm O'Kelly going over in the corner in the twenty-seventh minute. O'Gara landed a touchline conversion that drew thunderous applause and really marked his arrival on the international stage. He landed two penalties before the break, one coming after another inspirational drive by Wood up field, which resulted in Scotland going over the top in a ruck. O'Gara succeeded again with his kick and Ireland led 13–10 at the break.

'We started badly, but fellows stuck to their guns. There was a turning point in the second half for us where David Humphreys intercepted a pass from Gregor Townsend, the ball went to ground but he hacked it up the field and scored. We got a good try from Malcolm in the first half but that [Humphreys'] try was the turning point of the game really; the game was on a knife-edge until then and a lot of that was down to research. I did a lot of work on Gregor Townsend. We knew that when he ran from left to right, he often passed the ball inside blindly without looking, and he actually ran that line from left to right, and threw a blind pass inside which David Humphreys picked off and went the length of the field and scored.'

Humphreys was one of four Irish try scorers in the second half with Rob Henderson, Brian O'Driscoll and Wood – which drew the biggest ovation – also touching down.

Young Ireland was born. The Irish management's investment in youth reaped handsome rewards as the next two games against Italy and France also testified. 'It was a bit of a punt,' says O'Sullivan. 'There were a lot of new faces and trying to build something new. Obviously, if that failed or if things went wrong, you'd be back scratching your head. But the fact that it clicked early doors gave everybody the confidence to get on with it. That's very important if you take a punt like that to let new faces on the team or a new game-plan. If it clicks, it is the important thing because everybody believes it's the important thing to do. If it went pear-shaped, even though it's still the right thing to do, it's harder to convince people about it. So it was fortuitous that it went well for us at that time, trying to convince everybody we were on the right track and it was a good starting point for that reason.'

Next up was Italy, a bogey team for Ireland. Before the Azzurri entered the new Six Nations in 2000, Ireland had suffered some embarrassing defeats to them in friendlies. However, and maybe lucky for Ireland, Italy were going through a transitional period of their very own. But on a day when Ronan O'Gara could have kicked blindfolded at the posts and still not missed (he amassed thirty points in a flawless game), Ireland looked unstoppable, showing a high level of skill, pace and precision while the hard men still did the donkey work up front. Just like the last sixty minutes against Scotland, there was jauntiness to their step absent from previous Irish sides, and an insatiable appetite to attack from anywhere and from any distance.

Against Italy, O'Gara got the scoreboard ticking early on before the floodgates opened and Italy drowned in the tide. The first try was typical of the new-age Ireland: a sublime piece of skill from Peter Stringer, who flicked a pass behind his back to Keith Wood tearing in from the touch-line – the skipper broke the first tackle and stormed under the posts. Cue tumultuous roar for Irish rugby's most popular figure. Horgan and Dawson added two more tries and the dead-eyed kicking of O'Gara gave Ireland a 33–0 half-time lead. By full-time, Ireland had posted six tries in total, O'Driscoll, Dempsey and Horgan adding another three after the break to give a 60–13 victory.

These wins could hardly be called a false dawn at this stage in the championship and, when Ireland travelled to Paris in their next game and defeated the French – thanks to a Brian O'Driscoll hat-trick of tries – Ireland's best finish in the championship, a runners-up spot and a first four-match winning run since the Grand Slam winning year in 1948, seemed utterly attainable. Only Wales stood in the way.

Ireland–Wales is certainly the craziest fixture in world rugby, the 2000 match in Lansdowne producing an away win for the fourteenth time in seventeen seasons with Neil Jenkins' arrival in the second half, thwarting Ireland's chance of second place in the championship. Jenkins' two late penalties gave Wales a 21–19 win.

The 2001 'foot-and-mouth' Six Nations started off with wins away to Italy and at home to France in the spring before the competition restarted again in the autumn with a loss away to Scotland and a win away to Wales. England arrived intent on putting back-to-back Grand Slam defeats to Wales (1999) and Scotland (2000) behind them. But Ireland became the third Celtic country to deny England their Holy Grail.

'In fairness to Scotland, Wales and England, they had no games played, so when England came to Lansdowne Road they came in very cold. They were missing Lawrence Dallaglio and Martin Johnson – two key players in their pack – and, because of that, they were vulnerable. They tested our defence, but we were very lucky – they should probably have won that game a couple of times but they didn't have the composure and we scrambled very well. I think we were very lucky to win but it was still an important victory. It denied them a Grand Slam, which was something they'd been looking for for four or five years.'

The Gatland–O'Sullivan ticket looked like a winning combination, their reputations further embellished after a swashbuckling display – albeit in a loss – against the All Blacks in November 2001. A David Humphreys-inspired first half saw the home side lead 16–7 at the break, the out-half landing two penalties, a drop goal and a conversion.

So many encouraging cameos emerged under the floodlights at Lansdowne. Shane Horgan's tackle on Jonah Lomu seven minutes in, wrapping up the giant winger, allowing the home team to clear their lines; in the twelfth minute, Humphreys' quickly taken penalty, allowing Kevin Maggs score under the posts; a drop goal from Humphreys preceding some masterful touchline clearances from the Ballymena man; in the thirtieth minute, Horgan again smothering Lomu tackling him into touch; Humphreys landing a giant penalty just before half-time and a couple of minutes into injury-time, Humphreys pins the All Blacks' back inside their own 22. 'It was a phenomenal performance by Humphreys. Again, we caught the All Blacks cold with our attack; we ran the ball from places they didn't expect us and so on and we put ourselves particularly at the start of the second half in a very good position.'

Hickie's try after half-time put Ireland 21–7 in front. The build-up was very impressive with

Green giant: Arguably David Humphreys' finest performance in a green shirt came against the All Blacks in November 2001 at Lansdowne Road. 'It was a phenomenal performance by Humphreys,' says O'Sullivan.

great team-work involving Eric Miller and Brian O'Driscoll. Anthony Foley had just laid down another marker early in the second half when he sacked Andrew Mehrtens on his own 22 to win a scrum. 'Denis Hickie got a try based on a great break from a set-piece, that was then taken on by the forwards, Brian O'Driscoll squirmed out of a couple of tackles and put Denis Hickie in the corner. That put us into a match-winning position, about three minutes into the second half.

But, between the forty-fourth and seventy-fourth minutes, Ireland's defence collapsed and conceded five tries. As O'Sullivan says, Ireland weren't playing 'both sides of the football'. 'Unfortunately, as a team, we had developed our attack to a certain degree, but we hadn't developed defence, which was still very poor at that time. We didn't really have a very good system in place and, eventually, New Zealand just wore us down defensively. They held on to the football and scored some very soft tries, and really just beat us well in the end because we didn't have that capacity to defend. We had developed a capacity to attack at that stage which was new and exciting but there's two sides in football – when you have the ball and when you haven't and we were quite poor at it. The following year that was the most important thing when I became coach to make sure we could play both sides of the football.'

O'Sullivan became Ireland head coach soon after the defeat by the All Blacks and began his first full Six Nations campaign in some style. Wales were put to sword after which Graham Henry stepped down as head coach of the Principality. Young Munster's Paul O'Connell made his Ireland debut that Sunday afternoon, notching a try in the East Stand corner while David Humphreys – still favoured at out-half after an impressive Six Nations and autumn international series – scored twenty-two points in a whopping 54–10 victory. Geordan Murphy pitched in with two tries while David Wallace – so often on the fringes and seemingly lost in the wilderness of Irish rugby – came back to town to earn only his tenth cap. Munster legend Peter Clohessy earned his fiftieth.

It turned out to be a mixed Six Nations for O'Sullivan and Ireland, but at least there were more wins than losses. Though home wins against Wales, Scotland and Italy were not enough to temper the heavy defeats away to England and France or please the hardest-working coach (seventeen-hour working days) in the Six Nations.

In the autumn of 2002, O'Sullivan took his first big southern hemisphere scalp against world champions Australia. It proved to be match four in a record ten match-winning sequence that took his charges right up to a Grand Slam showdown against England in Lansdowne Road on 30 March 2003.

The Australian match saw the first signs of a new defensive system being implemented by Mike Ford come to fruition. The defensive system, so lacking against England and France in the 2002 Six Nations, looked watertight against Australia as Ireland celebrated their first win over the Wallabies in twenty-three years and first in Dublin in thirty-three years. The game also marked Brian O'Driscoll's first as skipper in the absence of the injured Keith Wood.

'The conditions were appalling,' recalls O'Sullivan. 'We were trying to develop our running game and, suddenly, we had to revert back to what we knew best which was basically keeping the ball and

Claw in Club 50: Young Munster's Peter Clohessy leads out Ireland on his fiftieth cap, with his son Luke (team mascot), before the 2002 Six Nations match against Wales at Lansdowne Road.

247

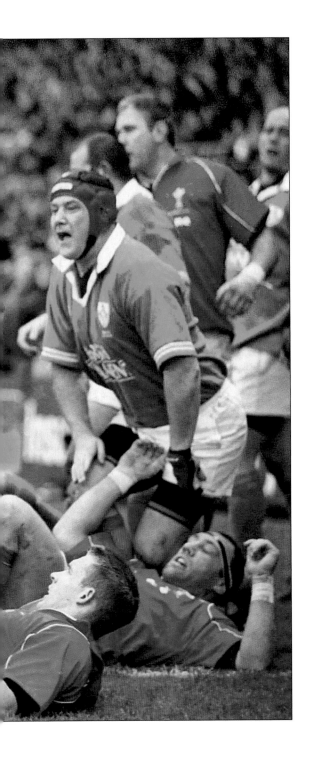

If you were a Young Munster man at Lansdowne Road on 3 February 2002, it would have ranked as one of your more memorable days at the Dublin 4 venue – and probably the biggest since 'the Cookies' epic All-Ireland League final win over St Mary's in front of 30,000 spectators in 1993.

Munster legend Peter Clohessy led the Ireland team out on the occasion of his fiftieth cap for his country, and while Lansdowne stood to acclaim the man affectionately known as 'Claw', it wasn't long before they were saluting the advent of another giant from Tom Clifford Park in Limerick.

Debutante Paul O'Connell marked his arrival on the international stage with a try in the twenty-fifth minute and, since that moment, the lock-forward has become the beating heart of both the Munster and Ireland sides. His try was taken from the Munster text book: from a penalty, David Humphreys kicked to the corner, and from the ensuing lineout O'Connell gathered and was driven over by the rest of the pack – a pack which included seven Munster men.

The day also marked Eddie O'Sullivan's first game as head coach, David Humphreys was man of the match kicking twenty-two points while twenty-five-year-old David Wallace got a recall from the international wilderness to earn only his tenth cap.

Ireland cantered to a 54–10 victory over an inept Wales and, afterwards, Graham Henry stepped down as their coach. Ireland's other tries came from Geordan Murphy (two), Denis Hickie, Keith Gleeson and Ronan O'Gara.

249

putting it in behind them in the wet conditions and, at the same time, not being afraid to move it if we had to. It wasn't a high-scoring game; we defended really, really well and that was the beginning in our belief of the defensive system, which has made a huge difference to our game.'

The Wallabies hardly got out of their own half in the opening forty minutes, their best chance came on ten minutes when George Gregan put Scott Staniforth down the wing. 'Their winger Staniforth looked set to score in the corner but Girvan [Dempsey] put in a superb last-gasp smothering tackle. A great memory, may I add.'

Then, Ireland took the lead and never looked back. O'Gara landed another penalty and his superb use of the boot kept the Wallabies pinned back inside their own half. The Irish pressure was relentless and the Irish defence resilient. In the driving wind and rain, O'Gara proved nerveless and, when he kicked his fourth penalty, gave Ireland a 12–3 half-time lead.

The Munster out-half kept adding on the points after the interval making it six out of six with twenty minutes to go. Ireland have been in winning positions before against the top teams only to tire in the final quarter and lose out, but there was no danger of that happening this time. Ireland beat the world champions 18–6.

It will be remembered as a boisterous celebration by the players and the supporters in the terraces who, drenched to the skin, hung around as long as possible as the team did a lap of honour with U2's 'A Beautiful Day' blasting from the speakers. 'They were the world champions and also we were playing them the following year in the World Cup. For that reason, it was important that we got a victory against them. Psychologically, that would stand us in good stead. We'd beaten Romania, Russia, Georgia, Australia, Fiji, Argentina and then the Six Nations which brought us on a run of ten games. That win gave us huge confidence going forward that season, but the next game we lost came against England in the Grand Slam match at Lansdowne Road.'

Pumped up, driven and mean, the 2003 England Grand Slam campaign set the tone for their most spectacular year in test rugby as they gobbled up every team north and south of the equator, including the little matter of the World Cup. When England came to Dublin, they not only set down a marker but delivered a message of defiance to the rest of world rugby. They also came to Dublin intent on putting to rest the hurt of losing three Grand Slam deciders in a row. Criticised for his team being one dimensional, Woodward's England on a beautiful spring Sunday, played a most perfect game of rugby, synchronising some powerful rugby up front with beautiful backline moves, all orchestrated by out-half Jonny Wilkinson. Lansdowne was home to a game of rugby and an England team that sent shivers down the spine of the Big Three in the southern hemisphere.

'We met England at the wrong time. That England was setting out their stall to win the World Cup and they realised they had a team that could win the World Cup and they put down one of their goals to win a Grand Slam. They'd lost three Grand Slams in four years, and this was a massive game for them. They had all their big men on board against us – Dallaglio, Johnson,

Thompson and their whole midfield. They really locked and loaded. They then went down to the southern hemisphere in the summer and beat New Zealand twice and Australia and went on to win the World Cup so that was probably the worst possible time to meet England for a Grand Slam.'

It had been fifty-five years since Ireland last played in a Grand Slam decider and expectations were getting ridiculously high amongst the public. If they had won it, it would have been the first Grand Slam captured in Lansdowne Road as well.

It started promisingly with a booming David Humphreys drop goal; then England hit their stride and ran roughshod over the Irish. The optimist in O'Sullivan still saw Ireland in with a chance midway through the second half. 'It was a strange game from our perspective – we gave up a very soft try, and I think if my memory serves me right there was about fifteen, twenty minutes in the second half, when we were only nine points behind and we had missed a couple of tries ourselves. It would have been a very interesting game if they had been nine points behind or even six points behind in the last twenty minutes. But, unfortunately, we needed to score and they got the crucial try which put the distance between us and they went on to win it easily. But it was a lot closer game than the scoreline suggests.'

Circle of friends: O'Sullivan tries to reassure his devastated troops that they aren't forty points worse off than England in world rugby. A Martin Johnson and Jonny Wilkinson-inspired England thumped Ireland 46–6 to win the 2003 Grand Slam at Lansdowne Road.

The post-match celebrations couldn't have contrasted more: England happy and relieved to have captured a first Grand Slam since 1995; Ireland gathered in a circle under the West Stand, O'Sullivan in the centre consoling his fallen heroes.

Still England didn't go overboard and conducted a very dignified lap of honour, Dallaglio and Wilkinson at one stage clutching roses in one hand and smiling and waving to the crowd with the other. Irish supporters, who remained behind, applauded what was a perfect England display. 'I was still disappointed to lose a Grand Slam, but I was actually quite happy with how we were developing as a team. We'd just been beaten by the next world champions who were pretty fired up for it. Our boys were obviously gutted. We went into the game, our eleventh game that season, and it would have been another record of going eleven games unbeaten and it would have been a Grand Slam. We just wanted to talk about the disappointment of losing a Grand Slam and, then, at the same time, try to put some sense into it. Like we just lost to a team – we didn't know it at the time – but we were pretty sure they were close to winning the World Cup. And we had to give ourselves credit. It wasn't a very bad performance, perhaps a harsh scoreline. That's when you get fellas focused on the positives of the game and it's important to do that at certain times. It's a salient moment, you keep the positives as well as the negatives. Just because you lose, everything isn't wrong, it's the same when you win, everything isn't right. It's to know what to focus on at the right time.'

Better days lay ahead – like the 2004 Triple Crown campaign that started with a win over Italy in a gale-force wind. A ludicrous day on which to play rugby but a professional Ireland performance nonetheless brought about a 18–0 win. 'It was a farce really in terms of conditions', says O'Sullivan.

A win over Wales and then England in Twickenham set up the prospect of a first Triple Crown in nineteen years. 'I had to keep them focused after Twickenham because we hadn't won anything. England were the world champions but we hadn't won a Triple Crown. We had to focus right on the Scotland match.'

Scotland's star had been on the fall, though, and their coach, Matt Williams, had been coach of Leinster. This game was huge from Ireland's perspective with the reward of a Triple Crown at the end of the rainbow. 'Probably, the important thing about that Scottish game was that for a lot of games we'd won up that – beating England [2004] or beating Australia – we were underdogs. It was the first time there was actually something on the line, a Triple Crown, and we were favourites, so it was coping with the favourites tag, there was a lot of pressure on the lads in front of the home crowd. The pressure was something new for the team. A lot of our victories up to that point were against teams we were supposed to lose to, so there was a little less pressure in those games. For that reason, it was a very satisfying victory in Lansdowne Road against Scotland. We did it in some style as well. We scored some beautiful tries in that game.'

Indeed, the DVD that came out shows a sequence of brilliantly choreographed tries from Ireland, that aspiring players might look at. 'And even when Scotland came back to level the

252

score, we didn't lose it, we didn't panic. We went down field, and David Wallace got a great try as did Peter Stringer and Gordon D'Arcy. We finished off the Scots in style. The Scots had a great record against Ireland up to 2002, and we had lost more games to them than we'd won. We hadn't beaten Scotland in Murrayfield for nineteen years until 2003 and the Scots were just trying to reverse a run of defeats, which was unusual for them. They were coming to Dublin and always fancied their chances against Ireland in Lansdowne. And, ironically, this was extra pressure because they felt they could upset the party – they're the best party-poopers in the world if they get a chance. For that reason, there was extra pressure there. Since I started coaching, they're one of the teams against whom we've never lost but they're always capable of beating you and you have to give them due respect. It's something for them that day too and, on top of that, they were being coached by Matt Williams who knew most of the Leinster players. So, all those little cameos were going on in the background. And that's why it was such an important victory.'

The moment David Humphreys hoofed the ball into the East Stand in injury-time, it kicked off incredible celebrations at Lansdowne Road. Nobody headed for the turnstiles, instead close to 45,000 Irish supporters remained inside the stadium to cheer the new golden generation as they did their lap of honour. 'The amazing thing was there was a lot of talk at this stage mainly in the newspapers that the Triple Crown didn't mean anything, that it was now all about Grand Slams and championships. I didn't know it to be honest, it wasn't for me to decide … I thought the reaction of the crowd in Lansdowne Road left nobody in any doubt that Triple Crowns are very important to everybody because the reaction around Lansdowne Road was phenomenal.'

O'Sullivan's favourite Lansdowne moment came when Ireland defeated South Africa for only the second time in their history in November 2004. It sticks out in his mind not only for it being O'Gara's finest hour in green, or the defensive unit that stuck together like super glue, but because there was a whole undercurrent going into the match. 'We had toured South Africa the previous June. It was the end of the season, we were very tired but we played pretty well. It was a very tough end of season tour. Jake [White – South Africa coach] made a few disparaging remarks on our way down there, but we didn't say anything about South Africa. We might have won a test there, we went very close, but we didn't win either of them. It was disappointing but we knew we were playing them in the autumn and I felt, leaving South Africa that June, that we had the beating of South Africa in Dublin. I was still quite happy with the performances.'

In Ireland, White continued to incite the Irish, insisting that only three of the current Irish side would make his starting fifteen. O'Sullivan stoked the embers, slamming the South African coach's remarks and giving an emotional defence of Ireland's proud rugby heritage. 'When they came up in November, Jake made some similar remarks, which were fairly disparaging, and I took great umbrage at them. I felt it was very unfair. I made it public, and that kind of kicked it off and there was a bit of blood in the water before the game started.'

The build-up was huge, not just because of White's remarks but because Ireland hadn't beaten the Springboks since 1965 and the feeling amongst the players was that they didn't do themselves justice during the 2004 summer tour. O'Sullivan acknowledges the contribution of the crowd that afternoon was vital. 'The crowd that day were incredible. There was an extra electric feel around the ground. Even when we were warming up we could feel it.'

South Africa saw their hopes of a first Grand Slam since 1961 dashed as Ronan O'Gara inspired Ireland to a 17–12 win. As one reporter cunningly put it: 'The twenty-seven-year-old out-half literally took the "spring" out of the Bokke.' The Munster fly-half scored all of Ireland's points including a cheeky tap-and-go try on twenty-one minutes and a sweet drop goal on thirty-four minutes.

O'Gara continued to torment the Boks in open play and from placed balls, but more pleasing for O'Sullivan was the resolute defence of his men particularly in the closing stages. 'We defended brilliantly. O'Gara gave a superb performance, scored all our points and got a cheeky try when they weren't looking. They were complaining about that after but, had they done it to us, I think people would have said we were stupid to turn our backs. O'Gara gave a phenomenal performance and, as I talked about being good on both sides of the football, we had to defend fantastically well and we did everything we had to do. And I remember the atmosphere building to a point where we couldn't really lose. I'll never forget the last ten minutes in that game because the crowd realised something special was on, they got louder and louder and louder. In the last couple of minutes, they ran a penalty near our line but didn't get over. It was unbelievable – I never felt any atmosphere like it. There was a great tackle made out in the corner, Foley turned over the ball and Stringer hoofed it into the East Stand. The whole place went beserk. Thinking about it now gives me goosepimples. For me, of all the games we've been involved in at Lansdowne Road that's the one that sticks in my mind the most. It was a great performance from us against a very good South African side who won the Tri Nations that year. That was one of our most complete performances. We didn't just defend but attacked brilliantly as well and stretched the South Africans all over the place.'

The year 2006 brought Eddie O'Sullivan his second Triple Crown success in three years and Ireland's eighth in total. The campaign never got off to the flyer expected, soaring after Munster's and Leinster's successful European Cup pool campaigns. Italy was first on the Six Nations itinerary – and arrived at Lansdowne Road on what would be the third last championship game at the ground. The Azzurri, under the stewardship of new coach, Pierre Berbizier, proved sticky opponents, providing plenty of threat in attack and were typically robust in the tackle and in the tight.

'We knew ourselves Italy were a lot better than other people were making them out to be. As assistant coach in 2000, I saw them as a very average team. But Italy very quickly got their feet under the table and became a very good side and they have improved every year. I knew at the beginning of 2006 that they were always a potential banana skin. We got results against them, but they've always been hard work. So, I wasn't too disappointed when we beat them at Lansdowne

Road, even though everyone was giving out about them, I thought it was a good start to the Six Nations for us, getting that one under our belt.'

Next up was a trip to Stade de France to take on the tournament favourites. Ireland gave the proverbial Jekyll and Hyde performance. The headless play of Ireland's first half in Paris was in stark contrast to the splendid demonstration of their skill and fitness levels after the break, but the thirty-two-point lead built up by France in the opening forty minutes was too big a gap to close after the interval, despite the heroism of Paul O'Connell, Brian O'Driscoll and Ronan O'Gara.

Wales were next on the Six Nations menu, arriving in Lansdowne Road under a dark cloud after the feel good spirit created during their flamboyant and thrilling 2005 Grand Slam triumph had been sapped from the squad with Mike Ruddock's sudden resignation. Newspapers were full of conjecture, rumour and story, many linking Ruddock's resignation to a player revolt instigated by senior players, including captain Gareth Thomas. One unnamed source labelled Ruddock's methods as being from the Dark Ages while skills coach, Scott Johnson, was allegedly making noises in the background pleading that he wasn't getting enough credit for their swashbuckling fifteen-man style of rugby that provided the most compelling narrative of the 2005 Six Nations. The players got their wish when Johnson took over as head coach for the remainder of a campaign that only deteriorated with a heavy loss to Ireland, a draw at home to Italy and a loss at home to France.

The week of Wales' internal strife coincided with their Six Nations trip to Dublin and, though a promising start seemed momentarily to gloss over their problems, Ireland scratched beneath their shallow veneer with a thoroughly professional yet uninspiring performance. O'Sullivan too was under some pressure trying to explain away the performance in Paris, but he pleaded for patience with the Irish public explaining that his team were trying to adapt to a new running/offloading/high-tempo game to keep up with the rest of the world.

Ireland kept their championship and Triple Crown ambitions on track with a comprehensive 31–5 win over Wales – tries from David Wallace, Shane Horgan and Peter Stringer as well as a sixteen-point haul from Ronan O'Gara overwhelming an uninspired Wales. 'The Welsh game was very important as well. The French game was a bit of an aberration. I didn't know what to make of it. At the end of the season, we probably realised we'd thrown away a Grand Slam. At that stage, nobody was talking about a Grand Slam – everybody was talking about us avoiding getting a hiding.'

Next up was a visit by Scotland, Ireland's last opponents for a Six Nations game at the old Lansdowne Road. The Scots arrived buoyed by their stunning Calcutta Cup win over England at Murrayfield – and opening weekend victory over France – and Ireland prepared themselves for a stern test. Their coach Frank Hadden introduced steel to their defence, a togetherness in the squad and a pride in the jersey, which had got lost somewhere after the 2003 World Cup. 'Conditions dominated the game and we had to slug out a very good victory against a very difficult Scottish team who were on a high themselves having beaten France and England. We would have loved it to have been a good fine day and have a great game of rugby. And I think

255

had it been a good fine day, we could have played some great rugby. It was a very good game by the half-backs who pinned them back in the corners and we used the conditions well.'

The game took on the spectre of a good old-fashioned penalty shootout between O'Gara and Scotland's Chris Peterson – O'Gara landed four penalties from five attempts in the first half to give Ireland a 12–9 lead at the interval while Peterson scored three from three. Conditions really deteriorated in the second half as the ball slipped from the players' grasp like a bar of soap. However, Ireland continued to dominate territorially and O'Gara cleverly played another tactically astute game, some might say a Munster game, pinning the Scots back inside their half and picking off the penalties when the opposition infringed. It was a ferociously physical contest, but very sporting. One cameo in the second half nicely illustrates the true old-fashioned all-Celtic fight between the sides when Jason White thundered into Jerry Flannery with a huge hit after the hooker felt like taking the ball forward in the loose. There was no remonstration from the Limerick hooker in his first Six Nations campaign; just a wink and smile in White's direction at the next scrum.

The Long Goodbye: Celtic cousins shake hands at the end of the last Six Nations match at the old Lansdowne Road on 11 March 2006. An old-fashioned stadium had just witnessed a classically old fashioned slog: no tries, big defences and two out-halves fighting it out in a virtual penalty shootout. Final score: Ronan O'Gara five penalties; Chris Paterson three penalties.

'In the first half, we played into the wind and rain, so it was hard. I knew coming up to half-time we were in control of the game that, bar a complete cock-up in the second half, we were going to win the game because all we had to do was play territory in these conditions and we knew we had the fire-power to wear Scotland down. It wasn't a classic game of rugby but it was a very satisfying victory. And, in the last four years, not losing any games to Scotland was very important. I thought we dug out a good victory. It wasn't very pretty but that's the way the cookie crumbles. The important thing was to get the result and head off to Twickenham for the Triple Crown decider.'

And what a Triple Crown decider. Lansdowne did not see it; it was 'Twickenham's Ball' as Ireland gave their most complete and gutsiest performance of the season, beating the world champions for the third year in a row. One of O'Sullivan's finest hours but, no doubt, he'd like to have won it in old Lansdowne.

'An old stadium like that with stands on both sides and no stand at the end, the wind can whip around the corners of the stand and create great difficulty for players. But I think there are only two guys who are able to work it better than anybody has – O'Gara and Humphreys. They've been phenomenally successful kicking the ball at Lansdowne Road whereas other kickers have struggled. In some ways that has helped O'Gara and Humphreys when they go into other stadiums where it might be difficult as well – they're well able to cope with windy conditions. They're a bit like the Irish golfers, they don't mind when the wind blows.'

257

Majella Smith

Groundsman

Majella Smith has worked as groundsman at Lansdowne Road since 1993 and, between the rugby and soccer games and summer concerts, his job is not an easy one. He'll wave a fond goodbye to one of the biggest front gardens in Dublin when the diggers move in for re-development, but his deep love for the ground and the games it has facilitated will live long in his memory.

He attended college for four years to study grass, attaining better scientific insights into ground preparation. Smith knows the weakest and better points of the ground and knows just the right time to apply surgery to it after all the wear and tear. 'Our rugby season starts in October and finishes second week in May. It's a heavy schedule of games that also include schools matches, club matches, Leinster play here in European Cup and Celtic League games – so it's in constant use all the time.'

The week leading into an international is his busiest time and, like any groundsman, he likes to have it presentable not only for the spectators but for the television cameras as well. 'We'd stripe the field out first. We know when the lads are coming in training. If there are any divots or locked out grass, we'd have to put it back the same for the next day. Then the Irish rugby team would come in on a Friday and do the Captain's Run and the visiting team would do its Captain's Run too. I'd stay back until that evening, turn the floodlights on, get the pitch up to scratch, presentable and mark it out and have everything ready for the following day. When there's a cold snap the grass doesn't look as well, but I always try to have it looking well for a rugby international, but in the winter temperatures go down and your growing season is more or less gone.

'Concerts cause an awful lot of damage to the pitch. In the summer, I would scarify the pitch and, by doing that, I get all the badness out of it. I sand it and seed it and you put a programme into place and let Mother Nature and the help of the irrigation system bring it back to full life. It's tough going and you always have to keep an eye on it to see if it gets diseases because when it's very warm, humidity comes into it and it becomes dewy.'

In recent years, he has received huge compliments from Ireland out-half Ronan O'Gara and visiting Number 10s like Jonny Wilkinson (England) or Stephen Jones (Wales). 'Most of the feedback would be from the players. The Irish team come in on a Tuesday and start to get a feel for the match on a Saturday. O'Gara and the lads would always pass a comment and the coaching staff would say it's excellent. They actually love it here. It's nice to be told something about the pitch but you're always going to get your critics as well, but the way I look at criticism is that it's news today and fish and chip paper tomorrow. I'd be my own worst critic. People say it was the best they ever saw it for the All Blacks match in November 2005. It was grand, but I always think there is more room for improvement that can be done to the pitch.'

In the 1980s, the field cut up rather easily and, in 2002, Smith was at the head of a pitch redevelopment plan committee that saw the ground undergo major surgery. Today scrums and heavy rucking leave few marks on the field on match day. 'The pitch can hold against the most ardent rucking. Since the 1970s and 1980s, the professionalism of groundsmen has come on too. There was no science and qualifications in the old days, but I believe the profile and structure of the pitch is very important. We reconstructed the pitch about four years ago because the old pitch had such a pan on it and it had 100 per cent meadow grass on it. Meadow grass is a shallow rooting grass and what happens is that when the players go for a scrum it tears out. We reconstructed it, we added fibre hair and mixed it through the roots and that holds the pitch very steady on the top.

'I love my work but I have my nightmares as well, but the golden rule is if I see people walking on my pitch, it's like a red rag to a bull! When Ulster beat Colomiers in the 1999 European Cup final, there were mass pitch invasions. I'd say 40,000 descended from the stands and terraces. It caused a lot of damage. It caused a lot of compaction because they all congregated around the West Stand and I have never in my life seen so many people taking chunks from the pitch and put them in their pockets.'

Ruairi Quinn
Labour Party Politician

As a fifteen year old running out at Lansdowne Road with the Blackrock Junior Cup team, Ruairi Quinn's initial impression of the stadium was its sheer enormity. He had previously watched the Rock's Senior Cup teams and Ireland there, but he had to blink twice to realise he was now in the centre of Irish rugby.

He says rugby became part of his life 'because my friends were interested in it', and describes himself as barely a competent player, but to play rugby in Blackrock, fitness was a prerequisite and Quinn was a supreme athlete – athletics was to dominate his life for the next three years where he became a champion schools athlete. 'Competitive team sports generate their own group dynamics and bonds of friendships,' he says and friends from his early days at St Michael's – Tom Crowe and later David Browne, Tony Amoroso, David Cantrell, Sean Kelly and Brian McLaughlin – were all on the Junior Cup team which took the field against Belvedere College that afternoon in 1961.

At the start of the season, the future leader of the Labour Party admittedly gave away some weight as a prop-forward but he persevered and worked his way onto the team and made it onto Lansdowne Road on Junior Cup final day. He'd arrived at the Mecca of Irish rugby and this was an occasion he was going to enjoy. 'We got as far as the final against Belvedere in March 1961 and we were defeated. That was the first time I played in Lansdowne Road. It's an incredible sensation to come onto the pitch. In the context of the time, this was an extraordinary place. I had been to international football matches and seen the Senior Cup team play there too. Even as a youngster in Michael's, we went to see football matches. This was following in the steps of fellows who were years older than me and I reckoned were mega-heroes and here I was out on the pitch. I thought the place was vast. And the height of stadium – as a fifteen year old, my only response was, "Wow!" I'd never been out of the country before at that time, never been on an aeroplane, and both the old stands, which are gone now, were vast as far as I was concerned. We actually changed in what was the Lansdowne Rugby Club pavilion and there was a tiny little open stand above it so we changed under the stand before the concrete terrace was put down.

'My abiding sense of the place was the smell of Wintergreen and the fear, the nervousness before a match. Then we lost the match and there was the whole sequence of coming back to the school and apologising for having lost. I steeled myself with the private resolution that I would never again lose a match.'

In fourth year, Quinn devoted all his extracurricular time to athletics, specialising in middle-distance running. Because his brother Conor was so interested in athletics, Ruairi became quite a keen runner and the disappointment of losing the Junior Cup final slowly began to dissipate. He says he didn't think in terms of the Senior Cup and came to the conclusion that his talent lay in athletics. 'I didn't really play rugby much after that. All of my energy was into running in fourth, fifth and sixth year.'

However, he didn't take his eye off the rugby entirely because, in Blackrock College, this sport was a religion. He kept abreast of the Senior Cup team's progress and, after Christmas, was inveigled into playing flanker on the Senior Cup team. 'I was asked by Brian McLoughlin and Fr Jerome Godfrey. Fr Godfrey was our trainer and coach, a Kerryman, known very affectionately as Goddo.'

It was an invitation too good to turn down but he was honest enough to admit to Brian and Fr Godfrey that his rugby skills might not be up to standard, but they assured him that his fitness would be of immense benefit to their back-row. 'I was doing something like a hundred miles a week between road running and training. So I could go forever but my rugby skills were not great. I was flattered to be asked. I had many friends on the team with whom I had been on the Junior Cup team.'

Quinn boarded in Blackrock in his final year and roomed with best friend David Cantrell. In the first cup game, Ruairi managed, in a late tackle on the High School out-half, to break Cantrell's arm. They made it to the final, but Cantrell more than anyone else wanted to play in

The 1964 SCT final, Rock v Terenure played in Lansdowne Road. Quinn is at the end of the lineout with David Cantrell and Brian McLoughlin in front of him.

the final at Lansdowne Road. 'The final was pencilled in for St Patrick's Day and David was still injured. Here I was sharing a room with him and all he wanted was to play.'

Then fate intervened. An outbreak of a flu epidemic meant the final had to be cancelled and re-arranged until after the Easter holidays at which stage David Cantrell was fully recovered. In the meantime, Ruairi had lost his place to Hugo Hynes, but then Hynes became ill on the eve of the match and Quinn was back on the team for the final. 'We barely got into the final. We were a desperate team but what we lacked in technical skill we made up for in self-belief. We also knew that, if we won the cup, it would be Blackrock College's fiftieth title. The Holy Ghost Fathers applied sports psychology techniques that were subsequently applied elsewhere.

Lansdowne Road has hosted every Leinster Senior Schools' Cup final since Blackrock College overcame Farra School 3–0 in 1887. The outbreak of two world wars may have forced the cancellation of all international fixtures, but the schools competitions continued. Blackrock College is synonymous with Leinster Senior Cup success having dominated the competition throughout its history – they have appeared in seventy-eight finals, winning sixty-five. Appropriately enough, Blackrock won the last Senior Cup final ever to be played in the current Lansdowne Road stadium.

Many Ireland internationals have captained winning Leinster Schools Cup sides down through the years. Some the most recent include: Mick Quinn, who led Newbridge College to a 19–5 win over Blackrock in 1970; Hugo MacNeill, who captained Blackrock to a cup in 1977 overcoming St Mary's College 24–12 after extra-time; Brendan Mullin, who captained the successful 1982 Blackrock team; and Denis Hickie skippered St Mary's to success over Clongowes after a replay in 1994.

Terenure College have claimed the title ten times. Amongst their famous alumni are the five Blaney brothers – John, James, Dermot, David and Brian. Except for 1996, there was a Blaney brother on the Terenure Senior Cup team every year from 1991 to 2000, with James and David captaining the College to cup success in 1992 and 1997.

'It was a highly contested match – we were playing against Terenure, a very strong school, and the end result was 3–0. I was playing wing-forward, David Cantrell was the other wing-forward, Brian McLaughlin was the lock. These were personal friends and there were two other guys from St Michael's Tim Crowe and David Browne on the team. This was three years later, so not an awful lot had happened to Lansdowne Road stadium, we changed in the same changing room, but I was that much older. I was back on the pitch determined to prove myself – and I did. There was one break and the ball went loose under the posts in our 22 and I scrambled over it, gave it an almighty punt right down the middle of the field. My sensation was of the roaring and the shouting and the enthusiasm and the game turned. We now had a scrum close to the Terenure line and Liam Hall went over on the blindside and scored and that was it – we were Leinster Schools Senior Cup champions.

'There were two incident that strike me very strongly of that day: at a time when old-style rugby rules applied (a try was three points and you could not bring on substitutes if someone went off injured), Brian McLaughlin, our lock-forward, got deeply concussed in the second half. Myself and David Cantrell took the decision, psychologically and emotionally, to keep Brian on the pitch because, if he went off, we would not only be a man down but we felt Brian's absence would possibly embolden Terenure. We were kind of half steering him a bit and he went into a scrum and he tried to bind with the other second-row forward Barney Mullin. Barney looked at him and saw his eyes turning like a slot machine and so it started to get panicky. With that, David Cantrell said to Barney, "Shut up, get in." This was eight minutes from full-time. I'll never forget the roar at the end.'

At the final whistle, Ruairi was overcome with emotion and collapsed to the ground both exhausted and elated as the supporters streamed on the field. The rugby player turned athlete turned rugby player again had breasted the tape in victory. 'That sensation for a teenage rugby player at that moment can be quite overwhelming. Absolutely overwhelming. Kids are more blasé now because they've had much more world experiences because of the holiday to Spain when they're twelve years of age or younger or getting in an aircraft. Life experiences compared to now – whatever about the past – were much less and the minute the game was over, I burst into tears. Brian McLaughlin was so concussed he was taken off the pitch immediately, and his mother never got to give him the cup which was the tradition then as it is now. Today, thankfully, he shows no signs of any residual damage!'

Other Lansdowne moments peppered a life you can certainly describe as less than ordinary. Quinn was vehemently opposed to the visit of the Springboks to Lansdowne Road in January 1970, and took part in the anti-apartheid march from the city centre to a demonstration outside Lansdowne Road on match day. 'I actually spoke that afternoon too. There was a lot of anger and a lot of emotion. There was a trailer organised in and around Newbridge Avenue. Kader Asmal was the organiser, I'd just come out of college and I had been very active in the Labour Party in southeast Dublin and member of the anti-apartheid movement and would have been a Youth Speak representative.'

He remembers Dick Spring playing against France, Wales and England in 1979 but, as a former flank-forward, he viewed Fergus Slattery as the supreme wing-forward of his time; the ultimate strategist on the rugby field. 'One thing I always remember from Lansdowne Road was the extraordinary ability of Fergus Slattery to read a football match. It was like watching a super chess player who could anticipate moves down and he seemed to be able to position himself in all the correct areas. That's the thing I never possessed. Fergus had the ability of a player to anticipate and read a game.

'I was there when we won the Triple Crown in 1982. There had been a general election the week before and I had just been elected. It was a Saturday after that election and I remember walking with my brother Conor and another friend from Sandymount to the match. I remember coming down by the Dodder Cross near Newbridge Avenue and different people saluting me and saying, "Well done" and all that. And we won the Triple Crown in the defining match against Scotland.'

As a politician, trying to help Ireland in the throes of an economic meltdown, Quinn envisioned how even the Triple Crown wins of the 1980s helped raise the esteem of a nation in a country beset with high unemployment, emigration and seemingly little hope. 'Unquestionably, the two Triple

Liberation Day: Delirious Ireland fans fill the Lansdowne pitch after Ciaran Fitzgerald's men clinched the 1982 Triple Crown. Quinn acknowledges that this Triple Crown win helped raise the esteem of the nation at a time when the country was beset with high unemployment, emigration and seemingly little hope.

Crowns helped lift the country. Sport in that sense does an awful lot for the well being and the sense of well being and also the sense if we can win it here we can win it elsewhere. I mean sport – and team sport in particular – is a terrific educational experience for young people – they learn how to play together, they learn how to win, they learn how to lose, there's always another day, there's always another chance to have another go at it. There's so much life experience associated with it that I can understand why. It doesn't really matter what the sport is – because you learn to co-operate, you learn that co-operation together means that if you're not selfish with the ball somebody can score and the glory goes to the team not to the individual.'

During the 1990s, the one player that stirred Quinn's imagination – and that of many others – was Simon Geoghegan, who on the few times he received the ball could electrify Lansdowne Road. 'Simon Geoghegan was just electric when he got the ball. He might get it three or four times in the whole match but then when he just took off it was unbelievable.'

An architect by profession, Quinn can see that, despite the ground's idiosyncrasies, the intimacy of the venue makes it a unique location on the international rugby fixture list. 'It's a bit of a hotch-potch now architecturally – the different stands were built at different times, but the intimacy of it is unlike the other stadia that have a running track around it. There's no space really; there's no *cordon sanitaire* between the football pitch playing field and the edge. I can recall being in the touchline seats and people coming in with their heavy-duty rugs to wrap over their knees and their little naggins of whiskey or hot toddies and sitting between the touchline and the metal barrier which surrounds the pitch. So you were really up beside the players and players were very physically close to the spectators. You were very conscious of the audience and the spectators. It was a great ground to watch a game of rugby in.'

268

Jonner O'Brien

VIP Gatekeeper

Jonner O'Brien has worked on the gate that divides the VIP car park and the entrance to West Stand for the last twenty years, and will be sad to see the passing of another famous Dublin landmark. He previously worked as a steward on Lansdowne's terraces but when he was asked to man the VIP gate, he jumped at the opportunity. He can look back wistfully and lovingly at the many great days at the ground. Jonner has seen the changing face of Irish rugby and can recount the many famous faces who passed through his gate for autumn internationals and Six Nations games. It's no surprise that his brush with sporting celebrity from his job has made many famous friends over the years with the surviving players from the Grand Slam side of 1948, to the famous Irish Lions of the 1950s and 1960s to the faces of the 1974 championship winning side, and the Triple Crown heroes of 1982 and 1985.

'There has been some famous faces going past going back to Willie John McBride to the present bunch of lads. What's nice is that a lot of the guys, who were big name players and who are now big shots in rugby, are still the most down-to-earth fellows you can meet. There is nothing snobbish about them. I always have a bit of craic and a few jokes with the likes of Tom Kiernan and Syd Millar. It's nice that they take the time to stop and have a chat. You never think that you would be so close to fellows like this. And it's the same with Eddie O'Sullivan and the team – I always wish them the best of luck as they go through and they seem to appreciate that.'

When the old Lansdowne Road disappears and new shining stadium is built in its place, O'Brien will miss the character of the former ground. 'I will be sad. I love going down there meeting these people and all of that will change. Something will be missing. By the time it is redeveloped, I might be too old for this game. It always gave you something to look forward to. Naturally, you feel some of that family feeling will be lost in the changes, but that's life. I'll miss it, but I could never forget it. I've loved every single minute.'

The View from the Box

Sean Diffley

Journalist, *Irish Independent*

Sean Diffley admits it wasn't easy being a young spectator attending games at Lansdowne Road, but the allure of the place was irresistible and the atmosphere too enchanting. From his early teens, as a student of Blackrock College in Dublin, it became a pilgrimage for the future *Irish Independent* rugby writer. 'First, there was the task of getting a terrace ticket for the match in Elvery's or Fox's and getting to Lansdowne Road no later than midday. Then, I used pick a decent spot under the East Stand, armed for the long wait with a sandwich or two and a naggin bottle of milk. As a stadium, you didn't see any faults with it – this was headquarters. This was the great cathedral of the game in Ireland.' He observed those pre-match rituals before each international in his younger days. For other home games, played in Ravenhill, he boarded a train to Belfast – there he caught the 1948 Grand Slam match against Wales.

Lansdowne Road has housed some of the most fascinating Leinster Schools duels since the very first final in the venue in 1887 when Sean's alma mater Blackrock, captained by James Walsh, beat Farra School 3–0. Sean attended his first Leinster Schools Senior Cup in 1943 when Blackrock, skippered by Barry Nolan, defeated St Mary's 9–6. 'When they won the cup, Barry was a very, very good scrum-half. After school, he went to the *Independent* and eventually became rugby correspondent until his retirement in 1970.'

With the suspension of the Five Nations for the duration of the Second World War, Sean's first experience of any type of international game came in 1945 when he viewed his first 'Overseas' opposition, a New Zealand Army XV who came to play Leinster at Lansdowne Road. 'They called themselves the New Zealand Kiwis, but they wore the All Blacks jerseys and were led by Charlie Saxton who had been a scrum-half during the war and he was their manager too. They played Leinster and Ulster and they played in England as well. They beat Ulster 10–9 in a splendid game at Ravenhill and, three days later, played Leinster at Lansdowne Road in a game that ended in a 10–10 draw – a magnificent match and a splendid performance by Leinster.'

Sean's writing career began as a freelance journalist and, as well as submitting material for various Irish newspapers, he worked in the Radio Éireann studios which, in the late 1940s and early 1950s, broadcasted from the GPO in O'Connell Street in Dublin.

Sean's elegant prose caught the eye of an editor in the *Irish Press* and, in 1958, he became athletics and rugby correspondent for the Press Group. 'I was, in fact, athletics and rugby correspondent for all the three papers – *Evening Press*, *Sunday Press* and *Irish Press*. And even when you went on an away trip or a Lions tour, you worked for the three titles. You also had to find a bloody phone, they didn't have the mobiles or the laptops in those days, but we got the copy through somehow. Then when I joined the *Indo* in 1973, I was also rugby correspondent for the *Sunday Independent* and the *Herald*; only gradually did they separate affairs and correspondents were appointed to all three titles.'

In the past, Sean Diffley described the 1948 Grand Slammers as 'the inimitables, the nonpareils', a side he adds that had excellent players, ones that fitted like gloves into every position. 'It was as if someone had sat down very deliberately, drafted a blueprint and found the ideal personnel to man every facet.' While extolling the virtues of Jack Kyle 'the natural genius in the side', Diffley says the most important person in the pack was Karl Mullen – the hooker's influence at set scrums and his ability to win ball against the head supplied Kyle with enough possession to show evidence of his repertoire of skills. 'In contrast to the game today, where the ball is predestined to go to the side which puts it into the set scrum, fifty years ago it was an even competition between the hookers. Then the hooker could use either foot, or both together, to hook the ball. He could launch himself, holding on grimly to his props, as far into the opposing scrum as possible. It was said in those days that Karl Mullen's feet were usually well implanted into the back row of the other side!'

Naturally enough, Jack Kyle, the superstar of the side, provides Diffley with his fondest memories, particularly Kyle's contribution to Ireland's remarkable run of success between 1948 and 1951. 'His

Karl Mullen, hooker supreme, tying his boot laces in the changing room before the 1951 Five Nations game against Wales. 'It was said in those days that Karl Mullen's feet were usually well implanted into the back-row of the other side!' says Diffley.

handling was magical and he took passes off his toes or over his head. His speed off the mark had opponents in constant trepidation. Above all, his brilliant individual bursts produced a succession of superb tries, many of which are still talked about today.'

Diffley's tales from the Lansdowne Road press box includes an Arthur McWeeney (*Irish Independent*) anecdote that emphasises the importance of Kyle to the Irish. McWeeney tells of sitting beside a Scottish journalist at the Ireland–England match at Lansdowne Road in 1949. 'The Scot was quiet and, viewing matters with detached interest, he turned to me and said, "You know, any international team with Kyle is pretty well bound to win." A sort of left-handed compliment but the point is taken. The win–loss ratio of the 1948 Grand Slam team, even by today's standards, was marvellous. They were lighter than all the other sides, but they were tremendously fast, the greyhound breed, tough guys as well, that's the combination of those three teams.'

Diffley vividly remembers Noel Henderson's try during the Australians' visit to Lansdowne in 1958. 'Henderson was coming to the end of his career and he got a pass from Dave Hewitt, and got clean away. But I remember he got slower and slower as he went and he scored eventually at the Havelock Square End!' Indeed, a photographer at the match, George Leech, caught up with Noel Henderson afterwards to pass judgement on the full-back's speed, or lack of. 'Do you know, Noel, I was on the halfway line when you took the pass for the try and I managed to get to the Havelock Square End behind the goal line and settle myself into position in time to take a picture of you scoring!'

Diffley recalls two games against the All Blacks where perhaps Ireland might have secured wins. 'In 1963, Ireland were leading late into the second half. There was a scrum under the committee box on the halfway line, near the touchline and, in those days, you didn't bring them out five yards, and so on. The scrum stayed out on the touchline, the referee blew and penalised the Irish scrum and Clarke kicked the penalty goal. And people wondered why Ireland were penalised. It was a mystery to everybody, even the players. Then, in 1973, Tom Grace got a try – Sid Going was the scrum-half who chased him to the line and if Barry McCann got the conversion we would have won, but the conversion was from the touchline a very tough one.'

Diffley was in Cardiff in 1972, the day the Welsh Rugby Union decided that their senior team would not travel to Dublin to fulfil their Five Nations fixture amid threats from paramilitary groups in Northern Ireland. Scotland soon followed Wales' decision; all in all it didn't go down well with the IRFU. Worse still, it was tough on the 1972 Ireland team on the cusp of winning a Grand Slam. 'I remember being in Cardiff in the hotel hanging around with the other reporters and upstairs the Welsh were discussing whether they'd come to Dublin or not. Eventually, they came down the stairs and said, "No, we're sorry, our people, our families are afraid and we won't travel." The Scots said the same. Ireland had beaten France 14–9 in Paris, the last match ever to be played at the Stade Colombes, and then outplayed England in Twickenham that year winning 16–12. There's no doubt about it – there was a Grand Slam there. The Welsh and Scots let us down. The RFU too held a press conference sometime afterwards somewhere in central London and I remember Terry O'Connor of the *Daily Mail* asking whether England were going to Dublin next year and the secretary of the RFU returned a defiant volley saying, "O'Connor, what do you think we are? Scaredy cats? Of course we're going. We have always fulfilled our fixtures – we even played in Lansdowne Road during the Irish Civil War and we have no intention of walking out of playing in Dublin."'

'The Welsh and the Scots were disgraceful. That has never been forgotten. England did arrive the following year, I was in the press box that day, and the applause went on and on and on. The English players and supporters were overwhelmed by the reception; it was quite one of the most magnificent afternoons in Lansdowne Road ever. The English players didn't wave to the crowd but they looked embarrassed; they stood in a huddle with their heads down. Then an English journalist turned to me and said, "We haven't a hope in hell of winning this match after that reception."'

Diffley has fond memories of Ireland's 1983 clash against France in Lansdowne Road on a day when Moss Finn scored two tries in a 22–15 win and Ollie Campbell kicked fourteen points. 'Ireland's veteran pack again proved their ability to meet the challenges of younger forwards, a team that went on to retain the championship. Ollie Campbell was chief scorer registering fifty-two points in the four matches to set a new Five Nations record, his fourteen penalty goals was also a new record for the championship and his twenty-one points against England equalled the international record by an Irishman in an international. An interesting fact about the 1983 championship is that, for the first time in Irish rugby history, the same fifteen players were used in the four championship matches.'

Diffley believes the 1985 Triple Crown winning side were marvellously skilful in an amateur era when teams did not get much opportunity to train with each other. 'Paul Dean and Michael Bradley, the new halves, forged a solid pairing and the emergence of Michael Kiernan as an accurate kicker had an important effect. He scored forty-seven points during the championship and his late drop goal against England won the match and brought Ireland a sixth Triple Crown. I don't think you can compare them to the Triple Crown sides of 2004 and 2006. In 1985, those guys trained two, three times a week, they weren't to meet until Thursday before an international. There was no opportunity to develop a squad to the extent they can today. Years back, I remember Tony O'Reilly would go out to Belvedere for a couple of days a week at lunch hour and have a run around the pitch because most of those guys were into work on a Monday.'

Diffley is still ever-present at Lansdowne Road games, and today marvels at the high skill levels of the players in the professional era which he says is good for the game. The stadium has packed in so many memories that Sean could pen a personal memoir on the ground. 'It has been one of the great cathedrals of the game of all the countries of all the stadia in rugby and I have been in all of them. It's the oldest. It was built by Lady Killanan's grandfather, Dudley D. Dunlop who actually started athletics in this country. It's now old and decrepit and it needs rebuilding, but there are solid memories of marvellous occasions there that should never be forgotten.'

277

Michael Kiernan waves his fist in the air to celebrate his winning drop goal against England which gave Ireland the 1985 Triple Crown at Lansdowne Road.

The build-up has been replayed a thousand times since, but it's still regarded as one of Lansdowne's great moments. The drop goal has often been called 'a Cork score' as Donal Lenihan, Michael Bradley (also in photo) and Kiernan were the main characters involved in its build-up and execution. Kiernan kicked his drop goal into the Havelock Square End of Lansdowne Road, but he must have been surprised at the amount of time and space he was given to execute his shot. Very few English defenders put pressure on him as the ball emerged from the ruck but Kiernan struck it with astonishing nonchalance and grace. It's not in the photo but Kiernan was wagging his finger at Keith Crossan as he ran back. About a minute earlier, Kiernan had told him that he might chance a drop goal. It was just as well Kiernan was on target for there was a two-man overlap on his right. The scorers in Ireland's 13–10 victory were Brendan Mullin (try) and Kiernan (two penalty goals and a drop goal).

Bill McLaren

Commentator

He brushed away a tear or two at Lansdowne Road on 4 March 2002 as he took the mike and the 'Cue Bill' from his producer for the last time at the old ground before breezing into his final commentary. The end was near, but not quite.

The PA announcer had just asked those present, particularly those closest to him in his commentary position in the Upper West Stand, to turn and salute the man – the 'Voice of Rugby' and Hawick's finest – wrapped in a blue and green tartan scarf. While water welled up in McLaren's eyes, he adds humorously enough that 'there might have been floods' after watching his bonny Scotland crash to a 43–22 defeat, courtesy of a Brian O'Driscoll hat-trick of tries.

He first hoisted himself up on the television gantry high above the old West Stand in the early 1950s and says he never changed his routine at Lansdowne Road up to that final commentary in 2002. Those watching and listening at home always got the benefits of his hours of homework during his unique commentaries and his broadcasts were never less than five star.

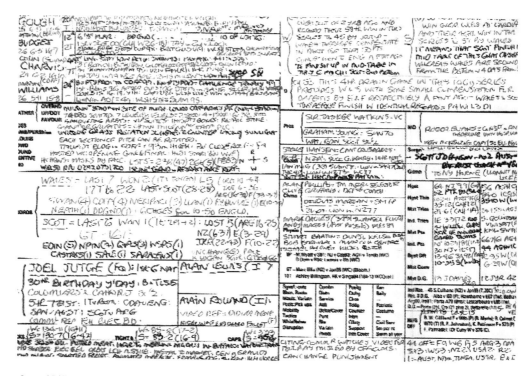

282

One of Bill McLaren's famous crib sheets: 'I spent all week filling in one of these sheets prior to every international on which I commentated. A tip from the late Richard Dimbleby gave me the idea and I never covered a major match without doing my research. As someone once said, 'Fail to prepare, prepare to fail.'

From the beginning of that week at his home in Hawick in the Scottish Borders, he had collated in his neat handwriting another famous A2 'crib sheet' brimful with information for Saturday's international at Lansdowne. Those crib sheets were a work of art, as fellow commentators later testified, containing all the facts and figures and data required for a major international.

The teacher in him made him prepare thoroughly, but he remembers getting the best nugget of advice from former BBC broadcaster Richard Dimbleby, who was said to have plenty of back up information at hand during a live broadcast. McLaren's famous A2 sheets were a miscellany of information comprising an introduction to the match, player profiles, statistics, results, and scorers from the previous eight internationals between the teams He might not have needed all of it, but he lived by the mantra 'fail to prepare, prepare to fail'. McLaren's crib sheet from his last Lansdowne match would probably make a few bob at auction today, but those who listened to the mellifluous tones of McLaren noticed an almost effortless quality to them. Yet, behind all this were hours of preparatory work.

He often captured a piece of individual brilliance with a turn of phrase as unique as the

Lansdowne atmosphere and that could only be fashioned in the McLaren School of Commentaries. His eye for detail was well known, but no one could describe a player's physique or movement better than Bill – they were drawn with an almost cartoon quality as Wales' Robert Howley found out when he was described as 'wiggling his way up-field like a baggy up a Border burn' in one match. That's Bill's favourite, a baggy being a small fish he used catch in his hands as a boy growing up in the Scottish Borders. And, on his first sighting of Ireland's Peter Stringer in Lansdowne (against Scotland in 2000), he commented 'the wee Corkman – catch him and you can make a wish'.

He sees the Irish and the Scots as kindred spirits, supporters who fused in song and merriment in the Dublin hostelries and on the well fermented terraces of Lansdowne on Five/Six Nations weekends.

Recalling his memories about the uniqueness of a Lansdowne Road international, you're expecting another *bon mot* to filter from the Master. 'Nobody seemed to take anything too seriously. The Irish had a philosophical attitude to their rugby and didn't have a wake if they lost.'

'Old, old fashioned and full of character' is McLaren's way of describing the stadium and he'll be terribly sad to see it go. 'The old-fashioned aspect of the ground I remember in the way they used to perch a television monitor for me just outside the window of my commentating box on top of the stand below, held on with bits of string. You wouldn't believe it if you saw it. I needed to have a monitor because it gave you a far better view of what was happening, so they said they'd hook one up for me – and hook it up they did! But the Irish sort of skidded along – they're wonderful.'

While a definite rapport existed between the Scots and Irish on the stands and terraces, McLaren believes both countries have a lot in common on the rugby field as well. 'During my days commenting, we [Scotland and Ireland] were always struggling for one thing, to beat England and France and the rest of them. Of course, the great thing was the Scots and Irish did get on well and that was seen on Lions tours, too, where the Scots and Irish blended so well.'

When hooked up in his commentary position whether by string or a more solid material, his observations couldn't help but be coloured by the charm of a Lansdowne occasion – particularly when Scotland and Ireland went at it on the field. 'It was different to anything I had done before – there was a lovely happy-go-lucky atmosphere there. I liked that because it was part and parcel of Scotland's approach to it as well, because Scotland, with the resources they had, were very similar to Ireland and always struggling against the colour as it were. There was a sameness there and a kind of bond between Scots and Irish people in the rugby field that didn't exist in relation to the other rugby countries.'

Even in the build-up to internationals, he found the Irish very approachable when he went along to their training sessions to practise his commentaries on the sidelines. He wasn't seen as some sort of a Scottish spy; the players had a great respect for him, some were even privileged to have him commentate on their training sessions. He remembers some Ireland squad sessions as

283

The voice of rugby: Bill McLaren in full flow during an international. 'I nearly had to get a taxi to get up to that commentary position in the old Lansdowne gantry.'

284

nothing more than light-hearted romps but he liked their attitude because it was redolent of the great old amateur days, when men held day jobs and rugby was only a game at the end of the day – and McLaren is a lover of the old way of life and tradition.

On a Thursday before a big match at Lansdowne, the tall, thin figure of McLaren could be spotted on the sidelines of the training pitch behind the East Stand taking notes, and giving running commentaries of the players as they went through their drills. He liked to memorise names and physiques and faces, and he wasn't satisfied until he knew each player before they left the ground. He left nothing to chance. 'Some of the players might remember me standing on a muddy touchline behind the East Stand, wind howling or rain pouring down my neck, making notes about a player or two.' He wrote in his autobiography: 'There was a very good reason why I took such meticulous care to get it right: if I ever identified a player incorrectly in my commentary, I was really, really angry with myself. Identification is the number one priority for commentators and, in my view, it is almost inexcusable to get it wrong.'

While he sometimes looked on at an Ireland squad with amusement during training, on match day, he discovered a different Irish team suffused with unyielding passion and an unquenchable desire to win. 'The Irish were deadly serious about wanting to win; get them on the field and even when they were struggling a bit, they took a hell of a lot of beating. There was always a feeling that, although each country wanted to win – and Scotland and Ireland each wanted to win desperately – at the same time it wasn't the end of the world if they didn't – that was the kind of attitude and it was different to when they played England or France or any of the others – there's a certain difference to the whole build up of a Scotland–Ireland game.'

He loved the open-air commentary positions and Lansdowne's television gantry in the old West Stand as they offered him a panoramic view of events on the field, but trying to get there in the first place offered its own difficulties – and dangers. 'I nearly had to get a taxi to get up to that commentary position!' he laughs. 'It was a rare experience to try and get to the old Lansdowne Road commentary position. You were glad to get there but you often wondered how you were going to get back down again. It was a great place to broadcast from. I loved Lansdowne Road because the venue was an ideal spot especially from a commentary point of view. I got a clear view of what was going on and everybody was so helpful – there wasn't a time when I asked for help of some kind and it wasn't provided immediately. It was simply wonderful.'

The hospitality and general homage paid to Bill was warming but there was no protection from the arctic conditions that often greeted him high above the West Stand. 'I felt that being able to feel how cold it was, or trying to keep dry in driving rain, was part of the experience. The conditions and the general atmosphere were a factor in the game to both players and crowd, after all, and I wanted to share their perception of the afternoon as fully as possible.' His perceptions never suffered and, while his style was unique, there was great insight in his commentaries. His cogent analysis always caught the ear – clear, articulate, conversant.

There were certain Irish players he will never forget – Jack Kyle, Willie John McBride and Mike Gibson in particular provided some of his best commentating moments and he was privileged to witness them play. He remembers that Kyle played against Scotland on ten occasions and was never on a losing side, and he quips that 'we got fed up of seeing him'. 'Scotland should have gone out and played Ireland each armed with a double barrelled shotgun because that seemed to me the only way to sort out Jackie Kyle!'

He believes that he had never seen a more complete out-half and, to this day, stands by this assessment, even when today's Number 10s carry more and more responsibility and kudos. 'He was the guy who caused us so much trouble. The thing about Jackie Kyle was he made it all look so easy. He was just a class act from beginning to end and there's no doubt he lorded over his era of Irish rugby football.

'He struck me as being a complete player. You wouldn't call him a bruising tackler, not the stand out fly-half who would tackle in a physical way, but he was really a gifted footballer. He had burning acceleration – he burned the grass when he got the ball. He was an absolute joy to watch because, apart from anything else, he's a lovely man and a great guy to get along with. And these are all important aspects as well. He was the player oppositions went out to mark. From Scotland's point of view, when they played Ireland their number one target was Jackie Kyle because he was just a gifted practitioner – he could torture a full-back with the placement of his kicking which was brilliant. Flank-forwards used get special injections to help cope with Jackie Kyle! You could almost hear Scottish, Welsh and English flank-forwards saying, "Oh God, not

285

'He had a heart as big as an outhouse.' McLaren's view of Willie John McBride seen here halting the progress of France's Paul Biermouret in Lansdowne, 1973. Ireland triumphed 6–4.

286

him again!" He was a great player but, of course, the great beauty about Jackie Kyle was he was such a monument for Ireland, the ideal type of rugby player.'

He saw Willie John McBride as a dominant figure of his time, a rock, the likes of whom you need in every side, like a modern-day Paul O'Connell. 'If you thought of Irish forward play, you thought of Willie John McBride. As a young commentator, to see Willie John McBride at close quarters was something special. When it came to heart and inspirational ability, he was different and there's no doubt that he had an awful lot to do with Irish resurgence at the time. He wasn't a gifted tactician but when the foot had to be put down and the extra mile put on, he would be the boy to do it. He had a heart as big as an outhouse. There's no doubt Willie John would be right there at the top of your list. He would still be running, and tackling and knocking people over at the end as he would at the beginning.'

McLaren speaks in the same awed tones of Mike Gibson as of Kyle, describing him as one of Ireland's greatest and most versatile backs and as the most complete all-round player of his time. Gibson was picked on McLaren's famous World XV at inside-centre alongside Danie Gerber of South Africa. 'You could stick him in anywhere in any fifteen and he would do a job. If you stuck him in at hooker, he would still win some ball against the head. He was that sort of player, a very astute fellow, very bright and you could see people listening to him with their mouths open, because he was so technically sharp, but there's no doubt that he was one of the most complete footballers I have ever seen.'

Gibson and Brian O'Driscoll are often put up for comparison, but McLaren sees them as different kinds of players. 'I think Gibson was probably more tactically astute. Gibson would recognise what was possible on the field more quickly – in the instant as it were. O'Driscoll is another one you'd need a double-barrelled shotgun to deal with. He is so adept. He is one of the quickest off his mark that I have ever seen. If you're down to mark him – you've got to do it like a bit of flypaper because if you leave him for just a split second, he's gone. And that type of player simply lifts a game. And with that type of flaring pace, he's liable to erupt at any time. It's a just a sheer delight when it happens.'

McLaren was there the day Ireland won their first ever Triple Crown at Lansdowne and will never forget the performance of Ollie Campbell who kicked all of Ireland's points against his beloved Scotland. McLaren liked to call him Ollie the Boot. 'It was one of the greatest goal-kicking performances that I have ever seen. Lansdowne Road on a wet windy day was such a test for goal-kickers. You can't get a bigger test than that. That day, Ollie Campbell was something really magical – there is no other word for it really. To have slotted the ball through the wind as he did was extraordinary from the point of view of artistry and touch and guidance. There's no doubt I marked him out that day as one of the all time great goal kickers. It surprised you in a way because when you looked at Ollie, he always looked in need of a good meal!'

Another Irish player McLaren liked watching was Fergus Slattery, who also made it onto his World XV. 'Slattery frightened the daylights out of stand-off halves. There's no doubt certain flank-forwards did put a little bit of apprehension into the minds of opposing stand-off halves. If they could do that and cause the opposing stand-off half to play below his form, he's done a good job. Slattery tore around the pitch like a demented buffalo! When Slattery tackled you, you'd think the Empire State building had fallen on you!'

One of McLaren's greatest moments was seeing Scotland win the Triple Crown in Lansdowne Road in 1984. The Scotland team was led by a former pupil of his from his days as a teacher in Hawick, Colin Deans. 'It seemed we hadn't won it since 1803! Colin's a very nice lad as well, so he was a good example for Scottish rugby and he was a very special type of hooker because he was desperately quick off his mark and that gave him an added edge as it were. Every now and then, there comes a moment when the whole country stands up to cheer and when that happens it's a wonderful feeling. That was us in 1984 and we went on to win the Grand Slam in Murrayfield a fortnight later. Ireland and Scotland have had their share of that kind of success. When it comes along, it's an absolute delight for the whole country because the whole country erupts.'

There was unbridled joy felt for Scottish supporters that day and McLaren remembers Scotland coach Jim Telfer going up to the television commentary position and singing 'Flower of Scotland' with himself and Dougie Donnelly. 'That must have been pretty awful for people having to listen to that!'

He was half-serious, but no one ever turned down the volume when McLaren was at full throttle.

287

Charlie Mulqueen

Journalist, *Irish Examiner*

At St Munchin's College, Corbally in Limerick, rugby was the word in the schoolyard. That hasn't changed, but kids' heroes evolve with the times. While a student at Munster's rugby nursery, Charlie Mulqueen grew up listening to the feats of 1948 Grand Slammers and Triple Crown 49ers and, of course, the majesty of Jack Kyle – the most complete Number 10 of all time. In the schoolyard or on the street, with a rugby ball in hand, everybody wanted to be Jack Kyle.

Charlie travelled to Lansdowne Road for the first time on 10 March 1956 to watch the Ulster magician at close hand. After reading and listening to tales of the red-haired Queen's and NIFC player, a mythology had blossomed around the Belfast boy and Mulqueen wanted to see the real deal. Kyle was nearing his end, his best years perhaps gone, but Mulqueen witnessed the out-half's one and only drop goal in an Irish shirt in the 1956 test against Wales. 'Wales had a terrific team: Cliff Morgan was playing out-half, Jackie played on for two more years but he was really coming to the end of his career. He got a loose ball around the forty-five-yard line, and put it over left-footed for his one and only drop goal for Ireland. Ireland won; everybody was wildly excited, the usual way a Lansdowne win ends.'

The Welsh had believed it was just a formality, of turning up and winning the Triple Crown, but Ireland had other ideas. 'The Triple Crown in those days was huge. I remember Con Houlihan writing, "Why do we place so much significance in the Triple Crown when France don't play in the Triple Crown?" He had a point; and subsequent events have proved him right. Because, nowadays, it is all about the Grand Slam and the championship and very little about the Triple Crown, even though we make a song and dance out of it when we win it. The championship in those days didn't seem to matter that much simply because France weren't around all that long as a serious force.'

Charlie, born into and nurtured in Munster's proud rugby heritage, naturally kept a close eye on the Munster boys, and remembers blindside flanker Marnie Cunningham touching down in an 11–3 win (Cecil Pedlow supplied the conversion and drop goal). 'Marnie came from Cork but subsequently quit rugby and became a priest. The late Tim McGrath (Garryowen) and Tony O'Sullivan (Galwegians) were unheralded at the time and, with Marnie, they comprised the Irish back-row. They destroyed Cliff Morgan and protected Jackie Kyle and did what a good back-row should do for his out-half.'

While never seeing Kyle in his prime, Mulqueen says the Ulster man's biggest match was in Ravenhill in 1953 (against France) when he scored a try. 'I never saw Kyle in his heyday. I grew up being told Jackie Kyle was the greatest player of all time. He had his biggest match in Ravenhill when Arthur McWeeney [of the *Irish Independent*] wrote his famous intro. It was a play on the novel *The Scarlet Pimpernel* and went: "They seek him here, they seek him there, those French they seek him everywhere, that paragon of craft and guile, the damned elusive Jackie Kyle." It was a brilliant intro.'

Mulqueen, the student, had an uncanny knack of picking some of Ireland's best days at Lansdowne and, against France in 1959, the Irish, who had been written off again, conspired to do the unexpected. Charlie's day became extra special through the acquisition of a Lansdowne memento after his trip to Dublin. 'In my final year in school, Lucien Mias brought a great team to Lansdowne Road for the Grand Slam and Ireland again were no-hopers. I knew Mickey English [Ireland out-half] because my brother Joe was very friendly with him, and Mickey used come to our house when I was a kid. He dropped a goal and the ball dropped into my arms, literally, in the schoolboy area behind the goalposts in the Lansdowne Road end. That's how I remember it – it was a left-footed drop goal. Ireland won 9–5.'

Ireland looked just as formidable on paper. Led by the famous triumvirate front-row of Syd Millar, Gordon Wood and Ronnie Dawson, other great names populated Lansdowne including Mulqueen favourite Bill Mulcahy (lock), back-rowers Tony O'Sullivan and Noel Murphy while the marquee backs included Dave Hewitt and Noel Henderson, who made his final appearance that afternoon against France for Ireland. The cause célèbre of the time, Tony O'Reilly, lined out on the wing. 'O'Reilly was the golden boy but I never really rated him – he never really played great for Ireland, he was more of a Lions than an Irish man. That day a different fellow on the wing for France called Jean Dupuis, who, to me, seemed to nutmeg O'Reilly, except he personally did it – not the ball. He was so small he seemed to run between O'Reilly's legs for a try! O'Reilly was played in the centre and the wing but Ireland rarely got the value out of him that was apparent on Lions tours.

'Noel [Murphy] was a great leader and he upset the opposition, not only by his play, but because he never stopped talking. I played against him at Munster club level. I should know! The real class act in those days was little David Hewitt – one of the famous Hewitts from Belfast – he was a fantastic player. The Lions team was picked the weekend after that match, and we'd have had nobody on it until we beat the powerful French team. Then a whole pile of them got on including the entire front row, 'Noisy' Noel Murphy, O'Reilly – who went on to score a record number of tries on the tour – and David Hewitt.'

Charlie didn't start covering rugby at Lansdowne until the mid-1960s, and was perched in the old press box in the East Stand the day Gareth Edwards dropped his non-goal on 9 March 1968. Edwards' effort was deemed good by referee M.H. Titcombe, but his decision evoked an angry reaction from the Lansdowne supporters. 'Edwards dropped a goal but it wasn't a goal – instead it was like an overdrawn golf shot. The referee pulled away in the belief that the ball was going to hold its line but, like a pulled five iron, it drifted and drifted until it swung well left of the post. That day, Mick and Tom Doyle were playing together – Mick got the winning try while I remember Johnny Moroney from Clogheen, County Tipperary, made his debut on the wing and finished the match unbeknownst himself with a broken leg.'

In 1969, against France at Lansdowne Road, the big noise in Irish rugby circles, Mike Gibson, could not play. At the time, Moroney, Barry McGann and Mike Gibson would have been battling for the out-half position but, on that day, because the selectors wanted to play both of them, Moroney played on the wing and McGann slotted in at out-half. 'Johnny set a new Irish record on the day; he

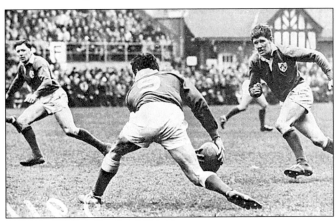

Irish wing-forwards (and brothers) Mick (left) and Tommy Doyle in action against Gareth Edwards at Lansdowne in 1968. Ireland won 9–6.

scored a try, a conversion and three penalty goals in a fourteen-point haul. Barry McGann dropped a great goal in front of the East Stand into the Havelock Square End and Ireland won 17–9.'

Johnny Moroney's record broke the previous record in 1949 by Barney Mullan and that same season saw the very first replacement on an Irish rugby team when the injured Roger Young was replaced by fellow Ulster-man Colin Grimshaw. 'Ireland beat England 17–15. That was the year subs were allowed for the first time but we must call them replacements in the strange idiom that is rugby.'

Mulqueen will never forget the standing ovation that greeted John Pullin's England team that ran onto Lansdowne Road in 1973. 'I cried at that match; we were all crying. Remember these were very taut times and England travelled over in difficult circumstances and received the warmest welcome I ever witnessed for a team. An incredible moment.'

If there were tears in 1973, then utter disbelief beset the press box when Wales came to Dublin in 1978 looking for a hat-trick of Triple Crowns. 'That one is famous for the late tackle of J.P.R. Williams. He has since preached the virtues of fair play and when asked about it he said it was a

professional foul. It was a dirty match. Wales were at their mightiest with Williams, Barry John, Mervyn Davies, Alan Martin, but they wouldn't be nancy boys themselves – they were no angels. People like Willie Duggan, Moss Keane and Philip Orr – a few of them wouldn't be renowned for standing back and letting the prisoners away. Wardie was great – he scored twelve points that day and Johnny Moroney scored a try, but I had great time for Willie Duggan, Moss [Keane], Pa Whelan and Philip Orr. Duggan stood up to them. He wouldn't take any crap.

'I found the 1985 Triple Crown far more exciting than the one in 1982 – no disrespect to anyone involved. In 1982, Campbell kicked six penalties and a drop goal to beat Scotland, in 1985, Michael Kiernan's drop goal was fantastic.

D–Day, 30 March 1985: Ireland players Willie Anderson, left, Jim McCoy and Michael Bradley celebrate winning the Triple Crown at the final whistle.

The build-up was real Roy of the Rovers stuff with Brian Spillane and Donal Lenihan and Michael Bradley all on the ball. Everything had to be done precisely or else it was all up.'

Since 1995, Mulqueen has seen huge changes in Irish and world rugby but Lansdowne remains the same – charming and old and full of nostalgia but praises the feats of those who pull on the green of Ireland. 'There have always been valleys in Irish rugby – there would have to be. We are a small country with a very limited number of players because of the GAA situation. If there was no such thing as Gaelic football, we'd take on the world and hammer them.'

Mulqueen enjoyed the camaraderie in the press box in the old days and has seen huge change in how rugby games are covered. He developed long-lasting friendships; and, as a journalist, Mulqueen still calls a match as he sees it, an authoritative voice, whose prose bristles in a reader's hand. 'When I was in the *Limerick Leader*, Dermot Russell was in the *Examiner* and we were great friends; we travelled around together a lot covering both golf and rugby. In those days, I used to look up to guys like Arthur McWeeney who was with the *Independent* and his brother Paul, in *The Irish Times*. I was in awe of the two of them. I grew to know Paul very, very well. He was a great character. Ned Van Esbeck, Sean Diffley, Karl Johnson (God be good to him), Fred Cogley – we're all great friends. There was great respect. I was only a young fellow but, as the years went by, I grew to know them very well and I was proud to know them well. Different era too – there were no laptops, no faxes, no emails, but all the deadlines were kept and some of the prose, if I may say so, was perfect.

'Mervyn Jenkins, a great full-back for Wales and the Lions worked for *The Sunday Times* and he was a giant amongst writers, and I enjoyed his company in Lansdowne and abroad. He made his rugby writing his career and so did one or two others. But what really annoyed me was when the Welsh team of the 1980s broke up and suddenly all became "journalists", even though they had never trained as journalists. Suddenly, the press box instead of being populated by the likes of McWeeney, Diffley, and so on, we were meeting up with Mervyn Davies, Barry John and Phil Bennett. Then John Jeffrey arrived from Scotland. Some people might not give a damn about that sort of thing, but I always felt a bit miffed that these guys could go overnight from being rugby players at the age of thirty to become a journalist at the age of thirty-one. And it's still going on. One of the great Welsh players at that time was Gerald Davies. Now he made journalism his career; it's his livelihood and so did a predecessor of his, Clem Thomas. Now, when they stopped playing, they became genuine journalists and made a living from it. But so many of the others are part-timers. A lot of them have to have their copy ghosted and that really takes me to the fair. Some of them can't express themselves, and very often what you're reading is the view of the ghost rather than the "writer".'

Peter O'Reilly

Journalist, The Sunday Times

He might not remember the day itself, but Peter O'Reilly will take his father's word for it that he was in Lansdowne Road on 8 February 1969, when Tom Kiernan's Ireland defeated England 17–15; tries from Barry Bresnihan and Noel Murphy keeping Ireland in the hunt for a first Grand Slam since 1948. A season of rich promise saw Ireland defeat Australia in an autumn international and this was followed by wins over France, England and Scotland before Wales spoiled the Grand Slam party in the final game of the championship, with a 24–11 win in Cardiff.

He says it would have been nice to remember some of those games peopled by legends Kiernan, Mike Gibson, Willie John McBride and Noel Murphy, however, the Belvedere student does remember the college's back-to-back Leinster Schools Senior Cup wins in 1971 and 1972. 'They won the 1971 cup against PBC Bray 14–11, and the 1972 final against Terenure 20–10 – those were great days. I was very young at the time, but the sense of excitement those wins generated was enormous.'

Ollie Campbell played on both cup sides

and, in 1976, made his Ireland debut against Australia at Lansdowne Road. O'Reilly headed to the North Terrace accompanied by his good friend Michael Campbell, Ollie's younger brother. O'Reilly thought that his lack of height might prevent him getting a clear view of the twenty-one-year-old Campbell in action so he brought a prop to help him get a better view. 'I brought along an orange box crate because my old man had advised me to bring something to stand on, thinking I wouldn't be able to see. But Lansdowne was half-empty. I remember sitting on the crate and watching Ollie miss a succession of penalties and then suffer the indignity of being replaced as goal kicker by Jon Robbie who was the scrum-half. I just remember standing behind the goalposts as Ollie was kicking but the ball never sailed between the posts. You'd remember stuff like seeing the Aussies green shorts as a bit odd, but they'd very tanned legs and Ollie looked so white! He kept missing and you couldn't help but hear the groans and then feeling terribly sorry for him. I felt sorry for his brother as much as anything else. It was 1979 before Ollie came back into it. Four years seems like an eternity and especially when you were a young player as Ollie was then.

'Robbie had played on the High School team that beat Belvedere in 1973 – I do remember being at that game too when Belvedere were going for a three in a row. That's another real memory and I remember the disappointment because Belvo were expected to beat High School.'

Though reluctant to bring up his own memories of playing on the ground, O'Reilly lined up opposite future Irish internationals Brendan Mullin and Neil Francis in the Leinster Schools Junior Cup final in 1979. Blackrock won 4–0, with Mullin, the star out-half and Francis, a precocious second-row. O'Reilly stood at first centre. 'I remember the next day when we gobbled up all the newspaper reports. Even though we'd lost, you wanted to see if you were mentioned and what the reporter had said about your team. I remember late in the day somebody said, "Con Houlihan has a full page on the match on the back of the *Evening Press*." People were then running out to get the *Press*. There were loads of pictures and stuff like that and Con had a 1,500-word piece on the game. But it was one of Con's colour pieces, very little about the match. It was all about how empty the old East Stand was and he was talking about the view of the pigeon towers in Dublin Bay. I think the only guy who got a mention was Conor Hickey on our team and that was because his brother [David] played for the Dubs!'

The year Ollie Campbell left Belvedere, O'Reilly entered the senior school, but Campbell never forgot where it all began for him and returned to help out the junior side on their road to the 1979 final in Lansdowne. 'Nick Hickey, Conor Hickey's brother, was doing a lot of coaching with us as well and Ollie came down to do a lot of sessions coming up to the cup matches and during the cup campaign. I remember he showed us a couple of very simple backline moves and we were thrilled with that. It was 1979 and Tony Ward was the Number 10 on the Ireland team, and Ollie was trying to get on the tour to Australia that summer. I remember this was his last chance to get on the tour. We went to watch him in a cup match against Monkstown and we had a training session down in Anglesea Road afterwards. I remember him playing really well. Then he came down to train us. When he got on the tour and then got on the test side, I watched the test matches where he scored nineteen points in Ballymore. I was in third year at school at the time. He was definitely a hero for all of us.'

Even better days lay ahead for Campbell, and his Belvedere supporters got plenty of cheer when Campbell steered Ireland to victory over Scotland in 1982 to land the Triple Crown. 'I went religiously to the games with Michael Campbell and a few others. Michael used keep it quiet that he was Ollie's brother but, by ten o'clock at night, everyone would find out! Because of those successes, the 1980s are remembered fondly. Ireland's form would have been up and down as well. That 1985 team could have gone on and done more; that was a bit of a disappointment.'

One of O'Reilly's highlights of the early 1990s was the World Cup semi-final between Australia and New Zealand at Lansdowne. 'I do remember that, and Campese, in particular, for three very important reasons. Firstly, he didn't face the Haka, but instead went down to the corner of the East Stand and South Terrace. Secondly, he backed up such an affront to the Haka then by scoring one amazing try on a diagonal run. And, thirdly, he gave this amazing pass over his head for Tim Horan for a try; he dragged their winger out towards the touchline and then popped the ball back inside and Horan scored near the back of the posts. It was odd because you didn't have that manic roar because the Kiwi and Aussie supporters who were there tended to watch and take it in, so you didn't get that madness you would have for an Ireland game. It was quite a grey old day at Lansdowne but it was lit up by Campese. Lynagh, too, was world class.'

One of O'Reilly's first big assignments when he took up a post at the *Sunday Tribune* in 1996 was to cover the autumn international that year between Ireland and Australia. From Ireland's perspective, it is regarded as the one that got away. They just about beat Ireland that day; Lynagh was gone at that stage and David Knox was out-half. 'It was my first international as a full-time reporter, my first live Saturday game. It's different watching a game, when you've got a deadline to keep. From a professional point of view, it's easier to report when the result is obvious before the end or early in the second half. I remember having mixed feelings about my first big international from a work point of view. It could have been an Irish victory and that was exciting. And, at the same time, I wanted the whole thing to be sorted out, wanted someone to do something decisive to decide the game so as to know which line to take for my report. Because you had to start your report as soon as possible.

'There was this nagging possibility that the Aussies were going to come back into it at the end, and then they did. I remember George Gregan made the scoring pass and there were a doubt about whether it was legal or not. It might have been a shade forward and David Knox has admitted that subsequently because he has watched it a few times on video. I just remember when Knox scored behind the posts at the Lansdowne Road end he was mobbed by his team-mates and that was sort of a moral victory for Ireland because the Wallabies, who had some world-class players in that team, were so relieved to have beaten Ireland. Saying this was a positive thing in

Famous Five: Shane Horgan, Peter Stringer, Simon Easterby, Ronan O'Gara and John Hayes. Ireland's five new rugby caps for the Scotland game on 18 February 2000.

298

itself because we were still thinking that way in those days and we would have had far too much respect for southern hemisphere teams.'

O'Reilly reported on the match that kick-started a new era for Irish rugby: Ireland–Scotland in 2000. He had seen and reported the humiliation and fall-out from the 1999 World Cup loss to Argentina in Lens, but the arrival of Eddie O'Sullivan and Warren Gatland's decision to plump for untried players at test level against the reigning Five Nations champions was the start of something brave, something new. The style was evolving with more ball going to hand, the width of park was being explored and suddenly the Irish press core had so many positives to write about the team and Irish rugby. 'I remember that kind of trend developing; Ireland suddenly getting the ball wide whereas Warren Gatland's approach up until then had been to use the forwards to try to get some momentum.'

Still, they turned to each other in the press box after twenty minutes with a look that said 'same old story'. Then, in the second half, the game was turned on its head and then Irish rugby's metamorphosis began. 'It was going the way all Scottish games went. Scotland scored early and were ten points up by the twentieth minute, and we're there thinking, "Here goes another one." A decision went our way after the break. Mike Mullins was on as a replacement full-back; he knocked the ball on but the ref was playing advantage to the Scots and it seemed like only a matter of seconds later, when the ball was hacked downfield by David Humphreys who got the touchdown. In any case, it was the turning point of, not just that game, but everything in Irish rugby in the last few years. Definitely, if we had lost that game, Gatland subsequently admitted that he would have resigned. It's incredible how much can hinge on a refereeing decision.'

If the trend towards total rugby was in full swing in 2000, then the apex of their flash-and-dash style was fully realised against South Africa in November, albeit it in a 28–18 loss. 'To give you an example of how it had changed, I would pick Tyrone Howe's try against South Africa in November 2000. It was an off the top lineout ball; there was no one taking it in and driving on. It was straight down to Peter Stringer, to David Humphreys, who was on as a sub, and maybe two passes – one miss pass, another a skip pass and straight to Tyrone Howe who scored in the left corner at the Lansdowne Road end.'

The Springboks shell-shocked by the emergence of an energetic Ireland capable of starting and moving a ball from anywhere (something coach Harry Viljoen was bringing to the South African game as he tried to implement a vision of total rugby), the Irish onslaught kept Viljoen

Chester Williams of South Africa chases Tyrone Howe of Ireland in the 2000 autumn international. 'To give you an example of how it [Ireland's style] changed, I would pick Tyrone Howe's try against Sooth Africa in November 2000,' says O'Reilly.

(in his first tour in charge of the Springboks) on his toes. Brian O'Driscoll was causing havoc around midfield so Viljoen pulled his Number 8 out of the lineout and crammed up the midfield.

'It was the whole idea of Ireland producing that sort of width and speed against a southern hemisphere team that seemed a bit unrealistic. It got to the stage where the South Africans pulled someone out of the lineout and put an extra centre in – they put André Vos in the centre as an extra defender on O'Driscoll basically. From a stage in 1997 when Ireland's only hope of victory came from forwards scoring as many tries as backs or when most of our points came from placed kicks, suddenly we had a situation where Ireland were scoring tries out wide. It was a bit of revolution and Eddie O'Sullivan deserves credit because when he came into the job, he brought something with him. He wasn't a yes man – he helped revolutionise the way Ireland played the game.

'There have been so many great tries, most of them by backs since 2000. I remember ones from the 1980s because they were so infrequent and because you're young you remember more. I suppose it's a testament to the way Ireland have gone; that they score so many that it's the older ones that stand out in your memory.'

He remembers nothing but complaints and a constant moan from the travelling Australian press core when they sat into their seats on a wet and windy November in 2002. The 1999 world champions were in town and, with the inclement conditions and the Aussies missing a few key players, the time seemed ripe for an upset. Ireland monopolised possession, dominated the line-out and defended ceaselessly. 'I remember the Aussie journos, who don't like being beaten as much as their rugby players don't like been beaten, were complaining about the conditions and about the pitch. The field had been reseeded or re-laid shortly before that and it wasn't draining as well but IRFU admitted as much. At the time, it didn't really matter. Ireland showed that they were able to play a bit more football than they had played in the past. They may not have gone the whole way in that our tight five forwards don't have the same footballing ability in that area of the pitch. But Ireland were able to keep their composure.'

Defence coach Mike Ford had just come in for that 2002 Six Nations but Ireland shipped five tries in both away games against France and England that spring. There were moments in that campaign when Ford wondered if the players were going to buy into his system, because they were slow to adapt. However, against the Wallabies in November, he saw the fruits of his labours materialise when Ireland started to believe in what he was preaching. 'Inevitably there were periods when Ireland were put under intense pressure and I think the impact Mike Ford had made as a defence coach became clear in that game. It wasn't just down to the conditions and that it was a tryless game; it was down to great defence on both sides and for once in that situation Ireland's defence seemed to be superior to the then world champions.'

O'Reilly wrote *The Full Bag of Chips*, a richly textured narrative focusing on Ireland's previous six Triple Crown wins and book-ended by the side's entire 2004 campaign – the title coming from Eddie O'Sullivan's colourful phraseology of what the Triple Crown is. When Scotland came to

Lansdowne for what was Ireland's Triple Crown match, O'Reilly was particularly delighted that Matt Williams' men came to fight tooth and nail and try at least to become Ireland's party-poopers. It was good from a writer's perspective too that the campaign would not be just remembered for Ireland's win at Twickenham and that winning in Lansdowne Road, a vibrant stadium that particular afternoon, was the perfect setting to lift a Triple Crown. 'What I liked about that day was the fact that Ireland were made to work for their win. It could have seemed like the Triple Crown was effectively the story of Ireland winning in Twickenham, and then two easy wins against Wales and Scotland.

'In terms of being an Irish rugby supporter and also from a professional point of view in terms of trying to make that a more interesting book – because I was planning the book already at that stage – it was good all round that Scotland had turned up. I think it was Alistair Hogg who scored a try early in the second half and there was a possibility that Scotland would rain on Ireland's parade and that Matt Williams of all people was going to overturn Ireland, having left Leinster. My favourite memory is of David Wallace's try just before the break because he broke about three or four tackles to get over the line – he just showed incredible power and strength. At that stage, he kind of calmed the crowd slightly. Eddie O'Sullivan said he'd make a great running back in the NFL. The scenes at the final whistle were spontaneous. I think Irish rugby supporters had all tapped into the Munster thing and so many people had enjoyed the away trips and had enjoyed being identified in some small way with success up to a point.

'Leinster and Munster had won the Celtic League. Outside of the Celtic League there had been no real tangible success. Although it wasn't a Grand Slam or a championship, 2004 meant something to an Irish rugby public. Our traditions are about things like Triple Crowns and, because they have been so few and far between, I suppose they take on a certain value. People stayed around in the stadium afterwards because they wanted to enjoy it and were sick of being gallant losers. Here was a bit of success, so why not celebrate?'

Another moment that sticks out in O'Reilly's mind in very recent memory is Ireland's win over England in 2005 – the first back-to-back victories over England since the 1993 and 1994 Five Nations wins. The win in 2005 consigned England to their worst championship run since 1987 (they had already lost to Wales and France). O'Driscoll's try on fifty-eight minutes – his first in six tests against the English – swung the match in Ireland's favour, but the build-up and the execution impressed O'Reilly greatly. It started with a deft incision in midfield by Hickie, and after the ball was recycled, Geordan Murphy dummied past Charlie Hodgson, played a beautiful cut out pass to O'Driscoll who danced in along the right touchline for his twenty-sixth test try – overtaking Hickie in the Ireland try record stakes again.

'There didn't seem to be a lot of space for players in Lansdowne that day because these guys all know each other so well having studied each other and played against each other so often. The line that Geordan Murphy ran managed to give O'Driscoll just an extra inch or two of space which

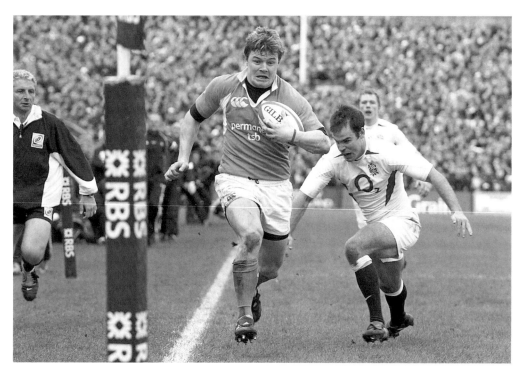

White line fever: Brian O'Driscoll beats Charlie Hodgson of England on his way to scoring a try in the 2005 Six Nations at Lansdowne Road. 'That was special – that would go down as one of the more memorable tries scored in Lansdowne Road,' says O'Reilly.

you needed. It was a bit of balancing act along the line. That was special – that would have to go down as one of the more memorable tries scored in Lansdowne Road. There are loads of photographs of him running past the old Wanderers Pavilion, which is one of the more well known landmarks in world rugby.'

O'Gara's conversion made it 19–13, a scoreline similar to the 2004 test in Twickenham. O'Gara, superb throughout, missed a penalty and drop goal before England began to dominate possession for the last fifteen minutes. Matt Dawson came on to revive the England attack, but Denis Hickie was called upon twice to tackle Mark Cueto and Josh Lewsey only metres from the Irish line. Ireland's defensive line held on, but only just, and perhaps with a friendly nod from Hickie to referee Jonathan Kaplan and the tireless work of Johnny O'Connor, the Irish held on in another home humdinger.

After an unconvincing start to the 2006 Six Nations campaign against Italy and the harum-scarum display in the loss to France, Ireland started their Triple Crown quest with the final three games of the tournament. When the Triple Crown was won in Twickenham, a piece by O'Reilly appeared in *The Sunday Times* the morning after: 'At half-time in Paris, Eddie O'Sullivan looked a dead man walking. Now he can savour an unlikely crowning glory.'

O'Sullivan was assured of a place in the history books after a second Triple Crown win in three seasons, and O'Reilly's opening paragraph sums up the inner delight of O'Sullivan who, after an autumn of poor results and talk of dissent within the camp, and that he had lost the dressing room, his second Triple Crown quashed all theories. 'At some stage late last night, Eddie O'Sullivan will have found a high stool in a quietish corner, lit a cheroot and celebrated his second Triple Crown – one perhaps not as aesthetically pleasing as 2004 but probably more personally satisfying.'

It was a Triple Crown that might have surprised many people given the pressure the coach was under and the question marks hanging over the performance, against Italy and France. 'The Triple Crown wouldn't have been as much of a surprise as the previous one,' says O'Reilly. 'By now, public and press are almost demanding or expecting a certain amount of success from Irish teams or a certain amount of consistency from Irish teams. Ireland beating England for the third year in a row (second time in Twickenham) doesn't happen very often. Beating Scotland and Wales at Lansdowne Road was no real surprise, although I suppose people would have seen Wales as a better side than us, based on the 2005 Six Nations but, again, you'd expect to beat them at home especially when they had so many injuries and disputes since Mike Ruddock's resignation. So it came down to winning in Twickenham really – that was a pretty special moment. It was different because it happened away from Lansdowne as well. There's a different sort of feeling to it.'

O'Reilly submitted his last copy on a Six Nations game from Lansdowne Road on 11 February 2006 as the rain rattled on the West Stand where the press box is situated (Ireland beat Scotland 15–4). But he was impressed by the level of sentiment the Scots expressed for the ground. 'I remember *The Scotsman* on Saturday produced a two-page spread on Lansdowne memories – the very fact Scotland reckoned it was that notable a moment shows how special Lansdowne is. Fenway Park in Boston is the oldest ballpark in American professional baseball. It's an incredibly evocative place of bygone times – it has got ivy growing on the redbrick walls ... Lansdowne has got a bit of that because of where it is situated. It's placed in a lovely part of Dublin. It'll always have special memories and in some respects it's part of your childhood. From a professional point of view, I can't say I'm going to miss the place terribly. I'm looking forward to better facilities.

'It has some of its idiosyncrasies. Rugby is an all-weather game, and you wonder sometimes whether it should be played under roofs because there's bit of rain; you don't want to homogenise the thing completely. I can understand when Irish players are frustrated when their game is no longer about booting it up in the sky and trying to terrorise teams; that when they want to play a bit of football that their home ground advantage is almost taken away from them.'

303

Acknowledgements

Tracing Lansdowne's Road's greatest matches and moments has been a journey of sorts. And along this immensely satisfying but sometimes difficult voyage, a number of people have lightened the load, and their assistance and co-operation has been immense.

To all those I have interviewed for the book – players and coaches, past and present, and to all other interviewees who took time out from their busy schedules to talk to me – my heartfelt thanks for your time, openness and co-operation. Without your insights and candour we wouldn't have had a record of your deeds and exploits from the world's oldest rugby ground.

A special mention to my editor at Hodder Headline Ireland, Claire Rourke, who, from day one, has been hugely supportive of *Lansdowne Through the Years.* Her energy, dynamism, encouragement and understanding have been of immense value over the past eight months.

To Hugh Farrelly, a great wit and writer, thank you.

Edmund Van Esbeck was the rugby voice I grew up with, and his knowledge, fairness and superb ability to read a game was always worth reading, and I am humbled that Edmund agreed to write the foreword to this book.

Peter O'Reilly of *The Sunday Times* was hugely encouraging when I told him I was pursuing this project. I told him of this book in the aftermath of Leinster's Celtic League win over Ospreys at Lansdowne Road in April 2006, on a night when Dubliner Eric Miller played his last home game for his province. Peter has always been there at the end of a phone to offer his help. A sincere thank you.

To Edmund and Peter, a special thanks also for allowing me dip in out of their books.

A special mention, too, to Michael Daly for guiding me through the history of his beloved club Lansdowne FC, and who showed a special interest in the book from the beginning.

There is one person where special thanks is overdue, and it's to a man who made the rocky road to full-time sports writing seem smoother; a man who possesses a brilliant mind and who is a superb sports editor and has always encouraged me in my writing. His name is Tony Leen of the *Irish Examiner* and I will never forget what he has done for me in the world of sports journalism. The *Examiner*'s Tom Ahern, Declan Colley, Bob Lester and Colm O'Connor have always been hugely supportive since I first began sending work into Academy Street in my early days as a sportswriter. To Paddy Maloney, Paul McCarthy, Declan Ryan, Sue Crosbie and Anne Kearney much gratitude for putting up with me late into the evening in the *Examiner* library, and to Joe Healy as well, thank you.

Thanks also to Liam O'Regan of the *Southern Star*, who was the first editor to publish my local match reports when I was a teenager.

Special thanks also to Dr Larry Jordan of Christian Brothers College who gave me 'my break'!

Special mention, too, to Karl Richardson of the IRFU for helping organise interviews.

A very special thank you to my family who have shown an interest since the book's genesis: To my parents, John and Marie, my sister Yvonne, brother-in-law Mark Southern (a massive Martin Johnson fan!) and brothers Paul and Austin and Karen O'Donovan, your support has been unwavering since I cobbled together the first sentence for this book.

To Steven O'Connor, who read parts of the manuscript and who offered sound opinion, my utmost thanks. To good mates, Gearoid O'Brien, Paul Sheehan and Niall Sweetnam – your support of this project has been unwavering from the beginning. And to Gina Cullen, a wonderful person – my heartfelt thanks for the kindness you've shown me down through the years.

Photograph Permissions

The author and publisher would like to thank the following for allowing the use of their copyrighted material in *Lansdowne Through the Years*.

Inpho Photography: 67; 221 • **Inpho/Allsport**: 248–49 • **Inpho/Billy Stickland**: 7; 13; 14; 16; 19; 31; 38; 63; 89; 112; 130; 146; 151; 169; 181; 192; 197; 214; 243; 247; 267; 271; 278–79; 299 • **Inpho/Andrew Paton**: 24; 78; 155; 166; 246 • **Inpho/Patrick Bolger**: 32–3; 34; 42; 136; 140–41; 176–77; 213; 251 • **Inpho/Lorraine O'Sullivan**: 36; 147; 148; 209 • **Inpho/Tom Honan**: 76; 82 • **Inpho/Morgan Treacy**: 84; 139; 231; 302 • **Inpho/Dan Sheridan**: 133; 256

Colorsport: 3; 11; 29; 101; 128; 186; 194; 200; 280 • **Colorsport/Andrew Cowie**: 190; 236

The Irish Examiner: 1; 68; 94; 100; 121; 198; 203

Sportsfile/Ray McManus: page 27; 60; 159; 292 • **Sportsfile/Matt Browne**: 46; 298 • **Sportsfile/Brendan Moran**: 116 • **Sportsfile/Brian Lawless**: 240

Empics: 49; 51; 123; 144; 182 • **Paul Faith/PA/Empics**: 244 • **Steve Mitchell/Empics Sports Photo Agency**: 174 • **Chris Bacon/PA/Empics**: 178 • **SMG/Empics/SMG**: 284

Getty Images: 217 • **David Rogers/Getty Images**: ii • **William Vanderson/Picture Post/Getty Images**: 54; 56; 275 • **Richard Heathcote/Getty Images**: 87 • **Gabriel Bouys/AFP/Getty Images**: 218 • **Peter Muhly/AFP/Getty Images**: 93; 235 • **David Cannon/Allsport**: 118–19 • **Dave Rogers/Allsport**: 208 • **Mike Hewitt /Allsport**: 210–11 • **Simon Bruty/Allsport**: 222 • **Central Press/Hulton Archive/Getty Images**: 224

Bertie O'Hanlon: 104

The Irish Times: 126–7; 264–65

The author and publisher have endeavoured to contact all copyright holders. If any images used in this book have been reproduced without permission, we would like to rectify this in future editions and encourage owners of copyright not acknowledged to contact us.